Charles Seale-Hayne Library
University of Plymouth
(01752) 588 588
LibraryandITenquiries@plymouth.ac.uk

THE NEW EUROPEAN AUTOMOBILE INDUSTRY

The New European Automobile Industry

Peter Wells

and

Michael Rawlinson

St. Martin's Press

First published in Great Britain 1994 by
THE MACMILLAN PRESS LTD
Houndmills, Basingstoke, Hampshire RG21 2XS
and London
Companies and representatives
throughout the world

A catalogue record for this book is available
from the British Library.

ISBN 0-333-58822-3

Printed in Great Britain by
Antony Rowe Ltd
Chippenham, Wiltshire

First published in the United States of America 1994 by
Scholarly and Reference Division,
ST. MARTIN'S PRESS, INC.,
175 Fifth Avenue,
New York, N.Y. 10010

ISBN 0-312-12238-1

Library of Congress Cataloging-in-Publication Data
Wells, Peter, Dr.
The new European automobile industry / Peter Wells and Michael
Rawlinson.
p. cm.
Includes bibliographical references and index.
ISBN 0-312-12238-1
1. Automobile industry and trade—Europe.   I. Rawlinson, Michael.
II. Title.
HD9710.E82W37   1994
338.4'76292'094—dc20
                                        94-20533
                                            CIP

Contents

List of Tables

List of Figures

Acknowledgements

This book is the result of two years of research work conducted by the authors while at the Centre for Automotive Industry Research (CAIR) in Cardiff. Our first debt, therefore, is to Professor Garel Rhys, who established the Centre and appointed us to our posts, and who has provided continued support and encouragement. Equally, we are indebted to the firms that provided Foundations for our initial periods of employment: Automotive Products (now part of the BBA Group); and Ford of Great Britain.

We are further grateful to the many firms and organisations that have funded various research projects at CAIR over the past three years. Much of the book draws directly or indirectly on this work, or is from specific contracts which provided the impetus to develop greater knowledge in certain areas. Of course, colleagues at CAIR who have joined us to conduct research projects deserve credit too, especially our fellow researcher Paul Nieuwenhuis.

Our greatest thanks, however, go to the automotive industry itself. Across Europe, the people in this industry have been welcoming, friendly, helpful and supportive. They have given their time and information freely, and without their contribution this book would not be possible.

PETER WELLS
MICHAEL RAWLINSON

Postscript

As this book was being prepared for publication two significant events occurred in the structure of the European automotive industry which deserve further comment: the purchase of Rover by BMW; and the dissolution of the alliance between Renault and Volvo.

The Renault alliance with Volvo was thwarted by the refusal of Swedish shareholders to accept the deal as presented by the then Chairman. The main concern was that the French firm could not be adequately valued while it remained in state hands, and that it was not acceptable that a French state company should own a significant proportion of an independent Swedish company. The failure to agree terms shows just how difficult it is to translate the economic logic of rationalisation and international mergers to the 'real world' of shareholders and vested interests. Renault and Volvo are now in the process of dismantling the various elements of the alliance, including the joint purchasing operations which had been established. Both are likely to look for new partners and new institutional arrangements for securing partnership.

The purchase by BMW of 80 per cent of the shares of Rover from BAe for £800m came as a surprise to many industry figures. While much comment and analysis has been devoted to the industrial logic of the acquisition, and the position with Honda following the purchase, it is clear from statements from both Rover and BMW that the most immediate and primary reasons for the purchase lie in the increased market opportunities which may be exploited. BMW is in a good position to increase Rover sales in Germany and the USA, major markets where the Rover presence is currently small or non-existent. In this context, then, the purchase is not about the spatial restructuring of productive capacity. Indeed, it is easy to forget just how expensive and time-consuming it is to establish a dealer network; certainly Rover was constrained from expanding sales outside the UK by the lack of an appropriate network.

It is clear that there are similarities between the two firms, in terms of overall scale and in terms of the model ranges currently produced. BMW is more orientated towards larger 'executive' saloons where the only Rover product (the 800 Series) is not a significant competitor. Rover is more orientated towards medium and smaller vehicles – the majority of which are based on Honda designs. The most obvious point of product overlap is the Rover 600 and BMW 3 Series. Both are recent introductions, and of course the Rover 600 also has to face competition from the Honda equivalent, the Accord. At present, there is no intention to cut any Rover products, but production of the 600 Series may be under threat in the longer term. Much also depends upon the product development strategy of the new BMW–Rover. The most likely outcome is that, in the medium to longer term, the brand names of the two firms will be retained but that areas of overlap will be reduced. Perhaps the UK firm will concentrate more on the smaller and medium sized vehicles and on the Landrover operation, but will also contribute to BMW vehicle designs.

Aside from the marketing benefits, BMW has purchased some key areas of expertise where it is currently weaker than many competitor firms, and where Rover is thought to have some genuine competitive advantages. These include off-road and four-wheel drive-vehicles (Landrover), small vehicles, front-wheel drive, and interior design and packaging. Given that new model development costs can range from £600m to £1b, it is clear that BMW has achieved a very low cost entry into key technologies and key market segments with considerable growth potential.

The position for Honda is less clear. The Japanese firm currently has licence agreements for many of the components used on Rover vehicles. The Rover 200/400 Series, the 600 Series and the 800 Series are all Honda designs which have been modified by Rover. It is unlikely that Honda will stop the licences, as they are a source of revenue for the firm. Honda is also dependent upon Rover for the supply of major body panels to its Swindon assembly plant, and is very likely to invest in its own press shop in the medium term.

Both of these cases illustrate the volatility of strategic alliances; they tend to be an unstable form of business organisation. This does not mean they are without value to the firms concerned. In the case of the Honda–Rover alliance both firms benefited. Rover gained many insights into Japanese production methods, shop-floor organisation, and design practices in the fifteen-year relationship with Honda. The Japanese firm gained access to the UK market and suppliers, and considerable licence revenues from Rover sales of Honda products.

With the purchase of Rover by BMW, the last major UK-owned automotive firm passed into foreign hands. Yet the reaction of many industry and union figures was muted. This in itself is an indication of the extent to which attitudes have changed in the UK automotive industry.

April 1994   PETER WELLS
                                              MICHAEL RAWLINSON

1 Introduction

1.1 THE SIGNIFICANCE OF THE AUTOMOTIVE INDUSTRY

The automotive industry is one of the stereotypes for academic research. From sociologists concerned with changing working practices and labour management relations, through geographers with interests in the spatial distribution of industry and employment, to economists concerned with questions about levels of integration, scale and scope economies, and macro-trade issues – all these disciplines draw on the automotive sector. The continuing fascination of the sector is perhaps due to the way in which it is seen as a paradigm of wider social and economic phenomena. There are three main reasons why the sector is of continuing significance: (i) economic; (ii) organisational; and (iii) environmental. It is for these reasons that we make no apologies for returning to the automotive sector here.

Economic

It remains significant in terms of employment, contribution to national gross domestic product (GDP), and trade for many European countries. In terms of the twelve member states of the European Community, for example, the automotive sector as a whole accounted for 10 per cent of manufacturing output. In total, including the retail, distribution and service sectors, the automotive sector may account for as much as 20 per cent of GDP in Germany, and has certainly been the 'power-house' behind the German economic growth record. One official estimate concluded that Germany accounted for 36 per cent of all European employment within the wider category of 'transport industries' (NACE 35/36, which includes aerospace, shipbuilding and railway stock), and the largest single firm was Daimler-Benz with 376 000 employees. In 1991 the automotive sector in the European Community (EC) contributed about ECU22bn trade surplus, although the balance for the car sector was only about ECU2bn (CEC, 1991, 1992). Western Europe as a whole (i.e. including Scandanavia) currently accounts for 28 per cent of world automotive production and 33 per cent of world automotive markets. Thus in simple economic terms the industry is of strategic importance to Europe. Moreover, the companies concerned are among the global giants. At a wider level the contribution of the automotive industry as a provider of means of transport to the economy and society is incalculable, though critics would say that the costs also are incalculable. Policy-makers at local, national and international levels are developing a range of initiatives to foster competitiveness in the sector, and with the arrival of Japanese 'transplant' operations in the EC, the intensely political nature of the sector has risen to the fore. Protectionist sentiments remain strong, notably in France and Italy, while European Commission attempts to remove protection and subsidy in the sector are likely to conflict with local and national attempts to retain current employment. Equally, the EC is acting as a funding and co-ordinating mechanism for a wide range of initiatives under the 'Drive' and 'Prometheus' programmes, which seek to develop new technology applications in vehicles and traffic management systems.

At a personal level the car remains the most important consumer durable, a purchase which carries great symbolic and cultural significance beyond its functional role as a means of transport. Car ownership levels in the USA have now reached 600 per 1000 of the population; in most of industrialised Europe levels range from 350 to 500 cars per 1000 of the population, with Germany having the highest ownership rates.

Organisational

The automotive sector has undergone profound shifts in terms of geographical and organisational structure over the past ten years. During the 1980s, Western automotive firms sought radical changes, both in terms of external organisational linkages (international strategic alliances and the development of new supply chain structures, for example) and internal linkages (teamworking, network management structures, flexibility and so on). Despite its long traditions in mass production, the industry is seen to be pioneering some of these developments in working practices and corporate networking grouped around the twin themes of flexibility and economies of scope. At times these changes have been turbulent: most notably, strikes at key Renault and Ford plants brought both companies to a standstill in the later 1980s and early 1990s, but in general it is remarkable just how many job losses and changes to work organisation have occurred without open union–management conflict. With some exceptions, it is evident that the automotive industry is expanding in what may be termed the European Community periphery – those countries at the edges of the EC, both within and outside. Thus Spain, Portugal, Turkey and Algeria all have expanding automotive industries. Even the Republic of Ireland, which has no vehicle assembly operations, now boasts a growing automotive components industry.

Environmental

The sector also lies at the heart of the 'green debate' (Elkington and Hailes, 1988; Elkington, 1990; Nieuwenhuis *et al.*, 1992). Its products, the methods used to produce them, and their subsequent use and disposal raise fundamental questions for those concerned with environmental damage. The automotive sector in this sense typifies the dilemma of modern industrialised societies – the products are vital for the functioning of these economies, and yet they also yield enormous costs in terms of environmental damage, wasted resources, and personal injury and death. The costs of car usage to society include the consumption of scarce resources (petroleum, steel, rubber, land for roads and car parks, etc.) and the associated costs of obtaining those products; the problem of pollution – especially exhaust emissions; traffic congestion; and health and safety generally. In the UK about 5000 people die and over 300 000 are injured on the roads every year, at a direct cost of some £5bn and untold emotional cost. The production of cars itself is problematic – the energy costs are high, for example, while it is only recently that water-based paints have been developed to replace inorganic, solvent-based paints. Perhaps the most interesting developments have been with respect to vehicle life and subsequent disposal. On the one hand, progress in steel technology and the use of non-ferrous products such as aluminium has allowed vehicle manufactures to set new standards in rust prevention – thus extending vehicle life. Anti-corrosion warranties are now frequently extended to six years, and the vehicle is expected to be free from structurally significant rust for ten years. The diversity of vehicle testing in Europe (from the stringent German 'TUV' to virtually non-existent testing in France) will slowly be eliminated, thus raising the importance of the 'long-life car' as a strategy. On the other hand, a number of firms, notably in Germany where the pressure for change is greatest, have announced schemes to recycle their own vehicles. At present these schemes are relatively small demonstration projects, or at the planning stage. However, BMW and others now claim their vehicles are being designed to be recycled – for example, by reducing the variety of plastics they contain, and by using parts made from recycled materials.

These three themes will recur throughout the book as important, though sometimes contradictory, forces for change in the sector. Underpinning them is a process of technological change which some have characterised as 'de-maturity' (Abernathy, 1978). Thus, for example, the development of sophisticated engine management systems has been enabled by advances in rugged electronics and sensors capable of surviving the hostile environment of the engine, but has also been prompted by legislation to improve engine emissions performance. At the same time, it has resulted in new entrants to the sector supply base, to a few firms dominating some areas of automotive electronics, and made new demands on automobile manufacturers in terms of understanding these new technologies. As Sieffert and Walzer (1984) point out, between 1969 and 1984 the number of standards relating to automobile performance and safety in the USA rose from 30 to nearly 100. Complex regulations with respect to noise, safety, fuel economy, emissions, and more recently recycling, have all served to increase the demands made on vehicle manufacturers when they design new cars – and in turn manufacturers have passed on the costs of some of those demands to their suppliers. The proliferating complexity of the car has meant that it is no longer possible for the vehicle assembler/ manufacturer to lead development in all areas, and this is a key facet of the creation of closer links with supplier firms. Seiffert and Walzer, writing in 1984, estimated that electronics had risen from 8.4 per cent of the cost of the average vehicle (1970) and projected 15.0 per cent by 1990, though they also pointed out that product innovations tend to be introduced incrementally, and that with vehicle electronics the critical problem area is usually the electronics/mechanics interface rather than the electronics itself. Thus in terms of the product and the processes used to make them, there is much that is new in the automobile industry, and some features which could be revolutionary.

The 'new' European automobile industry is being created out of the old, but also with the arrival of new firms. We are at a critical turning point in the sector, with wholesale changes being made to the organisation of the industry, methods of working, relationship to the market, and spatial structure. The shape of the 'new' industry is still emerging, but it is already clear that it will embody substantial differences from the industry that existed for much of the post-1945 period.

Moreover, the definition of Europe is growing over time as Scandinavian and former Communist Eastern European countries seek greater economic and political integration with the twelve EC countries. Consequently, much that is 'new' about the industry may be attributed to this expansion of the definition of Europe.

1.2 THE EUROPEAN AUTOMOBILE COMPONENTS INDUSTRY: A STUDY OF TWO SUPPLY CHAINS

Dicken (1988), in a short review paper, argues that industrial geography in the 1990s needs to embrace and integrate the separate traditions of enterprise geography and structuralism, while at the same time making a more powerful contribution to the realms of business and economics. We return to this theme in Chapter 2; here it is sufficient to note that we attempt to address much of the research agenda that Dicken provides in an eclectic theorisation of spatial economic change, and with an empirical study that has a clear focus on the supply chain as a whole rather than on core capitalist enterprises in isolation.

Clearly, no single text can hope to concern itself with all aspects of the automotive industry. The core of our study asks just one question:

What is the emerging spatial and economic structure of production and employment in the European automotive components sector in the light of new models of buyer–supplier relations?

Even answering this one question is itself an enormous task, but the task has been simplified in two ways. First, we are concerned only with automobile production, not with the diverse types of commercial vehicle. As we shall show later, there are clear overlaps between these two categories, especially at the level of the components industry, but they are also sufficiently different in a number of key parameters as to demand separate treatment. Second, the focus of the research is on two specific supply chains in the automobile components industry: first, that which links steel producers to the makers of pressed parts; and second, that which links friction materials producers to the makers of clutches and brakes. The focus of our attention on two specific supply chains enables us to explore the theme of changes being transmitted down (and up?) the supply chain as competition becomes more

systemic in character. To date most research has concentrated on the
vehicle assemblers themselves; we seek to redress that imbalance.
Many more research questions flow from our original point of
enquiry. Are new procurement regimes being developed by the
automotive assemblers? If so, what characterises them, how are they
different from each other and from previous procurement regimes? Is
vertical disintegration actually happening, at the level of the assemblers and that of the suppliers? How have changes in work organisation and production technology influenced procurement and the
spatial patterning of suppliers? Is a tiered structure emerging and are
new supplier practices being passed on down the supply chain?

Our starting point for analysis is theory. In Chapter 2 we address
different treatments of 'globalisation', and in particular seek to draw
out possible connections between the business/economics literature
and that of economic geography. At the same time technology is of key
significance. The automobile industry is one in which technological
change in both the product and production processes has become of
increasing significance. As we show later, technology, work organisation, and buyer–supplier relations are closely interrelated. In Chapter 3
we are concerned with the European automobile assemblers, as they
continue to be the primary stimulus for change in the components
sector. Again, the emphasis is on the components industry implications
of key changes under way, and the major concerns are issues such as
new quality measures, preferred supplier policies, and vertical disintegration strategies for each major automobile assembler.

Chapters 2, 3, and 4 give the main theoretical and empirical
dimensions of global competition in the automobile industry. Chapter
4 is both theoretical and descriptive, and seeks to provide an overview
of restructuring in the European automotive components industry.
Here we outline recent models of buyer–supplier relations, their
application with respect to the automobile components industry, and
appropriateness to specific technology areas. This review of available
evidence suggests to us that tiering and hierarchy are weakly developed
thus far in Europe, and indeed that vertical disintegration at the level of
the assemblers cannot be assumed to be the prevailing norm – witness,
for example, the increasing hold assemblers are seeking to obtain over
distribution outlets. It is clear that important changes are under way in
terms of the location of automotive components firms, with the former
East Germany and the rise of Spain and Portugal being of key interest
here. It is also clear that the industry is becoming more international in
structure, even in relatively traditional sub-sectors such as presswork.

Chapters 5, 6, 7 and 8 are the empirical core of our study. The two supply chains are considered in turn, with Chapters 5 and 6 dealing with the steel and presswork industries, and Chapters 7 and 8 the friction materials and brakes/clutches industries. Conclusions are drawn in each case as to the nature of relations between the structure of the industry, the product/process technology involved, and linkages with the assembler firms. Inevitably, these four chapters are uneven in content – indeed, this reflects one of the main points we are trying to make, that specific sub-sectors exhibit quite different characteristics. Thus, for example, the European steel pressings automobile components industry comprises at least 200 firms of significance, that for complete clutches only four firms, thus, the greater number of firms in the pressings sub-sector entails rather more research work in terms of identifying firms and products, conducting interviews and so on, and the greater complexity of the sector demands more space for description and explanation. In these empirical chapters a great diversity of material is integrated. We concentrate on the flow of materials, components, sub-assemblies and finished products through the industrial structure of the European components industry, and seek to identify the key stimuli to change in our two supply chains. It is apparent from this work that many of the key issues surrounding vertical disintegration, buyer–supplier relations, new production technology and so on are areas of considerable contention in which many firms with many (often conflicting) strategies are involved in a dynamic process of readjustment. As such, the future dimensions of the automotive industry cannot be read off a priori from an abstract model, though such a model may help us to identify the key determinants of change.

In Chapter 9 the 'introspective' world of buyer–supplier relations in specific technologies is counterbalanced by a much broader view of the automobile industry in Europe in the 1990s. The role of the state at local, national and international levels is reviewed with the emphasis on foreign direct investment (FDI) as a key mechanism of structural and spatial change in the sector. It is clear that the European Commission recognises the strategic significance of the European automotive industry (including non-indigenous firms such as Ford, GM, Nissan, etc.), while local authorities that are home to traditional concentrations of motor industry employment are increasingly concerned at the changes under way in the sector. The provisions of 1992's 'Open Europe' have been a core part of the political debate surrounding the automobile industry, while the Commission has undertaken a series of investigations into state subsidies at Rover, Toyota, Renault and Fiat.

In terms of the environmental impact of automotive production and use, no attempt at futurology is made, but the implications of these wider forces for the specific sub-sectors we have analysed will be brought out. Thus, for example, the balance of advantage in favour of using steel, aluminium or plastic for vehicle body parts is constantly changing in response to developments in the materials themselves, in production technology and in terms of market acceptance (see Wells and Rawlinson, 1994). So, while the future for any of these materials is difficult to predict, it is possible to say where the main points of contention will be.

Finally, in Chapter 10 we seek to bring together the various themes of the research and comment on the issue of how far generalised models of change can be applied in detailed sectoral analysis.

1.3 METHODOLOGY

It will be clear from the contents of this book that our research methodology has been biased away from quantitative and modelling techniques, and towards qualitative ones. That is to say, in general terms an intensive methodology has been used. In effect, we are presenting a case study of four sectors in two supply chains, bounded by time and space, from which we are seeking to elaborate more generalisable propositions about agency and outcome. Clearly, this is related to our theoretical understanding of the industry overall. None the less, we have tried to establish a framework which allows structural agents of change on the one hand, and micro-level change on the other. That is, we take a bounded view of social change in which key actors can and do influence outcomes (and not necessarily in the way that they intended), but their freedom to alter outcomes is constrained and patterned by wider structural forces over which they have no control.

It is in the nature of case study work that it seeks to develop detailed and comprehensive information on the subject in question, which generally entails a combination of empirical data and qualitative opinions from key actors obtained through interview. In the course of research for this book many firms and over a hundred individuals across Europe have been interviewed, generally using semi-structured questionnaires. Direct observation is important too, and a great many factories in both the components firms and the assemblers have been toured. In most cases, detailed profiles of firms have been developed using company reports, company product and process information brochures, financial and trade directories, site visits and interviews. In most cases senior management and directors were interviewed, not those closer to production activities – we cannot and do not therefore address issues such as the extent to which management and labour share the same understanding of work processes, strategic choices and so on. These methods allow the aggregate statistical material derived from governmental and industrial organisations to be given greater vitality and meaning. We are indebted to the industry as a whole for the openness with which we have been received; in practice only a handful of the many firms we contacted felt unable to contribute to the research. In part, this is due to careful selection of interview targets and the assiduous application of the 'right' procedures to obtain interviews, but it equally reflects an industry willing, even desperate, to learn. The legitimacy and neutrality bestowed upon us as researchers from a business school certainly helped, but without the co-operation of these firms the research would not have been possible.

Case study research also involves widespread reading to gain a 'feel' for the subject of research. In our case, we felt it was important to understand the underlying production and process technologies involved, as well as to keep up to date with ongoing changes in the industry as a whole. Thus, for example, in our research on the presswork sector we felt compelled to devote attention to press machine technology, die design and manufacture, and steel production and supply. This is particularly so because we are interested in the relations along the whole supply chain. Ultimately, a great deal of this material, derived from specialist journals, governmental publications, consultancy reports, newspapers, academic journals, books and interviews, is not used directly at all. None the less, the information obtained, together with that gathered through conversations with colleagues and other researchers, combines to provide a multifaceted understanding of the sector. The task of the researcher here is one of selection, in which pertinent information is presented to support the arguments offered.

As such, the work is inevitably biased. We have a bias towards English language publications: for example, our 'implicit' knowledge of the industry is strongest for the UK. Such biases cannot be eliminated, only acknowledged, and allowances made for them. Thus we have endeavoured to keep our perspective as 'European' as possible, and avoid insular concern with the UK alone – not least because the European components industry itself has emphatically shifted from being largely national in orientation to being international (see, for example, Carr, 1988, 1993; BCG, 1991).

Finally, on the subject of methodology, we must emphasise that case study research, and intensive research in general, is highly iterative in nature. That is, the research process cannot be considered linear, when a priori theory informs empirical research which subsequently proves or disproves generalised statements. Rather, the two areas of theory and practice (experienced empirical reality) interact over time. Theory is constantly adjusted in the face of new information, which in turn shapes the way in which we investigate and interpret the real world. This is especially true in the case here, where we are seeking to integrate the two different traditions of economic geography and business economics. In order partly to prevent a descent into hopeless relativism, we have imposed an order on this book which separates theory from empirical research – but this is not a reflection of the way the research itself was undertaken. The chronology implied in the structure of the book; with theoretical reflection followed by 'field' research followed by more theoretical reflection, is at best a gross simplification of the actual process of research.

2 Globalisation

2.1 INTRODUCTION

The literature on globalised or transnational firms derives from many traditions and has a long pedigree. The spatial extension of capitalist competition across territorial boundaries has been an historical feature of capitalist development generally. In the search for new markets, new labour and new production configurations, underpinned by the relentless drive for profits, crisis in the form of spatial restructuring appears to be the 'normal' condition for capitalism. In recent years, there is a general perception that not only has the intensity of competition increased, but also that there has been a fundamental change in the way global enterprises are structured.

In this chapter we seek to review the major theories relating to transnational corporations, and introduce some empirical material from the automotive industry to illustrate theoretical propositions. The term 'globalisation' is widely used these days but it is very imprecise. In many cases it is not clear whether globalisation is a stage of development at one end of a sequence of stages; or a process of transformation, or a mode of organisation. Neither is it clear whether globalisation refers to macroeconomic phenomenon or is really an extension of theories of the firm. Where globalisation is more overtly concerned with the firm, much of the debate is concerned with how far the globalised firm is different from the multinational, and how (and to what extent) the transition from one form to the other has been achieved. Thus we seek here to deconstruct prevalent theories on transnational corporations in order to elucidate their meaning and their limitations. First, we review aggregate evidence for the contention that global interdependence and economic integration have increased. Second, we delineate the development of the multinational firm and the key theoretical debates concerning the current structure of enterprises. We then seek to expand this discussion with general theories of spatial economic development and capitalism in historical perspective, drawing on the literature of economic geography. Subsequently, the highly influential 'lean firm' model of organisation and production is examined as this is explicitly concerned with the global automobile industry, and makes some important points regarding the

11

spatial structure of contemporary production. We conclude by indicating overlaps and discontinuities between these various approaches, paying particular attention to the parallels between regulationist (macro level) theory on the one hand, and lean firm (micro level) theory on the other. This lays the foundation for our perspective which seeks to analyse spatial economic change at the meso level, that is, looking at the diverse interrelations and linkages which create systems or constellations of firms. Thus, in our view, the stimuli to global competition are identifiable, but the form that they take cannot be predicted in advance as it depends upon the inheritance of practices, organisations, capabilities, sunk investments and so on which form a contingent environment within which each constellation of firms operates. Thus it is unlikely that any one 'globalised' paradigm firm will emerge. These themes are illustrated in Chapter 3, where we provide an empirical account of the European automobile assemblers (defined simply as vehicle assemblers in Europe regardless of their 'country of origin'), and where we argue that European firms are generally more on the 'receiving end' of globalisation.

None the less, we would not wish to say there was 'nothing new under the sun'. On the contrary, all the available evidence suggests a profound and irreversible shift in the global structure of many sectors, including the automobile industry. Even if the globalisation of firms in terms of their structure is highly variable, there can be little doubt that there has been an intensification or globalisation of competition in the automobile industry. Indeed, in terms of the stages of spatial extension, sales and marketing usually precede manufacturing investment, that is, the globalisation of competition and markets precedes and overlaps with the globalisation of production.

With the dissolution of the former Comecon Eastern Europe, there are now few locations in the world that are immune to global competition, and many are now being further integrated into wider production networks. In this context, globalisation is a process by which the internal and external organisational structures of the firm are reshaped, and ultimately reside in redefining the role, content and location of labour, but the causes of those changes reside more fundamentally in the capitalist economic system as a whole, the social relations of production, and the particular embodiment of characteristics which defines the firm. This reshaping appears to involve both an extension over space and a deepening of spatial interdependencies and integration, that is, the combination of both network and hierarchy.

2.2 AGGREGATE MEASURES OF GLOBALISATION

At the aggregate level, increased globalisation in its mercantalist form is measured by greater trade flows between countries. In terms of the spatial extension of production, globalisation is indicated by foreign direct investment (FDI) flows. While, historically, the USA has dominated such flows (Chandler, 1986), from the 1980s Japanese investment has come more to the fore, notably in key sectors such as finance (Thrift and Layshon, 1988), electronics, and automobiles (Dicken, 1988). While investment may substitute for trade, as is partially the case with Japanese automotive FDI into the USA, in general major trading links are also major FDI links – in the aggregate it would appear that trade and FDI growth are mutually supportive. While much of the literature on multinational firms has been concentrated on the role of such firms in the economies of developing countries, and the use of such locations as low cost re-export bases to advanced industrial nations (Grunwald and Flamm, 1985), these concerns have shifted more recently in the light of evidence which suggests that the majority of FDI from advanced industrial nations goes to other advanced industrial nations, leading to the notion of the 'triad' global economy of Europe, North America and Japan/Pacific Rim (Grey and McDermott, 1987; Hamill, 1988; Ohmae, 1985). Economic interpenetration, although unevenly developed, occurs chiefly between the 'triad' regions, though clearly Japan has a significant trade surplus with both the USA and Europe, while the extent of European and US penetration into Japanese markets and productive capital is still, by comparison, slight. In this process the dominance of the USA in terms of its share of world production, consumption and trade has declined, while that of Japan has steadily increased. This picture is especially true for automobiles, as we shall show in Chapter 3.

Japan was the driving force for international investment in the 1980s: the cumulative stock of Japanese FDI rose sevenfold in this period (Thomsen and Nicolaides, 1991), though other advanced industrial countries also showed significant increases. By the end of the 1980s Japanese FDI was about $50bn annually, amounting to 7 per cent of all Japanese private capital formation (Corker, 1991). An inevitable result of this is that FDI flows have become more significant for recipient nations. The UK, for example, a long-preferred investment location for Japanese and US capital, depended on FDI flows into the country for 25 per cent of all domestic capital formation in

1992 (Coopers and Lybrand Deloitte, 1991). The flow of FDI into the
UK by automobile manufacturers also has a long history, with Ford of
the USA establishing its first assembly plant in Trafford Park in 1911.
The Ford Dagenham plant, established in 1931, was built as a fully
integrated operation intended to mirror the Ford complex at River
Rouge in the USA, although in practice its productivity performance
has always been below that of the US plants (Womak *et al.*, 1990).
However, the recent surge of Japanese automobile manufacturing
investment into Europe has also featured the UK (Wells and
Rawlinson, 1993b), and is an important facet of the spatial restructuring process, which we shall review in the following chapter.

2.3 HIERARCHIES, MARKETS, AND INTERMEDIATE FORMS OF CORPORATE ORGANISATION

Chandler (1966, 1977) shows that the large multinational company is a
comparatively recent phenomenon, emerging in the later nineteenth
and early twentieth centuries, based on the cost advantages of constant
materials flow ensuring high capital utilisation. Industries which
tended to grow large and multinational were those where the
production technologies involved allowed high flow characteristics
from suppliers, through the factory, and on to distribution and sales,
which in turn demanded an administrative management cadre
organised in hierarchies to control the process overall. This gave rise
to the multi-unit, multi-functional firm in which functional processes
such as marketing, research, purchasing and so on were often
administratively and physically separate. Internal integration, or
control, was seen as being preferable to the purchase of the desired
inputs on the market. Typically, these firms grew first by integrating
forward into distribution and marketing and, second, by integrating
backwards into materials and components supply. The visible hand
was preferable to the Smithsian invisible hand. An important element
was the ability to serve local markets through local production, that is,
the production process could be divided functionally and spatially. As
Chandler (1986) argues, this model applied mainly to a few key
sectors, notably food, chemicals, petroleum, metals, machinery and
transportation equipment, and historically has been dominated by US
firms – in 1973, of the world's top 401 firms employing more than
20 000 people, 52.6 per cent were from the USA.

Chandlers' explanation draws heavily on the character of production technology and organisation. In brief, the benefits of integration and scale come only with the high capacity utilisation of a specific mix of technologies, but once achieved, significant unit price reductions (or higher profits) are possible and smaller competitors are squeezed out. However, the approach taken by Chandler essentially offers two alternatives: integration and control of the production process (including distribution and marketing), or resort to the market for materials and components supply. While this account does seem to capture the early phase of increasing vertical integration in the automobile industry (see Williams *et al.* (1991a) for a discussion of the early history of Ford), the bipolar reasoning and narrow neo-classical conception of the 'rational' firm fails to explain the diversity of real life corporate relations.

The transactions costs approach (Coase, 1937; Williamson, 1975, 1985; Teece, 1986) sought to modify the assumptions of neo-classical theory by allowing power relations and firm-specific competitive advantage to be introduced into a behaviouralist analysis. The transactions cost approach thus offered a third and more realistic alternative to absolute vertical integration or complete free market exchanges between equal parties (i.e. a mode of organisation between markets and hierarchies), and has been widely employed in the analysis of various forms of strategic alliance (Beamish and Banks, 1987.) and in terms of suppliers to primary firms (Blois, 1972.) In this analysis, firms are seeking to gain the advantages of vertical integration without the costs and risks of rigidity and ownership of assets through a form of 'vertical quasi-integration'. Typical costs of vertical integration would include disparities between productive capacities at various stages of the production process; lack of specialisation; inflexibility; an over-developed managerial and administrative cadre; and a lack of competitive pressure on captive suppliers of intermediate products (after Blois, 1972). However, as Blois argues, in reality there is not a limitless base of supplier firms (the market) which large firms may exploit at will. That is, the supply of products to a firm is not a simple market transaction. In this case, supplier firms are effectively integrated with the primary firm because of dependency (for a high proportion of sales), but the primary firm is also (to a varying degree) committed to its suppliers, who may have transaction-specific skills and competencies.

In general, the transactions costs approach can be seen as a modification of previous neo-classical economic treatments which attempts to explain inter- and intrafirm arrangements in conditions that do not allow perfect, free market explanations.

2.4 THE MULTINATIONAL AND THE INTERNATIONAL DIVISION OF LABOUR

In the previous section, the question of vertical integration was considered without any spatial content. Chandler (1986) takes the view that the multinational spread of large corporations derived first from these tendencies towards greater degrees of vertical integration. Put simply, the integrated corporation could mobilise the economies of scale established in its domestic market to enter non-domestic markets – at first with sales and later with investments in productive capacity.

Vernon (1966) sought to relate the international migration of capital to the stage of development of the product: as the product became more mature and the process technology more established, so production was transferred to low cost (principally low *labour* cost) locations outside core advanced industrial economies. The critical contribution of Vernon was to draw attention to the central place occupied by innovations and technology in the continued spatial expansion of multinational enterprise. This process coincided with a desire on behalf of developing countries to establish import substitution and export earning production as part of an overall growth strategy. This explanation of change showed clear sympathy with the empirical evidence then available, especially in key sectors such as semiconductors (Grunwald and Flamm, 1985; Henderson, 1989), leading to some analysts taking the view that a 'new international division of labour' was emerging (Froebel *et al.*, 1980) in which the developed 'North' systematically underdeveloped the South. Clearly, the development of such structures depends upon comparative labour costs and the importance of labour costs in the total share of added value. It is also more readily appropriate to those sectors where the product embodies a high value to transport cost ratio. Concurrently, a body of research was developed to testify to the increasing power and influence of large multinational firms compared with emergent nation states. More recent empirical research from a behaviouralist perspective has emphasised that this sequential, product-based, growth process occurs only to a limited extent, and that the life-cycle of the firm may be a better guide to internationalisation (Millington and Bayliss, 1990) because firms become more international as they gain and internalise experience in non-domestic operations (Johanson and Vahlne, 1977).

The transactions costs approach has also been used to provide explanations of spatial patterning in industrial development. Intermediate forms of organisation can be a requirement of market access and are often used to obtain cheaper production inputs (materials, components or labour) and to increase economies of scale (Auster, 1987; Harrigan, 1987).

In the automotive industry the spatial dimensions of quasi-vertical integration strategies in primary firms are observable in two main forms. First, there are international alliances, ranging from licence arrangements to equity joint ventures, for the production of automobiles. Historically this form of organisation has been a requirement of the governments of some countries – notably in Eastern Europe and parts of the Third World – and is a feature that is not confined to the automotive sector (Wells and Cooke, 1991). That is, large Western and Japanese firms have been disbarred from outright ownership of assets in some locations, and market access has been conditional on local production presence. Typically, this has resulted in outdated or 'previous generation' technology being utilised (for the case of Eastern Europe see, for example, EIU (1989a) either licensed or in some form of co-production. Second, quasi-vertical integration is increasingly prevalent between large assemblers and their suppliers, and is a prominent part of the Japanese *'Keiretsu'* structure of production (discussed more fully below in the context of the 'lean firm', and in Chapter 4), which has been associated with spatial clustering, as in the 'Toyota City' model.

2.5 COSTS AND MARKETS: THE DEATH OF THE MULTINATIONAL?

These approaches are similar in that they all take cost factors as the starting point for analysis of changes in the spatial organisation of production. While not denying the continuing and historical importance of costs in stimulating and directing spatial reorganisation, there is evidence that in some sectors at least (for example, military electronics and related products) the need for market proximity and the demands of co-ordination have prompted both the globalisation decision itself and the form that it takes. Equally, the role of technology appears to have changed. In high technology industries continuous product and process innovation have become the norm, and the importance of product price competition reduced. With curtailed product life-cycles there is insufficient time for the technology to mature and be spread in the manner which Vernon (1966) suggests. In particular, the integration of previously separate technologies has itself created enormous co-ordination difficulties for firms. In one sense, the cost element remains: for some products the cost of developing a new model or version is so high that it must be amortised on a world basis – telecommunications switches are a classic example. Moreover, as de Woot (1990) argues, in industries characterised by rapid technological change there is great pressure to introduce innovations into all major markets simultaneously. This is not to place technology as the overriding force for industrial and spatial restructuring, as Sayer and Morgan (1987) note, technological innovation does not constitute a necessary or sufficient basis for corporate success. Rather, it is the embodiment of technology into capital investment, that is, the accumulation of capital, which underpins structural change.

The automotive industry is not one that is usually characterised as being 'high technology'. Yet in many respects it is undergoing a process of de-maturity (Abernathy, 1978) under the impact of new technologies available from other sectors which have either transformed or replaced prevailing technologies. The pace of technological change appears to have increased in a number of component areas (for example brakes, engine management systems and materials) as electronics, servo-mechanisms, and new materials are introduced. This is immediately apparent when the product offerings of Eastern European firms such as Lada are seen on Western markets. Their very low price reflects not only low costs (and probably 'dumping' prices), but also their inability to compete with the specifications and quality of contemporary Western firms' products.

At the same time, there was concern that a process of de-industrialisation was under way in the advanced Western economies in which production (or more particularly, manufacture) was being replaced by service or tertiary economic activities, or, of course, by unemployment (Massey and Meagan, 1982). The traditional hierarchic multinational with its isolated branch plants was seen by some as a key cause of local economic decline (Hood and Young, 1982). In essence, the 'hollow corporation' can be seen as the logical end stage of multinational spread predicted upon low labour costs, as outlined above. In the hollow corporation, the firm itself does not undertake any production or assembly, but buys in all products. It is a marketing organisation. The argument goes one stage further in that US firms were being acquired and then 'hollowed' by overseas (principally Japanese) firms which retained key research and production activities in their domestic locations, but used the brand names and distribution channels of the acquired US firms to extend their share of that market.

In terms of organisational structure, it is claimed that hierarchy and vertical organisation based around functional stages of production are being replaced by flatter, more flexible management structures organised around market focus. Information technology has been a key enabling device (Child, 1987). Indeed, much of the analysis of globalisation from a business perspective emphasises the part played by more volatile, quality-sensitive markets (Boynton and Victor, 1991). At the same time, leading 'excellent' firms were said to be developing core competency strategies (Peters and Waterman, 1982) through change-of-ownership policies designed to divest firms of diversification portfolios and of integrated (owned) suppliers.

Business literature has been much preoccupied with the relationship between organisational form and competition. While some of the early contributions to the debate claimed a borderless world in which organisation, aided by appropriate technology, effectively destroyed space and the uniqueness of place (Levitt, 1983; Perlmutter and Heenan, 1986; Ohmae, 1990) – thus leading to the 'stateless' corporation – more recently a number of developments have sought to place the modern transnational as a hybrid form, somewhere between the idealised forms of the multinational and the globalised firm.

Some have identified industries and sectors where globalisation strategies have failed (Baden-Fuller and Stopford, 1991); others have asked more precisely what constitutes a global firm, and how it is measured (Hu, 1992). There is, consequently, a perception that not only does capital face difficult choices over the nature of organisational form in which global structures are just one option (Morrison *et al.*, 1991), but also even in hyper-flexible organisations new boundaries appear (Hirshhorn and Gilmore, 1992).

2.6   CORPORATE STRUCTURE AND STRATEGY

As noted above, Vernon was one of the first to draw attention to the role of technology in enabling and sustaining the growth of multinational enterprises. In essence, multinationals grow because they can appropriate and control technologies. By technologies we would here include both 'hard' technologies, such as specific products and processes, and 'soft' technologies, such as organisation practices. This is a critical point because it suggests that large multinational firms have grown because of their ability to internalise and disseminate innovations, including social innovations such as novel working methods on the shopfloor, or more efficient forms of management structure. However, under the Vernon model, innovations emanate from the centre, from the country of origin of the firm, and are spread down the corporate hierarchy to other locations. The strategy implications are simple: the multinational generates innovations at the centre and deploys them elsewhere to out-perform indigenous competitors.

The culmination of this mass production spatial strategy, at least in terms of the automotive industry, was the Ford 'World Car' strategy. In essence the strategy was very simple. The product development costs of a single model could be amortised over a greater production run if the car was designed to sell in all markets and produced 'locally'. In reality, the co-ordination effort required was too great for Ford, and the US and European versions ended up being almost entirely different despite superficial similarities, and the development time was far too long (Bloomfield, 1981, 1991). This concept has not been entirely abandoned: the Sierra replacement (the Mondeo) is conceived of as a world car, as is the GM Cavalier/Vectra. Moreover, as noted below, the Japanese have successfully employed a world car strategy from one production base for some time.

Porter (1980, 1985, 1986) sought to be more explicit about the competitive power of multinationals and the relationship between structure and competition. That is, while much of the above literature is concerned with the costs and benefits of market versus internalisation, the Porter analysis is concerned with the costs and benefits of internalisation in the process of competition between firms. While we might criticise this approach for assuming that corporate failure might simply be attributed to inadequate strategy, and for being insensitive to the broader corporate environment, the Porter analysis does highlight relative competitive advantage *vis-à-vis* competitors, in a manner similar to the Dunning (1988) concept of firm-specific advantage. This raises a difficult problem: how can core competency strategies (i.e. firm-specific advantage) be reconciled with the need for flexibility in more dynamic and volatile markets? In the real world of the automobile industry this problem is often met by hybrid strategies such as 'global niche' products, that is, by producing cars which sell in relatively low volumes across many markets (Mazda in particular has followed this course) from a small number of production locations. This enables some economies of scale to be realised while accommodating market fragmentation.

Equally, it is clear that the success of Japanese firms in penetrating overseas markets derives from the traditional route of exploiting domestic advantages to export into other markets – thus attacking established firms such as General Motors on their own ground. However, the Porter model does not allow an explanation of why some Japanese firms internationalised production ahead of others, or the form which that internationalisation has taken. Toyota were, until recently, able to serve world markets from one large (multi-plant) production base (Hill, 1989). That is, the globalisation of markets does not necessarily entail the globalisation of production, the single-location 'global factory' could serve just as well. The reasons why the firm had to undertake international investment in production facilities lie both within the domestic situation and in the political and economic consequences of their success in overseas markets, not simply with their competitive status *vis-à-vis* other firms in the industry. In other words, explanations of corporate structure and strategy have to move beyond considerations of the market, or of competitors, to the broader environment within which firms exist.

2.7 THE FIRM AND ITS ENVIRONMENT

A number of authors have sought to link internal corporate structure with external conditions. Dicken (1988) argues that internationalisation decisions will be shaped by both internal and external factors. 'Internal factors' are those pertaining to the domestic national environment, and 'external' to international conditions. In the case of the automotive industry, the international spread of Japanese production investment is a useful illustrative example.

In terms of the internal causes of internationalisation, evidence is now emerging that the very development of the distinctive Japanese production system itself contains key contradictions. The famous 'just-in-time' delivery system, for example, which requires many small loads of parts to be delivered frequently to assembly factories, generates external diseconomies in the form of increased congestion, with associated increases in other costs such as those incurred by drivers, fuel, etc., as well as broader social costs such as pollution. Moreover, as the Japanese economy prospered, so labour became scarcer, and more expensive. Table 2.1 illustrates average comparable wage costs in various countries, and shows clearly that Japanese wages have risen relative to others.

Changing external conditions at the international level also matter. The continuing (and even expanding) Japanese trade surplus has helped to generate protectionist sentiment in the EC and the USA. Notwithstanding the internal environmental contradictions noted above, Japanese cars were still competitive on landed cost with those produced by domestic firms in the USA and Europe in the early 1990s, yet Japanese automobile firms have pursued a vigorous policy of FDI. The need to be within protectionist barriers has clearly been a critical factor. Similarly, the rapidly rising relative value of the yen during the mid-1980s increased the pressure on Japanese firms. The desire to escape the vagaries of international currency fluctuations, and even to use such changes to advantage, creates a strong structural pressure to internationalise production facilities. At the same time, the destination of FDI at different spatial scales is also subject to these very broad 'environmental' conditions. In the case of UK, its prominent position as a major recipient of FDI can be attributed to several causes, of which the political support of successive Conservative governments over recent years, both through actual aid and through aggressive legislation curtailing the powers of trades unions, must count highly.

Table 2.1   Comparative total labour costs, selected countries, 1980, 1985 and 1990 (DM per hour)

Country	1980	1985	1990
Germany	26.92	33.95	41.87
Belgium	28.14	30.94	31.83
France	19.96	23.80	24.37
UK	14.95	22.54	23.95
Italy	17.15	27.86	30.84
The Netherlands	23.33	29.98	30.57
Sweden	28.60	36.97	40.45
Spain	12.63	22.88	27.78
USA	24.83	34.36	36.62
Japan	14.83	32.36	33.32

Source: VDA, 1990, p. 27.

That is, inward investment, especially where it carries novel ways of doing things, has an important ideological content (Garraghan and Stewart, 1991).

All of the above has led a number of analysts to conclude that the business strategy and structure literature needs to develop a clearer understanding of the way in which the environment structures and conditions the firm. That is, there is a failure in the literature to look into the realms of geography, sociology, psychology, economics and politics. We therefore discuss below some of the key features of the debate within economic geography which have parallelled and over-lapped with the debates within business structure and organisation.

2.8 FORDISM, POST-FORDISM, FLEXIBILITY AND SPATIAL DEVELOPMENT

The flexibility debate has been dominated by two major concerns. First, that about flexibility *within* firms, and second about flexibility *between* firms (Starkey *et al.*, 1991). Here we are mainly concerned with the latter form of flexibility. It is an issue we shall pursue further in Chapter 4, because external (between firms) flexibility clearly has a great bearing on the nature of relationships between components suppliers and their customers. This is not to deny the connections between internal and external flexibility, the point here is to review briefly the main points of the debate on flexibility and post-Fordism. In general, our view is that totalising concepts such as post-Fordism, while helpful in organising our understanding of major processes under way in contemporary society, are none the less premised on stereotypes and assume a bipolar or dualist form of reasoning which may obscure important transitionary or intermediate processes and forms of organisation. As several authors have recently noted, there are clear empirical difficulties in equating the recent past with a 'Fordist' mode of production (Williams *et al.*, 1991a; Lovering, 1990). Lewchuk (1987) demonstrates that the adoption of mass production in the UK motor industry was never comprehensive, and was certainly different in a number of respects from the US version of mass production (notably in terms of workers having a greater control over the production process in the case of the UK). The perspectives outlined below all share the 'stereotypical' view of Fordism, and all share the view that new productive strategies have been developed, aimed at serving a wider range of diverse markets fragmented in time and space (Kelly, 1983; Marginson *et al.*, 1988). As Sayer (1989) notes, in only a few sectors do the twin conditions of high volume and high variety output occur. In the case of the automotive industry it is easy to lose sight of the importance of high volumes of production.

2.8.1 Flexible specialisation

The Piore and Sabel (1984) analysis was based on the idea that the multinational and its power was on the wane; that small, flexible, high technology firms in spatially clustered complexes were better adapted to the more turbulent economic conditions of the 1990s, in which market competition was based on technological rather than price advantage (thus undermining economies of scale), and on rapidity of response (thus undermining the hierarchy organisation). That is, dynamic external environments (especially markets) were seen as being the primary cause of flexible specialisation, while new technologies were seen as providing the key enabling devices. This treatment is mainly concerned with flexibility between firms rather than the flexible firm model (Atkinson and Gregory, 1986) which is about internal (and especially labour) flexibility.

Piore and Sabel envisaged a 'second industrial divide' based on the re-emergence of craft-based, small and medium-sized enterprises in a process of industrial deconcentration, giving rise to new, cohesive, regional economies of mutually interrelated firms. New technologies combined with skilled artisan workers, and a network structure of firms were seen as providing a new model of economic growth. Critics have pointed to the political and ideological implications of placing industrial renaissance in the hands of entrepreneurial small firms (Pollert, 1988) while ignoring the intensely exploitative conditions that prevail in many small firms which remain outside the primary sector (Gerry, 1985; Rainnie, 1988). Even for Italy, the role model for the second industrial divide, Murray (1987) argues that there is little evidence of sophisticated technological and skill-based flexibility. Indeed, there is little conclusive evidence that large, primary firms are losing their dominance of the economy and their control over smaller enterprises. Even if markets are fragmenting and becoming more 'niched' (and even here the evidence is weak), there is little to show that large, mass-production firms have declined as a result. Indeed, in terms of the automotive industry, as we shall discuss in Chapter 3, it is notable that, first, small firms producing cars and commercial vehicles have steadily disappeared, either into insolvency or into large corporations; and second, that those large firms are themselves increasingly capable of meeting product diversification. The basic economics of production in the automotive industry have not changed enough to allow an automotive flexible specialised district to emerge. Imrie and Morris (1992) thus argue that large firms still dominate the economy, but that 'flexible response' is being developed in the context of volume production.

2.8.2 Flexible accumulation

The flexible accumulation approach developed by Scott (1988) sought to link industrial and spatial restructuring and, like Piore and Sabel (1984), envisaged the emergence of new 'Marshallian' districts premised on the replacement of the prevailing regime of Fordist accumulation which had been hegemonic at least since 1945. In this account Scott seeks to link the nature of the product (mass-produced commodity items); the nature of the production process and technology (assembly lines and dedicated equipment); and the nature of the labour process (Taylorised work definitions, job demarcation and formalised labour-management relations). This account also seeks to link with macroeconomic accounts of social control and change. The core of this approach is to link vertical disintegration into an 'extended division of labour' with forces for agglomeration and spatial proximity, based upon a spatial version of transactions costs analysis. As Lovering (1990) argues, this market driven analysis takes as its basis the assumption that in uncertain market conditions firms will adopt a strategy of vertical disintegration, and that firms are in a clear position to assess (as rational economic actors) the costs and benefits involved in disintegration strategies. It also assumes that the world outside the firm is effectively of no empirical significance.

Clearly, this account has some relevance for certain industries in certain places. In Scott's (1988) account of the development of Orange County, California it is shown that while at first a few large firms internalised many aspects of production in aerospace and electronics, as the size of the market expanded so the potential for disintegration arose. However, Scott provides no theoretical basis for extending the experience of that place and time to a generalised theory of flexible accumulation because it ignores the social and political context which forms a contingent environment within which real world firms exist. In the Orange County case, it ignores the vast sums diverted to military products by the US state as part of its broader strategy of becoming the 'global policeman'. Thus, as a model, it is denuded of specific historical realism.

Indeed, despite the widespread search for such dynamic, disintegrated, flexible accumulation districts there is little convincing evidence beyond a few key cases. That is, flexible accumulation, in so far as it exists, may be an exception rather than the rule. This caution is reinforced by a number of other observers who have questioned both the theoretical cogency and empirical accuracy of the Scott model (see, for example, Sayer, 1989; Morgan and Sayer, 1989; Amin and Robins, 1989). Certainly the model appears to have little direct relevance to the automotive industry. In the Toyota City case – perhaps the most well-known and well documented example of a spatially clustered and vertically disintegrated production complex in the automotive industry – the development dynamic was rather different. For example, Toyota City cannot be explained without reference to the use and control of labour by Toyota. First, and critically, organised and militant labour was defeated in a protracted confrontation in the late 1950s. Subsequently, a company union was formed and core workers were given lifetime contracts. The ability of Toyota to offer such contracts was dependent upon two features: constantly expanding output and productivity; and the ability to employ workers outside mainstream production – for example, in the supply base – as their jobs were removed in the assembly process. Since the 1950s, therefore, there has always been a strong pressure towards vertical disintegration in order to ensure that core workers were kept to a minimum. It is also apparent that Japanese firms, especially Toyota, faced capital shortages and were reluctant to invest in equipment (Cusumano, 1985; Williams *et al.*, 1991b), and thus did not go through the process of vertical integration which characterised many Western firms. Ironically, the USA was largely responsible for this state of affairs. It was US post-war legislation that sought to break up the *zaibatsu* industrial conglomerate structure which had dominated in Japan, and which gave rise to the *keiretsu* structure that replaced it.

2.8.3 Post-Fordism and the regulation school

In the 1980s a body of work developed which, arguing from a macroeconomic perspective, contended that capitalist development could be periodised in the long run (Mandel, 1979; Aglietta, 1979, 1982; Lipietz, 1984). In part, this body of work arose in response to the perceived weaknesses of behaviouralist 'geography of enterprise' approaches (de Smidt and Wever, 1990) which critics saw as ignoring the structural conditions (and especially capital–labour relations) that shaped spatial change (Walker, 1989). In regulation theory two key concepts have been developed: the regime of accumulation; and the mode of regulation. The regime of accumulation operates at the micro level and is concerned with the social relations of production, while the mode of regulation operates at the macro level and is concerned with the structure of consumption. Over long periods of time the regime of accumulation and the mode of regulation act together to support the process of capitalist development. That is to say, there is, at a broad level, synchrony between corporate organisation, technology, working practices, the role of organised labour and the nature of state intervention, all of which combine to provide the conditions for continued capital accumulation. It should be stressed that these are social relationships built around the structure of daily practice acting to recreate the conditions for successful accumulation. A key insight from this perspective is that, over the 1980s, the hegemony of the prevailing regime of accumulation gave way to a rather different set of relationships – that is, there was an ongoing transition from Fordism to post-Fordism.

The development of Fordism was predicted as a result of the major productivity gains which accrued upon the adoption of mass production methods. Thus at the level of the social conditions of production, the establishment of Fordism was generally held to contain a number of key features, most notably: flow line assembly of standardised, mass-produced products; a highly detailed and deskilled technical division of labour with very short work cycles; a hierarchic and bureaucratic production organisation with many layers of intermediate workers (i.e. supervisors, materials handling, quality inspection, work chasing and so on); an equally hierarchic, divisional, corporate structure of professional managers; and a concept of competition which was essentially based on stand-alone, individual firms. It is arguable that the Fordist stereotype was never fully established, especially outside the USA (see, for instance, Servan-Schrieber, 1968). Linking the regime of accumulation to the mode of regulation is the process of wage bargaining, because mass production must be accompanied by mass consumption. Ford's labour rate of $5 per day showed that, at the level of the firm, large real increases in wages could be offered because of the yields of higher productivity, and Ford thus acted as a benchmark around which other firms established their wages. As the Fordist regime developed, notably after the 1939–45 war, so the links between mass production and mass consumption became more universal and entrenched in state policy based on Keynsian demand management, and in corporatist political frameworks which allowed both organised labour and organised capital to shape policy provision.

In this analysis, the Fordist regime of accumulation was unable to sustain itself in the long run (see for example, Clarke, 1989), and various structural crises such as the dual emergence of high inflation rates and high unemployment were seen as being pivotal to the creation of new socioeconomic modes of governance. The post-Fordist project is to identify the emerging nature of the regime of accumulation that is supplanting Fordism (see, for instance, Cooke *et al.*, 1992). However, the theoretical approaches thus far offer little in terms of understanding the firm as an organisation beyond the issue of labour–capital relations. Some progress has been made with the concept of 'dynamic flexibility' (Klien, 1986) which seeks to enlarge the idea of flexibility from that of a narrow concern with short-term production variety. It is in this context that we turn to a highly influential account of the modern (post-Fordist) firm which also derives its inspiration from a study of the automotive industry.

2.9   THE LEAN FIRM

It is already apparent that globalisation represents an all-embracing term for a series of interrelated changes in corporate – labour relations, organisation, markets, and product across space. The insights from regulation theory suggest that many of these forces are beyond the power of individual organisations to influence or to withstand. However, it would be determinist to suggest that firms had no power to shape their own destiny.

A key dimension here is the 'lean firm' model. As promulgated by the authors, the lean firm model is an idealisation built around observations of actual practice (Womak *et al.*, 1990). It has come to capture, and be synonymous with, the idea of Japanese methods of organisation and working practices – although, in fact, the authors are careful not to equate 'Japanese' with 'lean'. The model has become highly influential, and its influences will occur frequently in the chapters on the components sector which follow. Indeed, the alacrity with which the model has been embraced by management in the industry is a key pointer to the political and ideological content of the work, as has been the character of some of the critiques of the model (Williams *et al.*, 1991a). It is therefore important to provide a summary of this work, how it was derived, its weaknesses, and its implications for the future.

In a summary paper, Jones (1990), one of the leading figures in the research programme which led to the lean production model being popularised, makes some strong claims for the productive superiority of the lean model, as Table 2.2 illustrates. These claims are broadly supported by related research, especially that on the links between product design and production engineering (Clark and Fujimoto, 1990). More importantly, Womak *et al.* (1990) argue that the lean production model, based in essence on the Toyota Production System (TPS), has been shown to be capable of relocation to the very different social milieu of the West.

Womak *et al.* consider that the lean firm is different in all aspects of its operation, but focus most clearly on R&D, production (final assembly), the supply infrastructure, and distribution to illustrate the key differences between archetypal mass production (more or less represented in Western firms) and lean production (most obviously shown by Toyota, and to a varying degree by other Japanese assemblers). Table 2.2 illustrates some of these key differences in performance. While it is possible to criticise the model on methodological grounds, and Womak *et al.* for their selective use of the data

Table 2.2   Comparative performance, automobile assemblers in Japan, America and Europe

	Japan	*North America*	*Europe*
Assembly hours/car	17	25	36
Defects/100 cars	60	82	97
Design lead time (months)	46	60	58
Engineering hrs/car (million)	1.7	3.1	3.0
Assembler stocks (days)	0.2	2.9	2.0
Supplier stocks (days)	1.5	8.1	16.3
Supplier/assembler	340	1500	1500

Source: Jones, 1990.

gathered in the International Motor Vehicle Programme (as do Williams *et al.*, 1991a), there can be little doubt that there were substantial performance differences in general between the Western automobile assemblers and those from Japan. More significantly, the International Motor Vehicle Programme survey revealed that (some) of the Japanese transplants in the USA were performing comparably with plants in Japan, and that Ford had in some instances improved its performance to match that of Japanese transplants. That is, they argue that the lean production model is capable of diffusion across organisational and national boundaries. In this, Womak *et al.* have some support from Florida and Kenny (1991) who argue that Japanese production practices and organisational forms have been uncoupled from Japanese culture and successfully transplanted to the USA.

One key weakness of the analysis by Womak *et al.* (1990) relates to the neglect of the shop-floor dimensions of lean production and the question of management control over the workforce, a critical issue for the application of lean production in Europe. Toyota management broke independent trade union existence in its plants in a prolonged strike during the 1950s, and this was crucial to their ability to pursue lean production around worker flexibility, intensification and lifetime employment. As Lewchuk (1987) shows, the primary concern for management in the UK motor industry throughout most of the post-1945 period has been control over the workforce in the context of a prolonged history of confrontation. This history is itself a barrier to further change in industrial relations at Ford (Starkey and McKinlay, 1989; Scherrer, 1991). Indeed, Lewchuk (1987) shows that the model of Fordism did not become fully established in the UK precisely because of its lack of 'fit' with the broader system of labour–capital relations. In part, the build-up of high inventory or 'just in case' production in many Western firms was a strategic decision designed to enable production to continue in the face of widespread unofficial industrial action at various points in the production system (see also Rhys, 1974). Some USA studies have been critical of the Japanese transplants in the USA, notably with respect to labour practices regarding recruitment and work intensity (Rehder, 1989; 1990; Newman, 1990).

While it is widely accepted that 'Japanisation' in some form is occurring (Oliver and Wilkenson, 1988), there is rather less agreement on its form and its implications for workers. For some, the Toyota Production System (TPS) and the lean production model represent not so much a departure from Fordism as a refinement of approach resulting in ever-increasing intensity of work and the appropriation by management of worker/shop floor innovations. Indeed, an examination of the writings of those involved in production engineering at Toyota when the firm was developing the TPS shows just how concerned the management were with eliminating any idle time for workers (Shingo, 1985; Shinohara, 1988). The approach was Taylorist in that it sought detailed analysis of each element of the production process via time and motion studies (we discuss the methodology further in Chapter 6). However, there were also important differences from Fordist practice: workers were integrated into a system of eliciting, codifying and establishing continuous improvement in the production process; and the whole production process operated on a low inventory which was vulnerable to industrial action – action which did not materialise because of the rather different place of trade unions in the Japanese economy in general and in Toyota in particular. None the less, some leading industry figures have raised the question of whether lean production exists at all (Wickins, 1993).

It could equally be argued that the lean production model ignores socio-spatial differentiation. Womak *et al.* (1990) consider that lean production is able to spread anywhere, given the commitment to make it work (despite their own historical discussion on the diffusion of Fordism which showed how only partial and distorted versions of Fordism became established outside the USA) (see also Servan-Schrieber, 1968). Womak *et al.* are thus dismissive of the experiments undertaken by Volvo in Sweden towards alternative forms of work organisation, the authors taking the view that the Volvo approach represents a retrograde step to craftworking. The key point about the Volvo experiments is that they made sense in their context, as we show below.

Several studies have drawn attention to the rather different approach to automobile assembly taken by Volvo in Sweden. At the outset it should be noted that the Volvo approach has been a limited experiment and in no way constitutes an entire production and marketing philosophy in the way that lean production does. None the less, as with TPS, the Volvo approach is firmly rooted in the prevailing social and political context of production. Experiments with alternatives to the paced assembly line were started in the early 1970s as a response to growing resistance from workers. Sweden could not import sufficient 'guestworkers' as many European firms did (although about 3000 Finns and Yugoslavs were to be found among the 8000 workers at Torslanda), to do the jobs that their domestic workers would not. With comparatively high levels of employment in the economy as a whole and a strong social welfare system, the Swedish vehicle assembler had to find appropriate ways to recruit and, more importantly, to retain workers (Berggren, 1989; Rehder, 1992). Typically, in the 1970s, Volvo faced absenteeism rates of 17 per cent and labour turnover rates of 30 per cent. For some, this response from Volvo (and indeed Saab) is a 'sociotechnical' corporate strategy (Bernstein, 1988). In the Kalmar plant, from 1974 onwards, Volvo developed a team assembly approach in which the production process was subdivided into twenty functional areas, each area having a team of fifteen or so people. Cycle times (the time taken by workers to do the tasks assigned) were increased from a typical 'Fordist' figure of about 1 minute to around 45 minutes. Experiments were also undertaken at other Volvo plants throughout Sweden, though the highest volume plants also had the most traditional work organisation (Hammarstrom and Lansbury, 1991). In 1992, these experiments were brought to an abrupt halt with the announced closure of both Kalmar and Udevella, with many observers regretting their demise (Sandberg, 1993; Cressey, 1993).

2.10   CONCLUSIONS

At a corporate level, the changes from hierarchal multinational to networked global firm are clear enough in theory, but in practice a great diversity exists in structure and organisational form. However, in so far as globalisation proceeds, it becomes ever more difficult to talk about a 'British' or 'French' or 'Japanese' firm. Corporate boundaries are blurred by alliances and other relationships, and the functional aspects of the firm need no longer be defined within a spatial boundary so that production, purchasing, development, marketing, finance and so on may all be increasingly conducted across national boundaries rather than within them. In this context, the development of supranational economic units such as the EC and the North America Trading Agreement clearly contribute to and are stimulated by spatial economic integration (Rugman and Verbeke, 1990).

   If we return to the Porter (1986) analysis, we can see that globalisation is at least partly about the mechanisms by which firms internalise location-specific advantages and thereby make them mobile over space. This is clear in the case of Japanese firms. The critical issue then becomes how innovations (very broadly defined) are transmitted across the firm (Ghoshal and Nohria, 1991). The lean production system broadly evolved as a corporate response to the prevailing socioeconomic-technical environment in which firms operated. Toyota happened to find the most successful combination of strategies which, in seeking to address location specific problems rather than advantages, yielded enormous benefits for competitiveness both in the domestic market and internationally. The critical question then becomes, 'how do firms successfully transfer organisational and management techniques across boundaries and borders?' (Arias and Guillen, 1991; Ghoshal and Nohria, 1991). That is, globalisation is about the search for locations and structures which allow, first, the diffusion of knowledge from the centre and, second, the more general interchange of knowledge within and between the various elements of the firm.

Lean firm theory and regulation theory are somewhat different in perspective, but by integrating elements of the two we can begin to move towards a meso level theory of spatial economic change. Global localisation essentially involves the development of constellations of firms in new locations – although those constellations may be spatially extended. Regulation theory addresses the 'environment' into which new management and work organisation (lean production) techniques are introduced. New constellations of suppliers, and new relationships along the supply chain, are both key features of the transition to post-Fordist economic structures and thus form the subject of the research for this book.

3 Restructuring in the European Automotive Industry

3.1 INTRODUCTION

Few can be unaware of the rising tide of Japanese foreign direct investment (FDI) into Europe, where the automotive sector has had a prominent role. Indeed, for some this is part of a wider process of 'Japanisation' (Oliver and Wilkenson, 1989). This process has overlain an indigenous industry already undergoing profound competitive changes, which has prompted economic and spatial restructuring, including the widespread adoption of elements of the lean production model outlined in Chapter 2. Foreign direct investment, notably within Europe, has become an important feature of restructuring. Indeed, as Wells (1992) shows, European FDI grew from 20 per cent of total UK inward FDI in 1980 to 46 per cent by 1988, with the automobile industry playing a prominent role. This chapter seeks to identify some of the main dimensions of growth and decline in the European automobile industry, because it is changes occuring among the assemblers which dominate much of the subsequent change in the components industry. We start with an historical overview of production and markets in Europe before moving on to consider investments, closures and other structural changes in the sector in the late 1980s and early 1990s. Particular attention is given to Japanese FDI and the economic integration of Eastern Europe. A flexible definition of Europe is used, because in the longer term the countries of Eastern Europe and Scandanavia may well be integrated into a wider European Community alongside other peripheral countries such as Turkey, and in any case for some firms, integration across current EC boundaries is a reality at the present time.

In our account, we pay particular attention to spatial development patterns and the extent to which automobile assemblers are developing new methods of production and components sourcing. The evidence suggests that a broad European periphery is being developed by the European and Japanese firms, and that core locations long associated with automobile production are being relatively neglected. Of importance, alongside the basic issue of labour cost, seems to be the way in which new production locations are used to embody new forms of working practices, labour representation, management styles and production regimes – but it is equally clear that no one strategy emerges at the corporate level. The Rover Group, one of the most aggressive in terms of introducing new working practices, has concentrated on achieving changes within existing plants. General Motors (GM) appears to be using its new locations to exert pressure on workers in existing facilities. Mercedes and BMW have created greenfield sites with new working regimes, but they are within Germany (although they are also looking at investments outside Germany, as is Audi, which we shall discuss below). Moreover, there is little evidence to suggest a major increase in the spatial clustering of suppliers arising from the adoption of high-frequency, small-lot parts delivery on a just-in-time basis, an issue we shall explore further in Chapter 4. In fact, as the present chapter makes clear, much of the growth of new capacity at the level of the assemblers is spatially peripheral at national and European levels, tending to mitigate against clustering of suppliers. The adoption of flexible manufacturing and lean production, as with that of Fordism which preceded it, is highly uneven – the empirical dimensions of this book are testimony to the socially mediated way in which industrial transformations progess.

Overlaying the investments in new capacity across Europe is a developing over-capacity crisis in the industry at large, a crisis that has already resulted in closures of some existing plants. For German Volkswagen (VW) workers (and indeed Spanish workers at Seat – owned by VW) watching corporate investments flow to Eastern Europe, there is a concern that their long-term future is in some doubt. For German GM workers, there is the exemplar of new working practices in both vehicle assembly (at Eisenach in the former East Germany) and engine production (in Hungary). Moreover, all the German workers have been warned by the president of the VDA (the German motor industry federation) of the dangers of high wage demands and restrictive working practices (Done, 1992). For some analysts, the Europeanisation of production coupled with the decentralisation of bargaining represent an overt link between manufacturing strategy and labour relations (Mueller and Purcell, 1992). The productivity gap between German and other European automobile firms declined in the 1980s; in the UK and France productivity grew by 6 per cent per annum, in Spain it grew by 5 per cent, but in

Germany by only 2 per cent (Fisher, 1992a). As we show below, only Germany recorded significant increases in employment in the 1980s. Even the high-cost, high-specification vehicle assemblers such as BMW, Mercedes and Volvo, while continuing to invest in or near existing locations, have signalled their intentions to invest elsewhere or to alter radically existing working practices.

Of course, one of the benefits of being a multinational is the ability to 'play off' one location against another. Ford, for example, recently released figures to substantiate its claims that UK plants were underperforming compared with other European locations (see Table 3.13 on page 57), and used these to press for changes in working practices in existing Ford plants (Smith, 1990a) and at Jaguar (Smith, 1990b). GM made it quite clear that further investment in the UK, and specifically a new engine plant at Ellesmere Port, would be dependent upon new working practices and bargaining procedures being adopted by all the GM workers at Ellesmere Port, not just those at the proposed new facility (Gapper, 1989; Smith, 1989). A slightly different approach, used at Nissan UK, is to use the best perfoming plant in the group (wherever it is in the world) as the standard benchmark against which performance should be measured. Thus the Nissan UK press-shop performance is compared with the Nissan plant press-shop at Zama, Japan, on a range of performance measures such as die change times, output per head, quality levels and so on. Underpinning these demands for changes in working practices is ever rising capital intesity in the industry (Mueller and Purcell, 1992). As we show in the case of presswork (see Chapter 6), the high capital cost of new equipment demands continuous working if investment is to be economic.

3.2   GROWTH AND DECLINE IN EUROPEAN MARKETS AND PRODUCTION: THE GLOBAL CONTEXT

Tables 3.1 and 3.2 summarise aggregate changes in the share of automobile markets and production in Europe compared with other major world automotive production regions. These tables make clear the decline in the proportion of global production and markets accounted for by USA and North America. In 1946, the USA and Europe accounted for 93 per cent of world motor vehicle production, but by 1985 this had fallen to 54.2 per cent. During the same period, the total of automobiles in existence rose from 30.0m units to 368.5m units. Thus by 1985, in production terms, the three main ('triad')

Table 3.1   Global production of motor vehicles, 1946, 1970 and 1985
(percentage share)

	1946	1970	1985
North America	79.2	28.2	26.0
Western Europe	13.4	39.9	28.2
Eastern Europe	2.7	5.1	7.5
Japan	0.4	18.0	27.4
Others	4.3	8.8	10.9
Total	100.0	100.0	100.0

Source: Pemberton, 1988.

Table 3.2   Global markets for automobiles, 1960–85 (percentage share)

	1960	1965	1970	1975	1980	1985
North America	58.4	54.1	41.1	36.9	34.4	38.4
Western Europe	29.9	33.3	36.3	34.1	35.3	33.8
Eastern Europe	2.3	2.2	3.3	6.1	7.1	6.7
Japan	1.2	3.2	10.8	11.1	10.1	9.9
Others	8.2	7.2	8.5	11.8	13.0	11.2
Total	100.0	100.0	100.0	100.0	100.0	100.0

Source: Pemberton, 1988.

regions had roughly comparable levels of production, each accounting for just under a third of total world production. However, it is also clear that as early as 1970 the USA had lost its pre-eminence to Europe. In market terms, the decline of the importance of the USA is less marked. Overall, these figures reflect the growing impact of Japanese production on global markets through an aggressive export strategy. In the context of this book we are not able to discuss the impact of new entrants into the global automotive business from non-core countries such as Korea, who through Hyundai have made an impact on US and European markets (Hyun and Lee, 1989; Waitt, 1993).

European firms lost crucial export markets in the latter 1980s. Table 3.3 summarises unit sales in the USA for German automobile assemblers from 1982. As Fisher (1992b, 1992c) shows, German firms

Table 3.3   German car exports to the USA, 1982–91 (000s units)

	Audi	BMW	Mercedes	VW
1982	40	52	66	220
1983	55	62	76	218
1984	70	75	80	252
1985	70	87	90	295
1986	55	94	100	260
1987	31	80	93	221
1988	22	70	75	160
1989	20	62	79	150
1990	15	60	69	125
1991	12	53	58	112

Source: Fisher, 1992b.

saw their market share in the USA decline from a peak of 4.5 per cent in 1986 to 2.7 per cent in 1992, with Audi suffering the greatest collapse. The MVMA (1990) show that, in aggregate, German exports to the USA fell from 439 000 units in 1985 to 213 000 units in 1989, a 50 per cent drop in five years. The US market accounts for 10 per cent of total BMW sales (Done, 1992), and in order to escape German labour costs and unfavourable exchange rate movements the firm is considering investing in manufacturing operations in South Carolina (see Table 3.9 on page 49). A further consideration was to be inside the North America Free Trade Zone (Fisher, 1992b). Equally, much of Porsche's problems in the early 1990s can be attributed to a collapse of sales in the USA, which in 1986 took 68 per cent of output but in 1992 only 23 per cent (Peel, 1992). A similar effect has been felt by Jaguar (Done, 1991a), Mercedes, Rolls-Royce and Volvo (Taylor, 1991) as European luxury car manufacturers suffered declining competitiveness, a stagnant US market, and increasing pressure from Japanese firms entering their market segments.

More generally, statistics from the MVMA (1990) do give support for one facet of globalisation, and that is the increasing penetration of domestic markets by imports. In general, domestic markets have become more open, with indigenous producers less protected. Table 3.4 shows the share of domestic markets taken by imports from 1968 to 1989 in selected countries. The most extreme change is evidenced in the UK: in 1968 imports accounted for just 8.3 per cent of the market, but as domestic production declined and market size grew the share

Table 3.4   The proportion of new car registrations accounted for by imports, 1968 to 1989, selected countries

	France	West Germany	UK	Italy	Sweden	Japan	USA
1968	21.4	20.4	8.3	15.2	59.6	1.0	10.5
1969	24.3	20.4	10.4	20.3	58.3	0.8	11.3
1970	19.8	22.5	14.3	27.7	56.4	0.7	14.7
1971	20.2	25.2	19.3	26.4	56.8	0.7	15.1
1972	20.6	26.2	23.5	26.8	58.3	0.9	14.6
1973	20.8	25.9	27.4	26.8	57.0	1.1	15.2
1974	17.9	26.7	27.8	27.9	62.1	1.7	15.7
1975	20.3	24.9	33.2	31.4	64.2	1.6	18.2
1976	22.9	21.6	41.4	37.1	66.1	1.7	14.8
1977	22.2	21.1	45.3	36.3	69.1	1.7	18.3
1978	20.9	21.9	49.2	37.1	67.1	1.8	17.8
1979	21.7	23.2	56.3	38.3	65.8	1.2	22.6
1980	22.9	26.3	56.7	41.5	68.5	1.5	28.2
1981	28.1	25.3	55.7	40.9	64.9	1.3	28.8
1982	30.6	24.1	57.7	40.7	64.7	1.2	29.6
1983	32.7	24.4	56.9	36.6	62.8	1.1	27.5
1984	35.9	26.7	57.5	36.9	65.1	1.4	24.9
1985	36.6	27.2	58.1	40.0	66.8	1.6	27.6
1986	56.4	29.7	56.0	38.4	68.8	2.2	30.9
1987	36.1	29.2	51.7	39.5	21.7	3.0	39.9
1988	36.8	29.1	56.4	39.3	73.2	3.6	35.4
1989	38.1	30.2	57.0	42.2	74.5	4.1	35.9

Source: MVMA, 1990.

taken by imports had risen to 57.0 per cent by 1989. Not surprisingly, this process was the chief cause of decline in the UK automotive components industry (Amin and Smith, 1991). However, all the selected countries show growth in the share of imports, indicating a globalisation of competition – although it is also true that Japan is still to a large extent closed.

If we consider the share of domestic production devoted to exports, this has risen in most cases for the countries concerned over the same period. Thus in 1960 Japan exported only 4.2 per cent of production, but by the mid-1980s this reached a peak at 58.6 per cent. Subsequently, a combination of stronger domestic market demand and the growth of import-substituting production facilities in the US and Europe has reduced the share of domestic Japanese production that is exported. It is also worth noting the very low proportion of production traditionally exported from the USA, a reflection of the unsuitability of US cars for export and the global production capabilities of US firms. Indeed, the evidence in terms of export performance is very mixed, in that both Italy and the UK registered a long-term decline in exports as a proportion of domestic production up to 1989, while France showed little change. Sweden has consistently exported the majority of production, reflecting both the small size of the domestic market and the limited range of models produced by Volvo and Saab. In fact, it is the newer automotive production countries such as Brazil and Spain which have shown the greatest improvement in export performance. In the period from 1960 to 1989 Spanish exports grew from 0 per cent of production to 56.4 per cent, while those from Brazil grew from 0 per cent to a peak of 41.1 per cent in 1987 (see MVMA, 1990, p. 14).

The data in Table 3.5 should be treated with some caution, not least because of the ambiguous position occupied by kit assembly operations. It should be noted that the globalisation thesis is uncertain about exports. On the one hand, the development of a global manufacturing presence in key markets should reduce the need for exports, as in the case of Japanese firms investing in the USA. On the other, if true global synergy is to be achieved, greater trade flows

Table 3.5 The proportion of production directed to exports, selected countries, 1975–89 (percentage share)

	West Germany	France	UK	Italy	Sweden	Japan	USA
1975	50.8	53.5	40.7	49.0	68.7	40.0	9.5
1976	51.8	50.5	37.2	47.3	63.8	50.5	7.8
1977	51.2	52.4	35.8	44.7	76.7	54.5	7.5
1978	49.0	50.8	37.1	42.4	81.3	49.0	7.3
1979	40.8	52.7	37.2	43.7	86.3	50.2	8.8
1980	53.2	52.1	37.5	35.4	80.2	56.1	8.8
1981	54.5	53.4	32.5	33.7	81.0	56.6	8.1
1982	58.3	52.7	35.3	33.7	79.0	54.8	7.0
1983	56.4	54.5	26.2	35.2	79.4	53.2	7.9
1984	58.9	56.4	24.1	33.4	80.7	56.2	7.6
1985	61.6	58.5	22.9	32.4	76.6	57.9	8.1
1986	58.5	55.9	19.8	36.5	81.7	58.6	8.3
1987	56.0	55.1	21.4	37.4	79.2	57.1	8.9
1988	57.7	56.8	19.7	36.4	76.3	54.1	9.4
1989	59.6	55.7	26.1	55.2	79.1	48.5	11.4

Source: MVMA, 1990.

exports, as in the case of Japanese firms investing in the USA. On the may occur as firms alter their production base. To date there are few examples of firms undertaking the practice of product specialisation in certain locations, although Honda in the USA, for example, have exported some Civic models (a variant which is produced only in the USA) to Japan, and a number of the Japanese firms in the USA are said to be considering using their US facilities to export to Europe. We below consider the extent of production for individual outside the parent country firms.

Many commentators have pointed to the increasing share of markets accounted for by Japanese firms. Table 3.6 illustrates this general point, at least as far as unprotected markets are concerned. Thus in countries such as the Irish Republic, Finland and Denmark, which lack an indigenous industry to protect, the share of the total market accounted for by Japanese firms has risen over the period 1978–89. However, Table 3.6 also illustrates the existence of formal and informal trade aggrements and outright restrictions which have limited Japanese market share in key countries such as the UK, France, Spain, Italy and Germany. These limitations are one of the reasons why Japanese firms have sought to develop a manufacturing capacity within Europe, as we shall discuss below.

The massive declines in employment in the indigenous US motor industry have been well documented, but it is worth re-examining the

Table 3.6   Japanese market penetration, selected countries, 1981–89 (percentage market shares)

	1981	*1982*	*1983*	*1984*	*1985*	*1986*	*1987*	*1988*	*1989*
Denmark	24.2	25.3	31.1	32.7	31.8	35.1	32.6	32.8	31.7
Finland	33.0	35.3	40.0	37.9	39.4	40.4	41.1	41.4	38.9
France	2.6	2.9	2.7	3.0	3.0	2.9	2.9	2.9	2.3
West Germany	10.0	9.8	10.6	12.0	13.3	15.0	15.1	15.2	15.0
Republic of Ireland	29.7	16.9	30.0	27.4	33.8	43.4	43.9	44.0	40.0
Italy	0.1	0.1	0.2	0.2	0.2	0.5	0.7	1.0	1.5
The Netherlands	24.4	22.4	23.5	22.0	22.3	24.0	25.9	27.7	26.2
Spain	1.3	1.4	1.2	0.6	0.8	0.6	0.2	0.9	1.2
Sweden	13.7	15.2	15.2	15.0	16.1	20.9	21.7	25.5	24.8
UK	11.0	11.0	10.7	11.1	10.9	11.1	9.7	9.4	10.9
USA	21.8	22.6	20.9	18.3	20.1	20.8	21.3	19.9	19.4

Source: MVMA, 1990.

Japanese 'transplant' phenomenon in the USA and its impact on the existing industry, as for many people it represents a portent of things to come in Europe. As we comment elsewhere, it is unlikely that the experience of the USA will be replicated in Europe (Wells and Rawlinson, 1993b). By the mid-1990s, Japanese assembler transplant capacity in the USA reached 2.7 million units, and they had invested some $6bn in eleven sites (Mair *et al.*, 1988; Reid, 1990); if local production were combined with imports at their current level Japanese firms could take 35 per cent of the market (Mair *et al.*, 1988). The effect on the indigenous industry has been devastating. Rehder (1989) reported that the US General Accounting Office estimate that between 1985 and 1990 some 360 000 jobs would be lost in the US automobile industry. GM, perhaps the worst affected, closed five plants in 1990 and followed this with announcements in late 1991 that it intended to close a further twenty-one plants over the next four years at a cost of 70 000 jobs (or 18 per cent of the workforce). In 1991, GM recorded the largest corporate loss in US history, despite positive contributions from GM Europe of $7.087bn. Between 1976 and 1986 Ford closed seven of its fifteen US assembly plants, while employment fell from 234 000 to 181 000 (Bloomfield, 1991). Perhaps more important in terms of this book is the extent to which Japanese components firms or components imports have been used in the USA by Japanese assembler plants. Newman (1990) identifies 232 Japanese components firms operating in the USA, with 88 suppliers arriving in 1988 alone. Other estimates support this order of magnitude, the EIU (1989b) identifies 'over 300', with a combined investment of at least $6bn – that is, on the same scale as investment by the assemblers themselves. At the same time, the value of components imported from Japan rose from $2bn (1983) to $10bn (1990), with a projected (though probably pessimistic) rise to $17bn by 1995 (Newman, 1990).

As we shall discuss more fully below, the situation in Europe is different. Not only is the scale of investment smaller, there has not yet been a phase of inward investment by Japanese components firms to match that which occured in the USA.

3.3 GROWTH AND DECLINE WITHIN EUROPE: A NATIONAL LEVEL COMPARISON

The 1980s was a decade of extremes in the European automotive industry. The early part of the 1980s was dominated by stagnant markets and economic downturn. By the late 1980s, however, most firms could not produce enough vehicles to meet the demand that boomed across Europe. Due to favourable exchange rates and a buoyant US market in the period 1983–6, automobile assemblers were able to reap large profits from US sales. Firms such as Vauxhall and Renault, which had not made a profit for many years, began to do so at this time. Subsequently, recession once again hit the industry as, in first the US market and then in Europe, demand began to weaken. The unification of Germany in 1989 released a further rush of demand which to some extent masked the more general decline in European markets, but not all firms were able to capitalise on this event. Notably, it was the German assemblers who were able to sustain output. Table 3.7 shows production by country in the EC over the period 1960–90. It shows contrasting experiences at the national level.

The UK, despite recent increases in output, has yet to match the production levels recorded in 1960. Germany, by contrast, has shown a generalised pattern of growth as it has come to dominate the European automobile industry, closely followed by France. Both Spain and Italy have improved their positions relative to the UK over the period, with growth in Spain being especially dramatic. Indeed, in aggregate, Spain has probably the most modern automobile production infrastructure

Table 3.7 Automobile production in Europe by country, 1960–90 (000s)

	UK	France	West Germany	Italy	Spain
1960	1 352	1 175	1 816	595	10
1965	1 722	1 423	2 733	1 103	15
1970	1 640	2 458	3 527	1 719	450
1975	1 267	2 546	2 907	1 348	696
1980	923	2 938	3 520	1 445	1 028
1981	954	2 611	3 577	1 257	855
1982	887	2 777	3 761	1 297	927
1983	1 044	2 960	3 817	1 395	1 141
1984	908	2 713	3 790	1 439	1 176
1985	1 047	2 623	4 166	1 389	1 230
1986	1 018	2 773	4 310	1 652	1 281
1987	1 142	3 051	4 373	1 713	1 402
1988	1 226	3 223	4 346	1 884	1 497
1989	1 299	3 409	4 563	1 971	1 638
1990	1 295	3 294	4 660	1 874	1 679

Source: SMMT, 1991.

of all the European countries following investments in the 1970s (Ford, Valencia; GM, Zaragoza) and the 1980s (VW/Seat, Barcelona; Nissan Iberica, Barcelona).

The kit assembly of component parts manufactured elsewhere is an important feature of the European and global automobile industry. Actual assembly of vehicles is an important part of the total value added in production, and is also the most labour intensive. Historically, states such as Portugal and Spain have made local assembly a condition of market access. Moreover, transportation of fully finished vehicles can be expensive compared with so-called Completely knocked down (CKD) kits. Consequently, there is a considerable movement of vehicle kits across national boundaries, an issue we shall return to in Chapter 6. Here, the point to make is that virtually all the production in Belgium (with the notable exception of the Ford Mondeo model, which is made exclusively in Belgium), much of that in the Netherlands, and a high proportion of that in Spain and the UK, may be attributable to the assembly of kits. The proportion of local sourcing will vary, with a tendency to increase over time, but in general, kit assembly has not greatly supported the development of an indigenous components industry unless (as with Spain) government measures have been enacted to ensure local content.

The overall significance of the automobile industry to the economy in Europe is not easy to estimate. The Commission of the European Community CEC (1992) estimate at a very aggregate level that employment in transportation equipment fell from 3.23 million in 1980 to 2.59 million in 1990. These figure for NACE 35/36 includes aerospace (approximately 400 000 jobs); shipbuilding (223 000 jobs, 1980; 89 000, 1990); and railway stock (100 000 jobs, 1980; 65 000 jobs, 1990). However, ten of the top eleven transportation equipment firms are predominatly in the automotive sector. While aggregate statistics are not available it is probable that the strongest contrasts in performance in terms of employment are between Germany and the UK. The CEC (1991) consider that the European automobile sector lost 390 000 jobs between 1980 and 1987 (with total indirect losses amounting to nearer 600 000) but Germany actually increased employment by 68 000.

Estimates of employment at a national level give some insights into the problems involved in defining the industry and its economic importance. For France, Chambre Syndicate des Constructeurs d'Automobiles the (CSCA) estimate a total employment of 2.59 million in 1988, of which only 345 000 were actually involved in automobile construction and components suppply (CSCA, 1988) because they also include items such as traffic police, road construction, automotive sports and so on. The Verband Der Automobilindustrie, in contrast, take a more restricitve definition by identifying shop-floor workers and office workers in the constituent (member) firms, which in 1989 amounted to 753 000. Their figures exclude the vast majority of the components industry in Germany (only about 40 000 jobs are accounted for here) which are not members of the VDA. In the UK, a study conducted by the now-defunct Engineering Industry Training Board (EITB) suggested that employment in the sector overall had fallen from 488 000 in 1978 to 225 000 in 1987 (see SMMT, 1990) but, taking a wider definition, Society of Motor Manufacturers and Traders, the SMMT and Institute of Manpower Studies concluded that total motor industry employment in the UK was as shown in Table 3.8. Of the figures mentioned, those relating to trade (48 000) refer to people engaged in the distribution of UK-produced parts and vehicles only; the total retail employment in the industry is estimated at 300 000; and vehicle servicing and forecourt personnel account for a further 500 000.

Figures from the VDA (1990) give an interesting insight into changes in labour cost over the 1980s (see Table 2.1 in on page 22). This data shows that while comparative labour costs in Japan have risen steeply, and those in Germany and Sweden have remained high, the UK has become the lowest cost location of the sample countries, closely followed by France. The high labour costs in Germany have become a critical factor in the spatial restructuring of the European industry,

Table 3.8   Employment in the motor industry, UK, 1987 (000s)

Car production, including engines	120
Truck production, including engines	20
Bodies, trailers, caravans	10
Vehicle parts	139
Materials, capital goods suppliers	65
Total vehicles and parts	354
Vehicle distribution	48
Multiplier effect	200
Total	602

Source: SMMT, 1990.

equally the low costs of the UK have added to its attractiveness as an investment location. Underpinning and following the above aggregate changes at a European level has been a process of corporate spatial restructuring which we shall consider in the next section.

3.4 RESTRUCTURING WITHIN EUROPE: THE CORPORATE LEVEL

Underlying these macro-level changes has been a process of largely national consolidation as the number of indepentent vehicle assembly firms (both automobiles and trucks) has steadily reduced. Some firms have failed altogether; more commonly they have been acquired by larger enterprises and, to a greater or lesser extent, been subsumed within those organisations. This is not a recent phenomenon; there has been a steady erosion of the numbers of independent commercial vehicle manufacturers (Rhys, 1972) and small car-producers (Rhys, 1989).

In the UK, the Rover Group (now 80 per cent owned by BMW and 20 per cent owned by Honda) was created, largely through state involvement, out of a series of mergers and rationalisations which reached a peak in the late 1970s (Law, 1985; Williams *et al.*, 1987). Several plants were closed and famous names in the UK industry such as Standard-Triumph, Singer and Rootes ceased to exist. British Leyland closed sites in Canley, Abingdon and Solihull in an attempt to rationalise its product range and improve capacity utilisation, while its total output fell 55 per cent, from 916 000 units in 1972 to 405 000 in 1982. In Italy, Fiat has progressively acquired Lancia, Alfa and Ferrari, leaving only a few highly specialised producers such as De Thomaso outside their control. In Germany, VW acquired NSU and Audi; while in France, Peugeot and Citroën merged to create PSA (see Law, 1974, for an historical summary). More recently, the acquisitions of Jaguar and AC Cars by Ford, and Lotus and Saab by GM, illustrate two key points. On the one hand, smaller producers operating with restricted product ranges have found it increasingly difficult to compete with the large firms, especially as those large firms have sought to develop 'niche' vehicles to compete with the specialist producers. And the other hand, the larger firms have met customer resistance when attempting to break into more specialised markets, and are using their acqusitions as a means of market entry. The subsequent sale of Lotus by GM in 1993, after several years of losses, by perhaps also shows that market entry in this way is not necessarily straightforward.

The following sections present summary information on major structural changes in the European automobile industry.

3.4.1 Strategic alliances

Strategic alliances have become a central feature of the global automotive industry, taking many forms and involving all the major firms. Here, we cannot undertake a detailed analysis of the reasons for alliances, nor of all the linkages of this type in the industry, for such a task would be a book in itself. Suffice to say, that alliances have become a widely accepted means of furthering corporate strategy (Hamel *et al.*, 1989), and can be understood more generally as an intermediate corporate form which arises out of attempts to cope with rapid technological, regulatory and market change (Jorde and Teece, 1989; Cooke *et al.*, 1992). However, we can illustrate, with material from the European automobile industry, the strategic and spatial dimensions of alliances. The focus is on just three alliances: Rover/Honda in the UK; VW/Ford in Portugal; and the pan-European Volvo/Renault alliance. There are many other instances where firms have co-operated on specific product developments to achieve greater economies of scale: instances would include, for example, the Saab/Lancia joint development of a floorpan for executive saloons; and the Fiat/PSA joint development of the Fully Integrated Robotised (FIRE) engine.

The Rover/Honda linkage has historical precedents going back to 1921, when one of the firms which now constitutes Rover had an alliance with Isuzu in Japan. In 1978, Rover recognised the need for partnership linkages, and after a period of analysis Honda scored the most points as a likely partner (Bertodo, 1990). Rover needed to learn about project management, product planning, workforce organisation and supplier management – and Honda were considered to have the right 'fit' for those needs without totally overwhelming Rover. For Honda, the advantages were clear: access to European styling and design approaches, a low-risk entry route into the European market, and a means of accessing local suppliers quickly (via the Rover supply base). Bertodo describes the process as a 'vortex' in which after several 'laps' the alliance has progressed and deepened, moving from a conventional licence agreement (the Triumph 'Acclaim' was a licensed Honda 'Accord') to integrated production and development. Honda has continued to expand its production presence in the UK, with Swindon as the main location, and still holds 20 per cent of Rover.

The Ford/VW alliance to produce 7-seater vehicles in Setubal, Portugal is particularly interesting. As with other new capacity investments, the process of establishing the venture and deciding on the location was intensely political. Portugal was keen to get the investment, the largest ever single FDI in Portugal, in the face of competition from other locations. Some 4700 direct jobs are promised, with perhaps 10 000 additional indirect jobs and a net contribution to the Portugese balance of payments of £4bn in the six years to 2001 (Blum, 1991). The financial aid package will include £350m in cash grants (70 per cent from the EC and 30 per cent from Portugal), as well as a five-year tax exemption worth perhaps £40m. This was challenged by Matra of France which orginated the 7-seater vehicle type (sold as the Renault Espace) to be produced in Setubal (Dawkins and Blum, 1991). Much of the ultimate benefit to Portugal depends on local content. The more local suppliers are used, the greater the impact on employment and balance of payments. Under the terms of the joint venture, VW is designing the vehicle and Ford is organising the supply base. Ford has been already encouraged some of its other European suppliers to invest in Setubal. This sort of alliance is not quasi-vertical integration, but rather quasi-horizontal integration between two parties involved in the same stage of the production process of the same product.

The Renault/Volvo alliance is much more wide-ranging than the VW/Ford link in Portugal. Initially involving a complex equity and cash exchange it has now progressed to a full merger between the two firms. It embraces both the car and commercial vehicle operations of the two firms. Volvo paid FFr17.18bn ($3.5bn) in early 1991 for 20 per cent of Renault and 45 per cent of RVI (the Renault commercial vehicle division). Renault paid FFr11.3bn for 25 per cent of Volvo Car and 45 per cent of Volvo Truck. The background had been two years of increasingly poor financial performance as key markets collapsed and new model and investment costs rose. Nearly 5000 job losses in the total Swedish workforce of 26 000 were announced by Volvo in 1990 as a crisis measure to cut costs (Done, 1990), but the alliance with Renault marks an attempt to gain longer-term viability. Since the share swap, Volvo has underperformed compared with Renault, which showed a sharp improvment in profits in the early 1990s. Moves to gain synergy from the link between the two firms include pooling of components purchasing and quality control systems. Collectively, Volvo and Renault purchase about FFr51.2bn per annum in components, but to date far only about 15 per cent represent joint purchases from suppliers – the intention is to raise this level to 80 per cent. Volvo estimated that joint purchasing could save $141.6m per annum.

3.4.2 New investment

New investment patterns show that few European firms have established significant production facilities outside the EC and Western Europe in recent years, although a number of the German firms are considering further expansion in the USA, Mexico or Canada (see Table 3.9).

Table 3.9   Investment plans for the 1990s, EC firms outside Europe

Form	Location	Type of investment
VW	Mexico	DM1.5bn announced 1992 to expand facilities for new Golf/Jetta models. 60% increase to 390 000 units p.a.
VW	China	Proposed in 1991 to build new plant in Changchum, capacity of 150 000 p.a. by 1996.
VW	China	Investment of £150m 1985–90. Further £250m to produce 150 000 units p.a. by 1995. Joint venture.
VW	Taiwan	Announced 1991, 40% VW joint venture to produce 30 000 T4 Transporter vans p.a.
Audi	USA/Canada	Currently evaluating plans for production site for mid-1990s.
BMW	USA	Announced plan in 1992 to build production plant in South Carolina. $400m investment, capacity 70 000 p.a.
Mercedes	Mexico	Decided in 1993 to build kit assembly plant for W124 mid-range saloon.
Mercedes	Alabama	Decision in 1993 to construct plant for assembly of 4x4 vehicles.

Sources: Compiled from company reports, company press releases, and press reports.

Table 3.10 Investment plans for the 1990s within the EC, greenfield and existing facilities

Firm	Date	Location	Type of investment
Volvo	1989–91	Ghent Belgium	Assembly of 800 Series SKr2bn 200,000 p.a. capacity
GM	1990–2	Ellesmere Port, UK	£190m investment for V6 engine plant, 450 jobs. 135 000 units p.a., 500 000 cylinder heads p.a. 1m camshafts p.a.
GM	1990–1	Sweden	$1.15bn invested in purchase and subsequent support of 50% of Saab.
GM	1989	Portugal	$49m to produce electronic ignition systems. 500,000 units p.a., 500 jobs.
BMW	1986–90	Regensburg	DM1.6bn greenfield site. Output of 800 per day, 3-series cars.
BMW	1987	Wackersdorf	Purchase of land for recycling plant.
Mercedes	1992	Rastatt	DM2bn on new assembly plant. Capacity of 360 vehicles per day by 1996.
VW	1992–6	Europe	Total investments of DM82bn, mainly in Spain and Eastern Europe, of which DM51bn will be for new car production.
Seat	1992	Martorell	Pa69bn spent on new plant near Barcelona.
Seat	1992–9	Spain	Investment plan includes: Martorell Pa282.6bn Barcelona Pa210.5bn Pamplona Pa111.8bn El Prat Pa40.6bn Other Pa141.9bn Approximately 50/50 split between new model costs and new facilities.
Renault	1989	Douai	FFr1.73bn on new press-shop and assembly hall. New Renault R19. Capacity 350 000 pa.
Rover	1992	Cowley	New 800 series production lines, £200m invested.
Rover	1991–2	Swindon	2 new transfer presses, £54m.

Firm	Date	Location	Type of investment
Ford	1990	Spain	$68m on new plant to produce electronic ignition modules.
Ford	1990–9	UK	Plans to invest £2.6bn in UK plants.
Ford	1990	Bridgend	£500m Zeta engine facility.
Ford	1990	Köln, Germany	£225m Zeta engine facility.
Ford	1989	UK	Purchase of Jaguar for £1.75bn.
Ford	1986–90	Valencia, Spain	Pa60bn on upgrading facilities.
Ford	1991	Charleville, France	$65m on plastic components plant. 375 jobs. Includes FFr38m subsidy from French state.
Ford	1991	Dagenham	£91m on diesel engine production. Capacity of 1500 per day.
Ford	1991	Valencia, Spain	$1bn for new Sigma engine production. Capacity of 550 000 units p.a. by 1995.
Ford/VW	1992–6	Setubal, Portugal	£1.75bn for new plant to produce 7-seat vehicles. Capacity of 180 000 p.a. by 1996. One third subsidy from Portugal.
Ford	1992	Köln, Germany	$54,000 pilot dismantling plant
Fiat	1992	Italy	Total of $32bn to be spent to year 2002 on new plants, models, etc. Mainly in Italy.
Fiat	1991–4	Melfi	New plant, 450 000 cars p.a. and 7000 jobs.
Fiat	1993	Pratolla	Engine plant with capacity of 1m units p.a., 1300 jobs. The two investments will cost about L48,000bn combined.
Rover	1990	Birmingham	£200m on new K-series engine facility.
GM	1993	Germany	New engine plant. £300m.

Sources: Compiled from company reports, company press releases, and press reports.

Picking up investment levels in existing plants can be difficult, as such investment receives much less exposure than wholly new facilities. Equally, capacity may be increased by changing working practices. In 1990 GM introduced three-shift working at its Bochum plant in Germany. This created an additional 830 jobs and expanded capacity by 22 000 units per annum. At the same time, the firm introduced scaled-down holiday working at Russelshiem and Keiserslauten in a similar move to expand capacity. Table 3.10 shows major investments within the EC. Moreover, it is often difficult to separate tangible investment in new equipment, buildings and so on. from the intangible investment in people. Thus if new model X costs £1bn to develop, only part of that cost will be attributable to investment costs in new equipment and tooling, or the maintenance of existing equipment. Table 3.11 shows illustrative model development costs and, where known, the share attributable to new investment in production facilities. Typically, between a half and a third of new model costs go towards new equipment. Total development costs can be as high as £1bn, though a more typical figure is around £400m for an average model. However, as Table 3.11 suggests continued investment in existing facilities is very important and is a reflection of the high costs of attaining lean production. We return to this issue in presswork Chapter 6, discussing presswork where we show that new, high-volume and flexible press machines may cost in the region of £30m each. Here, it is sufficient to note that the investment demands of remaining competitive in the automobile industry are huge, and in

Table 3.11   Illustrative new model development costs

Firm	Model	Costs
Mercedes	200/400 Series	£130m on production facilities
Mercedes	New S-Class	DM3bn
VW	Passat (1981)	DM2.6bn
VW	Golf III	DM1.3bn
Rover	200/400 Series	£600m
Rover	800 Series	£240m including £130m on production facilities
Opel	New Astra	DM1.5bn
Renault	New R19	FFr5.8bn
Renault	Clio	FFr4.9bn

Source: Press reports.

some cases would appear to outweigh the ability of firms to raise sufficient funds. Perhaps the most outstanding case is Renault; in 1990 they spent FFr 15bn on investment, compared with FFr 7.3bn in 1988, yet in 1985 the net financial debt at FFr 61.9bn represented 55 per cent of total group sales. Other firms have announced major investment programmes. Fiat, in 1991, announced a ten-year capital programme of L40 000bn (about £32bn in total) over the following ten years; VW is to invest some DM82bn over five years from 1991. In this context there is strong pressure to reduce the investment bill by whatever means possible, as well as to improve operating margins. The recessionary conditions in the industry prevalent in the early 1990s, in which major markets fell by 20 per cent over 12 months, caused some retrenchment of investment plans. Whatever happens in the future there will be strong repercussions for the components industry: Investment costs may be lowered by placing more component development work and production with components suppliers; operating margins may be improved by out-sourcing more low-value-added work, and by reducing stocks and increasing quality. Per-unit costs may also be reduced by sourcing more components from low cost locations, while strategic alliances may enable joint purchasing of components to reap economies of scale.

In terms of the spatial patterning of investment, it is clear that the automobile assemblers have been seeking out new production locations in several significant instances. As Law (1974) shows, the post-1950 period saw a proliferation of assembly sites by European firms, almost entirely within national boundaries, as capacity was expanded to meet rising demand. In many instances, regional development policies played an important role in directing investment towards locations of high structural unemployment, typically coal and steel areas. Examples include the Rootes factory at Linwood, Scotland; VW at Emden and Saltzgitter; DAF at Born (The Netherlands); Ford at Saarlouis; and Alfa Romeo at Naples. More recently, the incidence of new capacity additions has been fewer, with closures of sites or partial rationalisation more obvious. In the cases of BMW and Mercedes, new sites are relatively close to their main production locations, though for both firms the decision to develop production facilities in the USA marks a significant change in policy. In 1993 Mercedes announced a decision not to proceed with the construction of a commercial vehicle factory in the former East Germany; at the same time, the firm announced its intention to build a new, small class of vehicle at a new site in Europe – in either Germany or the former

Czechoslovakia. The primary consideration in most firms, it appears has been where to implement rationalisation measures. Outright plant closures have thus far been relatively few, but may well accelerate in the future; it is illustrative that in 1993 VW announced that the old Seat plant in Barcelona might be closed.

3.4.3   Rationalisations and closures

The question of rationalisation is made more difficult by short-term measures introduced in the face of temporary market conditions which may obscure more fundamental, permanent changes. None the less, some interesting features emerge from Table 3.12, which summarises rationalisation in Europe. First, job losses in the UK were especially high in the 1980s (despite earlier job losses during the 1970s) at a time when GM Opel in Germany was fighting to establish three-shift working in its plants. Second, however, Renault and PSA have not been immune to the need to cut jobs; in the case of Fiat the figures are distorted somewhat by a state subsidy for redundancy, where the state pays the costs of retaining workers on the payroll. Third, it is noticeable that Ford has also started to reduce white-collar employment dramatically, having already taken out many jobs on the shop floor. Finally, it is clear that even the German firms have had to announce job losses recently: VW, BMW, Mercedes and Porsche have all cut their workforce to varying degrees – a further indication of the troubles the German industry is facing.

These rationalisations have not been confined to EC firms. Volvo and Saab (both based in Sweden) have both seen declines in profitability in the later 1980s while investment costs have risen steeply (see, for example, Done, 1990). One consequence was the purchase of 50 per cent of Saab by GM in 1990, with the immediate closure of the new assembly facility at Malmo – this will probably go down on record as the shortest-lived automobile production facility ever. This facility, as with the Volvo Udevella plant, was an experimental assembly operation to develop new working practices. A second consequence was the complex Renault/Volvo alliance which brings together both the car and commercial vehicle interests of the two firms in the previously discussed cross-shareholding arrangement. In part,the recession in the industry, reflecting broader economic problems in the EC and especially the UK, may be a significant cause of job loss.

Table 3.12   Rationalisations in the European automobile industry, 1991 and 1992

Firm	Location	Type of rationalisation
VW	Germany	To shed 12 500 jobs out of 130 000 over the period 1991–6.
Renault	France	Closed Billancourt (Paris) plant, 1991: 4000 jobs lost. 1992, announced plans to cut 3746 of 120 000 jobs in France.
Saab	Sweden	Over the period 1991 and 1992 total workforce cut by 30%. New assembly plant at Malmo (£250m investment) closed.
Jaguar	UK	From 12 800 employed (1988) to 8500 by the end of 1991. Six-week production halt. 4-day week from August 1991. Further job cuts to leave 7400 end 1991. End 1991, announced further 2000 job losses. August 1992, 700 jobs lost. September 1992, further 120 jobs lost. Jaguar lost £226m in 1991.
Rolls Royce	UK	1991 lost 1200 jobs (30% of total) to leave 3100. 3-day week for much of 1992. Sales fell about 50% in 1991/2. Further cuts to leave only 2100 jobs announced September 1992.
Lotus	UK	1991 workforce cut from 900 to 600. 1992 workforce reduced to 150. Elan production axed after only 2 years. Loss of £15.8m on turnover of £43.2m. Sold by GM 1993.
Fiat	Italy	Plans announced in 1992 for 10 300 job cuts. Prolonged short-time working in many plants. Closure of Desio plant in 1991 with 2500 jobs lost.
GM	Germany	Announced plan in 1992 to reduce 31 000 workforce by 6000 over period to 1997.
Mercedes	Germany	1992 announced plan to cut 10 000 jobs out of 183 000 total in wake of 5.8% pay agreement which would cost the firm DM600m in 1992.
BMW	Germany	1992 announced plan to shed 3000 jobs out of 62,000 in Germany.
Rover	UK	500 jobs out of Longbridge engine and gearbox plant. Total of 3500 jobs (12% of all Rover jobs) cut in 18 months to the end of 1991. Six-month pay freeze imposed October 1992.
Jensen	UK	Went into receivership August 1992.

Table 3.12 continues overleaf

Table 3.12 continued

Firm	Location	Type of rationalisation
Ginetta	UK	Went into receivership September 1992.
Mercedes	Germany	Extends holidays for workers, winter 1992. Output cut by 35 000 units. Parent company announces 40 000 jobs to go from 1993.
Volvo	Sweden	November 1992 announces the loss of 9500 jobs (10% of total truck and car) by 1995. Uddervalla (820 jobs) and Kalmar (800 jobs) plants closed. (Might also cut 1200 of 9000 jobs at Volvo Car BV, The Netherlands)
Saab	Sweden	November 1992 announces 1650 jobs to go at Trollhatten plant (20% of total), with 350 jobs elsewhere. Loss of $370m in 1992.
Porsche	Germany	1991/92 loss of $43m, sales down 26%. 1850 jobs (25% of total) cut 1992/93.
Ford	Europe	1991 plans to cut 2500 jobs among white collar workforce to 1994. Cut 10% of indirect workforce a year for 3 years. 512 jobs lost, Transit van plant in Southampton. By 1991 employment at Halewood (UK) down to 7500 from 1970s peak of 14 000. 3-day week at Halewood for much of 1992. Further job losses expected. 1991 net loss of $1.079bn. Other UK plants at Dagenham and Southampton went on to 3-day week towards end of 1992, when Ford announced a further 1550 job cuts in the UK following 2100 announced in February 1992. Assembly plants in Valencia (Spain) and Köln (Germany) also having a series of non-production days.

Sources: Compiled from company reports, company press releases, and press reports.

3.4.4   Productivity and work organisation

As the above data show, the changes in the spatial pattern of the European automobile industry are a complex outcome of investment in existing and new locations, and rationalisations of existing locations. Accompanying this has been a process of reshaping production practices at existing locations. Ford, who are well placed to assess productivity and other performance differences across

Europe, are a useful illustration, though they are by no means unique in seeking changes in working practices. In the case of Ford, the company released the figures shown in Table 3.13.

While there are complicating factors behind these figures, such as the difficulties of changing existing plant layout at Dagenham to meet new production organisation, or the relative costs of buying components (and differing degrees of vertical integration) in different locations, they do illustrate important differences in operating costs across Europe. In the UK, low total wage costs (i.e. hourly wage rates plus social costs – see Table 2.1 on page 22), combined with longer working hours, are insufficient to compensate for lower productivity per head. In Germany, high wage costs were offset by greater productivity, but not enough to match the overall (labour) cost per vehicle in Spain. Opel (GM) claimed in 1992 that it cost £260 per unit more to make its Vectra car in Russelsheim (Germany) compared with Luton (UK) (Fisher, 1992a). Equally, VW claimed (also in 1992) that the Polo model cost DM600 less per unit to make in Spain (in its Seat subsidiary) compared with its main plant at Wolfsburg, Germany. Given the very low margins on small, high-volume models, this is a

Table 3.13   Ford of Europe labour productivity and vehicle costs, 1989–91

Hours per vehicle	*1989*	*1990*	*1991 (forecast)*
Köln (Fiesta)	33.5	29.9	28.5
Valencia (Fiesta)	35.0	33.3	34.1
Dagenham (Fiesta)	59.4	52.2	40.0
Saarlouis (Escort)	29.5	33.9	32.5
Halewood (Escort)	58.7	63.8	43.0
Ghent (Transit)	48.7	45.7	45.1
Southampton (Transit)	70.4	73.2	64.0
Average hours worked per annum			
UK	1747	1 786	
Spain	1 731	n.a.	
Belgium	1 731	1 755	
Germany	1 590	1 612	
Labour and overhead costs (1991) Fiesta (per unit) ($s)			
Dagenham	1 344		
Köln	1 084		
Valencia	992		

Source: Ford of Europe.

significant difference. All the above suggests that the decentralisation of automobile production away from traditional locations is at least partly attributable to cost considerations, although, as we argue below, the adoption of new capital–labour relations and working practices has also featured significantly. A number of firms have used new plants in close proximity to existing factories to develop new working practices. The Volvo case has already been discussed; other examples include Mercedes at Rastatt (Germany) and BMW at Regensburg (Germany). The Regensburg plant, for example, is in a relatively rural area in a small town of 130 000 people. Here BMW have introduced a novel team-based shift system which allows 30 per cent more working time than their conventional shift system. So, shifts in productivity capacity, both within national boundaries and across them, are being used to reorganise the production process, but so too are changes occuring in existing plants. Rover in the UK is perhaps the most 'advanced' among the indigenous European assembly firms in operating lean working practices (Smith, 1992a, 1992b), including removing job demarcations, giving common terms and conditions for all workers, and provisions for worker–task flexibility. Ultimately, the problems of many existing plants will not reside in working practices or union – management relations so much as in physical layout and location. As we shall show in Chapter 4, the shift in productive investment away from Germany by the assemblers is being matched by a switch in their sourcing patterns, again with a view to using more suppliers outside Germany, even for their remaining German production.

3.5 JAPANESE INWARD INVESTMENT

Of all the influences on the changing structure of the European automobile industry, Japanese inward investment is probably the most visible and the most contentious. On the one hand, other EC member states regard, to varying degrees, the arrival of Japanese volume assembly operations in the UK as a major threat to their established producers. On the other hand, within the UK, critics have questioned the economic benefits thought to accrue to the Britain from playing host to Japanese inward investment (Garrahan and Stewart, 1991). At the EC level, debate has chiefly been concerned with two issues: local content; and the extent to which local (i.e. within the EC) production by Japanese firms should be counted against the total market share quota to be allowed to those firms. Both these issues will be explored more fully in Chapter 9. Here we concentrate on the nature of those investments currently in place or already announced, and the likely impact on components suppliers in Europe.

Japanese foreign direct investment into Europe has thus far been biased towards the UK (Thomsen and Nicolaides, 1991) both in general and in terms of the automotive industry (Jones and North, 1991). The UK has deliberately sought to attract such investment: the combination of clear political support, low wages, a much-restrained and less militant workforce than in previous times, and in some cases outright financial help, have secured considerable investment in the UK (de Jonquires, 1989; Oliver and Wilkenson, 1989). We argue elsewhere that the emphasis in policy and academic research on Japanese inward investment is somewhat misplaced, in that such investment is still relatively small compared with the aggregate flows from Europe and the USA (Wells, 1992). However, in the context of the automotive industry it is clear that Japanese firms are continuing to build their presence in the UK and the rest of Europe through a mixture of direct greenfield investments and alliances. Tables 3.14 and

Table 3.14 Japanese automobile assemblers in the UK

Firm	Date	Location	Investment	Planned output (date)
Nissan	1986	Sunderland Phase 1 Phase 2	£620M	220 000 (1992) 400 000 (2000)
	1991	Cranfield R&D Centre	n.a.	Capable of working by 1995
Toyota	1990	Burnaston	£700	100 000 (1992) 200 000 (1998)
	1990	Shotton	£140	200 000 Engines (1998)
Honda	1989	Swindon	£60	100 000 Engines (1994)
	1991	Swindon	£300	100 000 (1994)

Sources: Compiled from company reports, company press releases, and press reports.

3.15 summarise the investments by Japanese automobile assemblers in the UK (Table 3.14), and the wider pattern of Japanese production in Europe to be expected by 1999 (Table 3.15).

Up to now, total investment is of the order of £1.8bn. Japanese firms in the UK have made two key commitments: to export a high proportion of output (to the rest of the EC) and to purchase a high proportion of parts locally (Griffiths, 1989). It is interesting to note that, thus far, the European operations of Japanese automobile firms can hardly be considered to be independent nodes within a global network. The Nissan technical centre in Brussels, for example, will be responsible for body, suspension, drive axles and trim for future European models, but not the core areas of powertrain and body platform. The embryonic development of research and technical centres, however, suggests a different logic from that of production. It is notable that these functions have been placed in Belgium and Germany (though Nissan also has a centre at Cranfield), echoing the recent Ford decision to shift move its UK-based R&D operations to Germany.

Table 3.15   Total possible automobile, light commercial vehicle, leisure and utility vehicle production by Japanese firms in Europe by 1999

Firm	Output	Type	Location
Nissan	400 000	Cars	UK
Toyota	300 000	Cars	UK
Honda	200 000	Cars	UK
GM–Isuzu	100 000	Light CVs, off-road vehicles	UK
Nissan	150 000	Light CVs, off-road vehicles	Spain
Toyota	100 000	Light CVs	Germany
Ford–Mazda	120 000	Cars	Germany
Volvo–Mitsubishi	200 000	Cars	The Netherlands
Suzuki	150 000	Cars, leisure, utility	Spain
Daihatsu–Piaggio	60 000	Light CVs	Italy
Total	1 830 000		

Sources: Author estimates.

Of most interest to this book is the second of the two main commitments, that to local purchase. Local content is difficult to define precisely, but in simple terms the UK sought agreement with the Japanese firms that 80 per cent of the ex-works cost of the vehicle would be contributed locally. How much of an impact this has on suppliers depends upon the amount of value accounted for by the assembler, and the definition of 'local'. Here we would note that Nissan in the UK is highly vertically integrated – having its own foundry, its own plastic-injection-moulding facility, and a captive supplier of small pressings on site, for example – so that much of the local content is accounted for by Nissan itself. Actual sourcing practices also vary greatly, with Honda largely using existing Rover suppliers in the UK, whereas Toyota and Nissan appear to be sourcing more widely. One recent estimate suggested that by 1999 the annual spending on components by Japanese assemblers will be over £4bn at current prices (EIU, 1992). Toyota estimate that their Burneston plant (UK) will spend about £700m per annum from 1995 on parts and components. Honda will use 138 suppliers to purchase parts for its Synchro mid-size passenger car to be built at its new Swindon plant, in the UK. Of these firms, 89 are located in the UK, 19 in France, 13 in Germany and 4 in Italy (EIU, 1992). This does not mean, however, that, in terms of ownership, the firms are British or German, etc. Inevitably, sourcing has become political too. A clear example was given to us in the course of our research. A Japanese assembler in the UK wrote to a UK component supplier saying that they considered the supplier the best in Europe and intended to use them as a source. Following lobbying from a rival French firm which involved govern-mental (ministerial) intervention, the UK supplier lost the contract. Japanese firms realise that access to other EC markets will be easier if they can source components from those markets.

The spatial dimension of these sourcing practices quite clearly does not replicate the 'Toyota City' phenomenon of tightly clustered suppliers in close proximity to the assembler firm in a vertically disintegrated production structure (Hill, 1989). In the US case, some clustering and regional level concentration was evident (Mair *et al.*, 1988; Glasmeier and McClusky, 1987) such that the seven US states which are host to the transplants also account for 79 per cent of Japanese automobile components firms. But this pattern hardly amounts to the massive production complex established at Toyota City. In the case of the UK, some clustering around Japanese assembly operations has been identified, but it is weakly developed. Thus Tighe

(1991) reports that in 1990 Nissan spent £280 million on UK-based suppliers, predominantly in the North East (where the Nissan plant is located), where £133 million went to twenty-three suppliers. Interestingly, a report on quality problems in the UK supply base serving Nissan suggests that Nissan may source more widely in the EC in future (NEDC, 1991). The Japanese firms appear to be happy to use this dispersed supply base, though there is an emerging strategy within the automotive components sector in Europe to develop decentralised warehousing in order to serve hybrid just-in-time systems (both Japanese and indigenous European). Typically, the new decentralised warehouse will actually constitute a sub-assembly operation as well. We return to the issue of just-in-time, and that of inward investment by Japanese components firms, in the Chapter 4. Here, the key point to note is that while Japanese assemblers may have new policies and practices with respect to the supply base, they are mainly using existing firms rather than encouraging a 'second wave' of Japanese components suppliers, as happened in the USA. The arrival of the Japanese assemblers certainly may make the geography of the supplier industry more complex, but is unlikely to yield new clustering. We shall return to the question of supply to the Japanese automobile assemblers in Europe in Chapter 4, where we shall discuss the likely scale of purchases and the spatial distribution of the supply bases used.

3.6   EASTERN EUROPE AND THE EC PERIPHERY

If Japan is the most important source of inward investment activity, then the most significant location for outward investment by the European automobile industry in recent years has been Eastern Europe, and an area we may term the extra-EC periphery (see Table 3.16 on page 64). Notwithstanding the unprecedented nature of the changes under way in the former Communist centralised economies of Eastern Europe as they move towards liberal democratic market status, the automobile industry has been at the forefront of investment and alliance relations in the region. In this section we review the transformation of Eastern Europe from the perspective of the automobile industry and consider what may portend for competition generally and the further development of the European components industry. In what follows, two key points should be borne in mind: first, that Eastern European developments need to be seen in the context of the EC periphery more generally; and second, that in many respects the corporate process of economic integration is preceding the political. Thus, just as Ford and General Motors could claim to have pan-European corporate organisation structures well ahead of the provisions of Open Europe which came into force at the end of 1992, so too have firms sought to integrate production across EC borders ahead of moves to include former COMECON countries and Yugoslavia within some extended form of EC.

There are clear differences emerging in the way in which firms co-ordinate spatially extensive production systems. In the case of GM, for instance, there has been a more intensive use of facilities within Germany (with the addition of a night shift and holiday working) alongside a decentralisation of assembly. Interestingly, parts of the production process, notably the increasingly capital-intensive pressings area, remain highly concentrated in Germany – the Eisenach plant, for example, will be supplied from existing pressings operations in (West) Germany and will not have its own press-shop – while the remaining labour-intensive assembly work is being spread more widely. Thus, components sets as a proportion of total production in Germany (i.e. kits which are assembled elsewhere) rose from 14.6 per cent (1985) to 28.6 per cent in 1990, even when the kit assembly operation in Eisenach is included in the German production figures. Compare this with the Fiat strategy in Poland, where the Italian firm has placed the entire production of a new model (the Cinquecento, a small car) in its recently-acquired FSO plant. This plant will serve both the local Polish market and markets in Western Europe, including Italy.

3.7 EUROPEAN AUTOMOBILE FIRMS: HOW GLOBAL? HOW LEAN?

Europe is a location for several global firms in the automobile sector, but European firms cannot, in general, be considered to be global. Perhaps the only exception to this is VW, although if all of Fiat's plans for Eastern Europe come to fruition then it too could attain global status.

Table 3.17 presents data on the proportion of production outside the parent country for all firms who had such production in the period 1985–89. Significant firms with no international production facilities in this period include Mitsubishi, Suzuki, Mercedes, VAZ Lada, Hyundai, Daihatsu, Isuzu, Rover, BMW, Kia, Zastava, Polski-Fiat,

Table 3.16   Investments in Eastern Europe and the EC periphery (excluding former Yugoslavia), 1989–92

Firm	Date	Location	Type of investment
VW	1990	Zwickau, Germany	DM3bn to produce Polo II. Capacity 250 000 p.a.
VW	1990	Cheminz, Germany	DM2bn for new engine facility. Capacity 400 000 p.a.
VW	1991	Former Czechoslovakia	Purchase of 31% of Skoda for DM620m, to rise to 70% by 1995. Ultimately plan to invest DM10bn. Cars, capacity 400 000 p.a. Engines, capacity 500 000 p.a.
VW	1991	Former Czechoslovakia	Alliance with BAZ. DM60m to produce 30 000 Passat cars p.a. DM900m to produce 400 000 gear boxes p.a.
GM	1991	Eisenach, Germany	DM1bn. Capacity for 150 000 cars p.a. Astra model.
GM	1989	Hungary	$215m cumulative on engine production, 400 000 units p.a. capacity. Kit assembly 15 000 units p.a.
GM	1992	Poland	Agreement with FSO. Scaled down proposal to assemble 10 000 cars p.a.
GM	1992	Finland	Assembly of 40 000 Calibra models p.a. by Saab–Velmet.
GM	1992	Turkey	Kit assembly, 15 000 units p.a.
GM	1989	Austria	£192m to develop gearbox production plant, capacity 800 000 units pa.
Fiat	1990	Poland	Alliance with FSM. Sole source of the Cinquecento. Capacity of 200 000 p.a.
Fiat	1992	Russia	A complex proposal which has changed greatly. Currently preparing an alliance with ELAZ to produce 300 000 cars p.a., investment of $2.6bn.
Fiat	1992	Algeria	Kit assembly, 30 000 units p.a.
Fiat	1992	Turkey	Alliance with Tofas. $900m investment. Capacity by 1996 of 100 000 units p.a.
Suzuki	1989	Hungary	Alliance with Autokonzern. $138m invested to produce 100 000 Swift models p.a.

Firm	Date	Location	Type of investment
Rover	1993	Bulgaria	Alliance with Vanio to produce 50 000 Maestro models p.a.
Citroën	1992	Hungary	FFr10bn to produce 300 000 gearboxes p.a. in alliance with Videoton.
Ford	1992	Poland	£28m investment, 1000 jobs to make seat covers.
Ford	1990	Hungary	$80m plant to produce ignition coils and fuel pumps.
Chrysler	1992	Austria	Alliance with Steyr to produce 40 000 Voyager models p.a. £330m invested, one-third subsidised.
Peugeot	1992	Poland	Kit assembly by FS Lubin, up to 10 000 units p.a. £36m investment, 405 model.
Ford	1992	Bulgaria	Alliance to produce 20 000 'pick-up' vehicles p.a.
Toyota	1993	Turkey	$325m proposed investment, 40% Toyota. Greenfield plant of 100 000 units p.a. capacity. 2000 jobs.
PSA	1993	Turkey	$350m proposed investment. Greenfield plant of 100 000 units p.a. capacity. 4000 jobs.

Sources: Compiled from company reports, company press releases, and press reports.

Daewoo, Saab, Skoda, Trabant, ZAZ Zaporojetz, Moskvitch, Wartburg, GAZ Volga, SEVEL, IMV, and Porsche.

First, with respect to Table 3.17, it is clear that Ford and GM are in a league of their own in terms of international production facilities. As their US operations have come under increasing pressure, so the overseas production facilities have become more significant. The rise in the proportion of external (i.e. outside the parent country) production is almost entirely attributable to declines in production volumes in the USA. The very low level of internationalisation of the Japanese firms is also apparent, because in most cases this period fails to capture the impact of so-called 'transplant' investment in the USA (but note the cases of Honda and Mazda, which were the first to invest in US production facilities). The figures for Renault and PSA are somewhat deceptive because much of their overseas production consists of the assembly of kits which are actually manufactured in France. The

Table 3.17   Proportion of production outside parent country, 1985–9
(percentage)

	1985	1986	1987	1988	1989
GM	31.0	33.7	35.7	38.2	42.0
Ford	56.7	55.5	54.8	57.3	58.6
Toyota	2.2	2.5	3.1	3.1	9.1
VW	32.1	31.9	30.8	34.5	31.5
Nissan	7.0	7.7	10.6	14.1	12.4
PSA	15.3	13.5	17.6	17.4	19.4
Renault	18.8	20.1	21.0	21.6	21.8
Chrysler	2.9	2.0	6.5	11.3	13.0
Fiat	8.7	8.2	10.1	8.4	8.0
Honda	1.3	18.8	25.0	30.0	27.8
Volvo	29.0	30.5	30.9	30.5	33.8
Mazda	0	0	0.5	15.6	18.3

Source: Calculated from MVMA, World Motor Vehicle Data, 1989–90.

figures for VW appear understated: again, it rather depends on how non-domestic production is defined. The EIU (1991) considered that in 1990 1.816m out of a total of 3.058m units were produced by VW in Germany: that is, about 40 per cent of production was outside the parent country. Finally, it is worth noting just how much the picture has changed after the period covered by the data. Japanese investments in the USA and Europe are coming on stream, while the opening up of Eastern Europe has provided the opportunity for a number of firms to expand their international presence while also leading to the end of independent existence for firms such as Skoda, Trabant and Wartburg. The impact on the European automobile industry of the enormous political and economic changes under way in Eastern Europe are discussed more fully below.

One of the main arguments of the 'globalisation' thesis is that production for and in the original domestic market is of decreasing significance. We have already shown that imports are taking an increasing share of all national markets, and that in general an increasing share of domestic production is being exported. However, an examination of this pattern at a corporate level reveals how far the Japanese firms are really 'novices' when it comes to global production.

However, it is probably true to say that European firms are seeking to emulate aspects of Japanese production methods, both in terms of shop-floor practice and in the wider conduct of the business – for example, in quality assurance, co-makership, just-in-time delivery, preferred suppliers and so on. On the other hand, the prevailing concern appears to be with costs *per se* rather than organisation, thus the adaptation of elements of lean production are in parallel with a process of labour rationalisation. In this concluding section we illustrate some of the changes currently under way in the organisation of European production in the automobile industry which will lead into the more specific discussion of changing relations with the components industry in the Chapter 4. Here we concentrate on changes that may be considered 'internal' to the firm. In Chapter 4 we show how these changes relate to new 'external' practices with respect to the supply base.

In an important report, the Boston Consulting Group (BCG, 1991) argued that European firms had some way to go before they could claim to be 'lean', but the report assumed that becoming lean was the critical aim and that it was really a question of management prerogative. The extent to which management may simply impose lean production on its workforce is, in reality, severely constrained. As we argue elsewhere (Rawlinson and Wells, 1992), the transition phase is mediated and negotiated in most instances, with a high degree of involvement at a shop-floor level. It could also be argued, with some justification, that rationalisation in the European automobile industry has been driven by traditional cost concerns pursued in a traditional manner (Mair, 1992). However, a number of assemblers have sought to use new peripheral locations to develop new working practices or to adapt existing practices as was discussed above. Most obvious is the case of Nissan in Sunderland, whose working practices have had much attention. While we recognise that claims of intensification of work and continuous surveillance may have some merit, our own experience inside the plant suggests that some critics have been blinded by their own theoretical perspective (notably Garraghan and Stewart, 1991). Certainly, for those shop-floor managers and team leaders who had previous experience of the motor industry, there was a sense of euphoria in Nissan – and this is not surprising. These people had the very best of equipment and a 'clean slate' on which to create the best possible working methods. Several commented to us that, unlike other firms, it was possible at Nissan to make decisions and implement changes quickly, to feel in control of the working environment. Indeed, we have argued elsewhere that changes in work organisation and practices depend greatly on the existing character of labour–management relations (Rawlinson and Wells, 1992).

It is clear that shop-floor production practices are more than just a question of managment rationality, but cannot be separated from the broader social context. While the lean production authors (Womak *et al.*, 1990) are dismissive of Volvo in Sweden and of their attempts to develop job-enrichment, it is interesting that GM, with their recent purchase of Saab, have not sought simply to impose changes. Saab, prior to the GM purchase, suffered a 25 per cent job turnover and a daily absenteeism rate of 10 per cent among blue collar workers (Done and Taylor, 1991), problems which have been a long term feature of automobile production in Sweden (Rhys, 1974). The changes introduced by GM, including team working, continuous training, merit-related pay and a 30 per cent cut in the workforce have cut staff turnover to 8 per cent and absenteeism to 5 per cent. Productivity rose from 85 labour hours per car to 60 labour hours per car. Significantly, Done and Taylor (1991) report that of hours contractually available, only 62.8 per cent were worked in Saab compared with 90.8 per cent at GM Continental in Belgium. Most of the difference was attributable to broader social costs: 3.3 per cent lost to military serive; 5.8 per cent to parental leave; and 7.8 per cent to non-automotive study leave. The attempts by Volvo to create more interesting work have to be seen in this light. The stabilisation of the workforce is a critical first step in establishing more efficient working methods.

In the context of this rather mixed conclusion, the implications for the European components industry are by no means clear. Certainly major changes are under way, but the impact those changes will have upon the supply base depends fundamentally upon the pre-existing structure of the supply base and the character of interfirm relations. It is to these issues which we now turn.

4 The European Components Industry: An Overview

4.1 INTRODUCTION

Here, we are simply concerned to provide a general background, both theoretical and empirical, to the more detailed discussions in the later empirical chapters. The automotive components industry is a substantial one in both employment and turnover terms, but there is also a widespread perception that it is a sector under threat for a number of reasons (BCG, 1991), leading to rationalisation, concentration and internationalisation (Carr, 1988, 1993). The following section describes the sector from the available literature and information sources. Thereafter, we move on to consider the main forces for restructuring the sector. Finally, we outline a key determinant of change in the sector – the extent to which new buyer–supplier relations are being established (Cole, 1988). Here we compare the theoretical and idealised model with the evidence for actual practice by the various vehicle assemblers and the components sector. In what emerges, it is clear that great diversity is shown in supplier policies by the vehicle assemblers, and that, for each assembler, diversity also exists according to the component under consideration.

4.2 SCALE, SCOPE AND STRUCTURE

What is the European automotive components industry? There is no one answer to this question, but here we attempt to segment and describe the industry and indicate where some of the boundaries may lie.

4.2.1 Scale

It is impossible to know the size of the industry in exact terms. There is no real agreement as to the number of firms, the value of the industry in terms of turnover, the number of people employed, or the extent to which various sectors such as steel, plastics, electronics and so on can be described as automotive. In many instances, automotive components firms are part of a larger group, either a parent automobile assembly firm (for example, ECIA owned by PSA; AC Rochester owned by GM), or a firm with wider interests (for example, Bendix within the Allied-Signal group). Indeed, such are the problems of identifying the exact proportion of turnover, employment and so on. accounted for by automotive components in these groups, that one well-informed report abandoned attempts to rank firms according to scale of involvement in the sector (see Sleigh, 1991). Official statistics only capture part of the overall industry, and only a part of automotive components in particular – especially in sub-sectors such as presswork (see Chapter 6) which have traditionally supplied inputs to several industrial sectors (in the case of presswork, for example, products are often supplied also to the construction, sanitary ware, white goods, electronics, and aerospace industries). Equally, in newer products such as engine management systems, the introduction of new technology also brings the involvement of new corporate actors – in this case Siemens and Hitachi for example – or the development of new related activities by established firms (for example, Bosch or Lucas).

In a major study for the European Commission, the Boston Consulting Group attempted to define the European components industry. Their analysis may be taken as a benchmark for the sector, but even so their findings should be treated with caution. At the aggregate level the study (BCG, 1991) found that automotive production down the supply chain was structured as shown in Table 4.1.

The value of the EC independent component production industry was estimated at Ecu79bn, employment at 950 000 (or 2.6 per cent total EC industrial employment), dominated by five countries (Germany, France, Italy, Spain and the UK), which accounted for 90 per cent of output and employment. These figures exclude captive suppliers to the automotive assemblers. The study estimated there were 3250 companies in total, but did not provide an explanation of the criteria used to select firms. Table 4.2, reproduced from Sleigh (1989) gives a reasonable estimate of the size composition of the European components industry.

As can be seen, Sleigh estimates about 1000 firms and total annual sales of $92bn. Lamming (1989a) estimates 1500 major suppliers in Europe, falling to less than 1000 over the next ten years. PRS (1985)

Table 4.1   Value added in the vehicle supply chain, Europe

Sector	Percentage value added
Materials	11
Processing industries	28
Independent component producers	21
Vehicle assemblers' own component producers	2
Vehicle assemblers' plants, components	13
Vehicle assemblers' plants, assembly	24

Source: BCG, 1991.

Table 4.2   Size distribution of the European automotive components industry, 1989

Turnover range ($m)	Number of firms	Total sales ($m)
Over 1000	17	44.8
500–999	18	13.0
200–499	21	6.7
100–199	11	1.7
25–99	13	0.9
Others in 25–99 range not contacted	80	18.0
10–24	100	3.3
1–10	740	3.7
Total	1000	92.0

Source: Sleigh, 1989.

identified some 6000 companies throughout Western Europe, though the quality of the information is suspect. Subsequently, the Economist Intelligence Unit (EIU) concentrates on the eighty leading components suppliers, identifies the country of the parent for each firm, and the principal country of manufacture in Europe (see Table 4.3).

Table 4.3　Ownership and principal production location for the leading European automobile components firms

	Parent location	Main manufacturing location
Germany	36	43
France	8	15
UK	8	9
Italy	7	8
Belgium	0	1
Spain	1	2
Sweden	1	1
Japan	2	n.a.
USA	16	n.a.
Total	80	80

Source:　Sleigh, 1991.

Table 4.3 indicates that, of the German components industry is dominant, both in terms of ownership and main production location. This view is reinforced by data from the BCG (1991) study. Table 4.4 summarises production, value added and employment in the five leading countries in Europe, which comprise 96 per cent of total employment.

Further support for the overall strength of the German components industry comes from Lamming (1989a) who provides the figures given in Table 4.5. However, with reference to Table 4.4, the key point to

Table 4.4　Production, value added and employment in the leading European automobile components countries, 1988

Country	Production, ECUbn, per cent		Value added, ECUbn, per cent		Employment 000s, per cent	
Germany	30.6	39.0	14.5	44.3	329.1	34.6
France	16.9	21.5	5.7	17.3	168.7	17.8
Italy	11.1	14.1	4.5	13.7	138.5	14.6
Spain	8.8	11.2	3.6	10.9	147.1	15.5
UK	8.2	10.5	3.3	10.2	132.6	14.0
Others	2.9	3.6	1.3	2.1	34.0	3.5
Total	78.5	100.0	32.7	100.0	950.0	100.0

Source:　BCG, 1991.

Table 4.5   The numbers of automotive components firms in European
             countries

Country	Major firms	Minor firms
Germany	450	5 000
France	400	1 500
Italy	250	1 000
UK	300	1 500
Spain	50	500
Others	50	500
Total	1 500	10 000

Source: Lamming, 1989a.

note is that German production accounts for 44.3 per cent of value
added, but only 34.6 per cent of employment in Europe, an indication
of both higher labour productivity and greater levels of technological
sophistication. Lamming, as a former purchaser for Jaguar, bases his
data on qualitative perceptions and in-depth working knowledge of the
supplier sector, rather than on direct measures such as turnover, again
because of the difficulties of arriving at sensible figures for many firms.
In terms of concentration, Lamming (1989a) estimates that the leading
twenty-five firms account for some 40 per cent of the overall original
equipment market. The BCG (1991) study found 138 firms employing
over 1000 people, and that these accounted for nearly half of all
employment.

The BCG study also provides some data on the differences at a
national level of industry structure (see Table 4.6). It is not easy to
reconcile these two sets of figures, except to note that the number of
firms rather depends upon how closely the industry is examined: those
firms providing aftermarket components, sub-components, production
equipment and so on are often more difficult to identify. In a recent
exercise the Black Country Development Corporation identified over
2000 firms in their area with an interest in the automotive sector.
Equally, in Chapter 6 we show that there is a substantial body of firms,
generally small, who are not classified by official statistics as being
automotive components producers yet who work almost entirely in
this area.

From Table 4.6 it can be inferred that the components industry in
Italy and Spain is characterised by a relatively high proportion of

Table 4.6   The numbers of automotive components firms by country

Country	Number of firms
Italy	1 000
Germany	600
Spain	450
France	400
UK	350
Belgium	150
Portugal	110
The Netherlands	80
Republic of Ireland	50
Greece	30
Denmark	25
Luxembourg	1

Source: BCG, 1991.

small firms. The UK and France have a cluster of large firms. Germany has a broad spread of firms in different size categories from the very large to the small, but is especially well represented in the medium-sized range (100–500 employees).

4.2.2   Scope

An additional complication in the automotive components sector is that the development of new materials and product technologies has meant that the sectoral composition of the sector has changed over time. Initially, the vast bulk of the components industry was involved in various forms of metal processing: casting, turning, pressing, welding and so on, or in vehicle electrics: lights, wiring, starter motors, alternators and so on. However, the progressive introduction of plastics, metals other than steel, ceramics, solid state electronics, hydraulics and other new technologies has been accompanied by the departure of some firms, the realignment of others, and the arrival of new firms. In this sense, technological change in materials, processes or products provides a hub around which industrial and spatial change may also occur. In some instances, spatial continuity is evident. The friction-materials producer, Mintex (part of the BBA group) has its main production location in Cleckheaton, Yorkshire which has historically been one of the centres of the UK textile industry. This location was chosen because the original friction material used, asbestos impregnated with a resin, was a woven product which required the skills and technologies of the textile industry. Now, asbestos has been all but replaced, but the firm remains in Cleckheaton and friction materials remain a prime interest.

Ultimately, these changes in technology are driven by a number of causes, notably state legislation on emissions, safety and so on, and more generally the shift in competition (in the new car market) from simple price per unit to more complex value and performance criteria. That is, vehicle assemblers are under continuous pressure to produce vehicles which are safer, quieter, use less fuel, pollute less, are more amenable to recycling, more comfortable, embody greater reliability, and offer greater specifications, while real price per unit has been falling (Seiffert and Walzer, 1984). This presents the assembler with very large costs in product development, and in practice no firm is able to encompass all of the technologies required to produce a car.

However, these trends make it more difficult to identify the automobile components industry, especially further down the supply chain where finished and semi-finished materials are concerned. They also have an impact on industry structure. Typically, for example, electronics applications have to replace mechanical technology which has matured over many years of mass production, and the mature technology is cheap and of known performance. Generally, hybrid solutions are sought, leading to the progressive and piecemeal introduction of electronics. This is bringing together firms with competencies in the relevant technologies, as we shall show in Chapter 8 which deals with clutches and brakes. An alternative approach, as seen with engine management systems, is to overlay the existing mechanical technology with electronics and software to improve efficiency. Anti-lock braking (ABS) and engine management systems (EMS) are probably the fastest growing areas of application for electronics in the vehicle, but others include air conditioning, steering, active suspension, displays and passive restraint systems. With additional in-vehicle features such as traffic guidance systems, it is possible that electronics will account for 20 per cent of vehicle cost by the year 2000. These trends are supporting general pressure for primary systems integrator suppliers to develop.

Lee (1989) asserts that by the year 2000 plastics may account for 30 per cent by weight of the finished vehicle, compared with 8 per cent at the beginning of the 1990s. Plastics are now being used even in high volume applications, most notably the Fiat Tipo tailgate, produced in volumes of well over 300 000 units per year. The introduction of new materials and products may be accompanied by the arrival of new firms, together with the exclusion of previous firms. Alternatively, firms with existing automotive components business may shed some areas and concentrate on others. A typical example is Lucas, which has disposed of its more established interests in high-volume vehicle instruments, lighting, alternators, starters and small motors in order to concentrate on (diesel) engine management systems, fuel injection units, braking and chassis systems, and body electronics. More broadly there is a corporate strategy in Lucas to reduce dependence on the automotive sector and the UK market altogether.

4.2.3 Structure

As we have intimated above, the European automotive components industry is dominated by large firms, often part of larger groups, but also comprises many smaller and medium sized firms which collectively account for a significant proportion of output and employment. At least in the case of the UK, it has been argued that the early 1980s period of economic downturn resulted in up to 30 per cent of existing automotive components factories closing and perhaps 40 per cent of jobs which exist in 1979 being lost (Amin and Smith, 1991). Several of the largest components suppliers are controlled by vehicle assemblers, an issue we shall discuss later with reference to vertical integration. Many of the largest firms have grown by acquisition, enhancing levels of concentration in the sector (IRES, 1991).

Of particular interest here is the question of tiering in the supply base. Studies of the Japanese automotive industry have clearly shown the existence of a layered system of suppliers. This model broadly accords with the descriptions of the Japanese automotive components industry from Hill (1989), Odaka *et al.* (1988), and Cusumano (1985). A number of points can be made with regard to this structure. First, the vehicle assembler only makes some 30 per cent by value of the parts in the vehicle, with the rest outsourced. Those items that are retained may be regarded as core activities. Typically, almost all firms seek to manufacture much of the basic body or structure of the vehicle, together with the powertrain (i.e. engine, gearbox and transmission). In Japanese firms the 'core' is more tightly defined, and levels of vertical integration are not high. Second, the number of primary (or direct) suppliers is relatively low. In the case of Mitsubishi, for example, the assembler has an equity interest in 38 of the 156 primary suppliers, and the remaining 118 are part of the wider Mitsubishi *kyoryokukai* (suppliers' club). This is a pervasive feature of the supply base in Japan, where most of the major suppliers are part owned by one or more vehicle assemblers (though usually this falls well short of a controlling percentage share of the equity). It is important because it illustrates the Japanese solution to the key problem of vertical integration through direct control; that of ensuring the efficiency of captive suppliers. Under this system, Japanese assemblers have considerable control but also some 'distance' between themselves and their suppliers. The *keiretsu* structure (a family of companies with cross-share foldings) also tends to prevent suppliers to one assembler being suppliers to another, although not all Japanese assemblers work within a *keiretsu* regime (for example, Honda) and there is some evidence to suggest that the 'exclusive' supply hierarchy is also breaking down. In Europe, by contrast, supplier firms tend to be either majority owned by assemblers or with no equity links at all. Third, it is notable that some supplies are still delivered direct from the secondary suppliers – these will tend to be low-value, high volume products such as washers where assemblers can hold high-stock levels at little cost.

Finally, the implication of the above model is that primary suppliers are often concerned with sub-assembly of particular parts rather than manufacture, which may take place within sub-suppliers. Moreover, the assembler expects primary suppliers to manage their own supply bases, passing on methods to measure and improve quality, speed of response and so on. Whereas in Europe the tendency has been for assemblers to undertake much of the detailed sub-assembly of components before they are installed in a vehicle, in Japan the tendency has been for suppliers to deliver complete sub-assembled modules. The structure of the supply chain is closely related to the nature of purchasing policies in Japan. In the case of Europe the implication is clear: if European assemblers (and indeed Japanese transplants in Europe) are going to emulate Japanese purchasing methods then a new, tiered structure will emerge. In this context, the characteristics of the Japanese purchasing model and the extent to which it differs from that in Europe is of critical significance, as is the degree to which that Japanese model may be adopted in Europe. Evidence from the US suggests that Japanese transplants have achieved similar quality levels to their domestic operations in terms of components supply, and that these transplants are performing better than domestic US assemblers in terms of components supply, but again differences emerge (Cusumano and Takeishi, 1991).

In later empirical chapters we show that, in Europe, the concepts of tiering and hierarchy in the supply base are not well established (although, see Turnbull *et al.*, 1993 who argue that the process is well under way in the UK). We show that the more likely general pattern is one of oligopolies at various stages down the supply chain, with many firms occupying an ambiguous position in terms of hierarchy. Indeed, there has been little systematic work on defining the characteristics of first-, second- and third-tier firms and the relationships between the various levels. While being a superficially attractive concept, the idea of tiering seems to us rather inappropriate. However, European assemblers are undoubtedly changing the way in which they manage the supply base relative to their own activities, which may include the development of some degree of tiering in the supply base, and it is to this issue which we now turn.

4.3   CHANGING PROCUREMENT REGIMES IN THE AUTOMOTIVE SECTOR

One of the implications of the wider adoption of some form of lean production is that assembler firms have to rely on their supply bases for a greater proportion of the value of the car than was hitherto the case. Jim Robinson, purchasing director for Toyota in the UK, says:

> It is Toyota's belief that business is now so complex that the long-term prosperity of the customer (i.e. the vehicle assembler) and the supplier are inextricably linked. The ongoing struggle for continual improvement in every aspect of business performance cannot be achieved in isolation from each other. With competition ever increasing the importance of customer/supplier partnership cannot be over-stressed. Ignore it at your peril. Survival is not compulsory! (Robinson, 1991, p. 4).

For the vehicle assemblers, competitive success depends upon, among other things, their ability to co-ordinate efficiently a system of suppliers. That is, competition is no longer between stand-alone enterprises but between constellations of secondary firms grouped around primary firms. In Japan, these constellations have had a degree of exclusivity, but in Europe the more likely outcome is competition between more or less interlocking constellations. It is in this context that we introduce the concept of the procurement regime, which will be discussed later. First, however, the issue of vertical disintegration must be considered as this determines the volume of business (at a given level of production) available to suppliers.

4.3.1 Vertical disintegration

Part of the major changes being made currently in the way in which products are designed and manufactured concern the relationships between firms involved in the production process. Elements of this were outlined in the previous chapter. With greater vertical disintegration it is apparent that the level of competition is shifting from the micro or individual firm level to the meso or system of firms level, and the way in which this 'system' is orchestrated by prime firms will play a crucial role in the competitive process (Wormald, 1989). This shift towards 'systemic' competition is happening in two ways. First, the large or prime firms, those which face final markets rather than supply intermediate goods, are developing global collaborative networks between themselves through a range of quasi-horizontal integration strategies. This is a key feature of the globalisation process overall, and was discussed in Chapter 2. Second, and more significantly for the automotive components industry, there has been a reappraisal of the management of the supply base, of those firms which mainly supply intermediate products to other firms rather than direct to the final product market. Here, vertical disintegration carries both advantages and disadvantages.

On the one hand, disintegration allows prime firms to shift product development responsibility on to suppliers, and enables much of the fixed costs in equipment to be made outside the assembler; it also allows the outsourcing of components and sub-assemblies which embody a high labour cost content and offers the possibility of capacity flexibility in the face of volatile demand for the final product (Shutt and Whittington, 1984; Rawlinson, 1991). Typically, the prime firm is large, unionised and carries a high overhead cost compared with the secondary firm, and vertical disintegration allows labour to be segmented into disparate and competing groups (Imrie and Morris, 1992; Shutt and Whittington, 1984). Moreover, for some products, it enables vehicle manufacturers to pass on warranty claims for defective products to the component supplier. Thus in this sense a 'lean' production system is one which allows variations in final demand to be passed on and absorbed within the wider supply base more rapidly than was previously the case – greater variable cost flexibility is achieved over a shorter time period than was previously the case. It also reduces fixed costs and overheads at the level of the assembler, or at least allows resources released from detailed component design to be deployed on key design areas and systems integration. In practice, large differences still exist in the European automobile industry in terms of the absolute level of vertical integration and the extent to which parts are designed in-house by the assemblers (Wormald, 1989). On the other hand, disintegration also means the relinquishing of control in some respects. Supplier firms may have knowledge and competencies beyond those of the assembler customer, or may be in a superior bargaining position for other reasons such as greater size or control of the supply of a particular component. External single sources are vulnerable to disruption from a wide variety of sources including labour unrest, equipment or production failure, and so on. The traditional response of the assemblers has been multiple sourcing strategies of various forms, enabling the prime firm to maintain a 'stable' of suppliers within each product area and play them off against each other. An alternative and historically favoured strategy has been integration, often by purchasing a previously independent supplier. Clearly, continued rationalisation in the supplier base, combined with the trend towards single sourcing (at least at the level of the individual plant or model) and the desire to reduce the complexities of managing a large supply base, have reduced the potential for prime firms to indulge in a strategy of multiple sourcing – though, as we shall illustrate later, the development of pan-European sourcing strategies may be understood as one attempt to reintroduce multiple sourcing.

We would argue that it is important to distinguish between subcontracting and component supply. With the latter the supplier provides complete sub-assembled units or products and will have a written contract with the assembler, often for the lifetime of the model. With the former there is often no actual contract exchanged, only a verbal agreement from the supplier to provide x number of parts at y unit cost over a (short) period of time or at a specified rate per day. It is also important to acknowledge the political dimension to sourcing patterns. For many years assemblers such as Rover, Jaguar and Ford sought to source components where they had their major manufacturing and market interests. Where assemblers have sought to enter non-domestic markets it has sometimes been expedient to purchase local components even where they are not 'competitive' with other sources.

Levels of vertical integration differ between firms and between global regions, as the study by the Boston Consulting Group (BCG,

1991) showed (see Table 4.7). Interestingly, the BCG study expected a substantial proportion of future growth in the automotive components sector to derive from greater levels of vertical disintegration, with the assumption that overall output would also rise. As we show in Chapter 6 and Chapter 8, assembler firms are highly selective about which activities are outsourced, and greater levels of vertical disintegration cannot be assumed in times of underutilisation of capacity when the assembler has facilities which directly compete with outside suppliers. Equally, in some areas, vertical integration has generally increased. Most notable in this regard have been the steps taken by a number of firms selling in the UK to gain control over distribution and retail outlets. Since 1989, Lancia, Alfa Romeo, Toyota, Seat and Nissan have all taken control of UK importers and wholesale distributors which were previously independent operators. These steps can be seen as both an attempt to capture the added value of retailing and finance provision and as a means of getting closer to information on the market. Under a lean rather than a mass production system, importing, distribution and sales become of greater strategic value.

A complicating factor is the issue of captive suppliers. In the BCG (1991) study three of the top twenty firms were owned by major vehicle manufacturers (Magneti Marelli by Fiat; ACG by GM; ECIA by PSA). Ford has considerable components production interests, notably in engine electronics and air-conditioning. GM has an explicit

Table 4.7   Comparative levels of vertical integration

Firm	Value added/sales, per cent	Value added/sales, including component divisions
Fiat	36	51
VW Group	60	60
Renault	55	60
Ford	40	55
GM	40	65
Mercedes	50	51
PSA	45	
Honda	42	
Mazda	32	
Toyota	38	
Nissan	34	

Source: BCG, 1991.

strategy to win more external (that is, non-GM) business for its Automotive Components Group, as has Magneti Marelli. For Magneti Marelli sales to the Fiat Group (the ultimate parent firm) account for 39 per cent of sales, PSA and Renault for 21 per cent, and other firms 40 per cent.

The impact of greater levels of vertical disintegration will depend upon where and how the business is placed. Currently, there is an observable trend among assemblers in Europe to source more in the UK (see Table 4.12 on page 93 for levels of purchasing in the early 1990s). This in turn will help shift the geography of the sector, making some locations more attractive for expansion or acquisition than others. The impact will also depend upon how the business is placed. If vertical disintegration is accompanied by a reduction of the numbers of direct suppliers, as seems to be the case, then a greater volume of work will be placed with a decreasingly number of primary suppliers. The extent to which that greater volume of work is passed on will in turn depend upon levels of vertical disintegration in primary suppliers. The BCG (1991) study is optimistic about the prospects for firms which cease to be primary suppliers, arguing that many will find a role as second- or third-tier suppliers. We have seen no evidence to support this view (see also Amin and Smith, 1991), and our own understanding of the presswork sector, for example, suggests that firms removed from the primary supply base may leave the automotive sector altogether, while those that remain will increase levels of integration by adding more downstream activities such as welding, painting and sub-assembly. So there will be both winners and losers from the process (Turnbull *et al.*, 1993).

There is little doubt that vehicle assemblers in Europe are trying to reduce the numbers of direct suppliers delivering to their plants. The data in Table 4.8, taken from a wide range of sources, may be regarded as illustrative. In most cases, assemblers in Europe have expressed an intention to reduce direct suppliers. Lamming (1989a) contends that typically 80 per cent of the suppliers to any one European assembler provide only 20 per cent of the supply value. However, the number of suppliers does not equate with the numbers of sites of suppliers. The major suppliers tend to be multi-locational, often international. If rationalisation in the supply base is achieved by acquisition, this may give the appearance of having reduced the number of direct suppliers (i.e. fewer names on the list of suppliers) without actually reducing the number of sites from which the assembler is supplied (i.e. only the names above the door are changed). So while Ford may intend to

Table 4.8   Numbers of direct suppliers, 1992

Firm	Number of suppliers
Nissan	195
Honda	155
Toyota	196
Ford	900
GM	2 000
Rover	1 500
Renault	700
PSA	1 500
VW–Audi	1 200
Seat	700
BMW	700
Mercedes	1 500
Volvo	500
Saab	500
Fiat	700

Source: Interviews, press reports.

reduce its supply base to 600 firms by 1995, it is highly unlikely that this will mean only 600 supplier manufacturing sites throughout Europe. Moreover, while there are considerable overlaps, each assembler has a different supply base. If each assembler is looking to maintain three suppliers in each of the 200 main product areas, as Lamming (1989a) suggests, then it is likely that four firms in each component product area will come to dominate. Indeed, this is already the case in the supply of clutches, as we shall show in Chapter 8. Oligopoly, regulated by the vehicle assemblers and by EC monopoly legislation, would appear to be the likely condition for much of the European components industry.

The question of how outsourcing is placed is also relevant. Brake systems are a useful illustration. Nissan in the UK source the entire brake system for their production of the Micra (introduced in 1993) from Lucas Girling. Ford, in contrast, for the Sierra replacement (the Mondeo, introduced in 1993) has Teves front brakes, Girling back brakes, and a Bosch ABS system. GM is often even more extreme: it will buy in components such as brake shoes, plates and so on and build the brakes itself. Thus while all firms buy in brakes, the way they do so is different. These differences are part of the overall effect of the procurement regime discussed below.

4.3.2 The procurement regime

The conventional scope of buyer–supplier literature fails to capture the richness and diversity of these new relationships. These approaches generally have an implicit conception of individual, one-to-one relations between a buyer (purchaser) and a supplier (salesperson). Theories of buyer–supplier relationships derived from a neo-classical economics viewpoint assume that the price mechanism of the market acts perfectly to determine product flows, and that firms act as equals on the market place (see Holmes, 1986 for a critique). Our research, and a reading of current analysis, suggests that the concept of a dynamic procurement regime is more useful in theorising prevalent changes in buyer–supplier relations. A procurement regime may be defined as the total ensemble of interactions which exist between a buyer firm and its suppliers. Such relationships go far beyond the issue of price alone to consider a broad range of interactions. However price continues to feature as a critical part of the equation. This important fact is illustrated in Figure 4.1 for the case of Toyota. Under the Toyota approach the eventual selling price of the vehicle is the starting point, which is then disaggregated into component parts. Given this price, suppliers then have to reduce costs to such a level that they can make a profit.

It is characteristic of Japanese assemblers, for example, that they send teams (typically comprising production engineers, quality experts and personnel from purchasing) into the supplier in order to help them achieve the quality levels demanded (although the ways in which they do this vary). While the buyer firm may have its own characteristic regime, the extent to which it fully embraces the supplier firm will depend upon factors such as relative market power, the possession of firm-specific technological capabilities, and the willingness of both parties to adapt. Toyota, for example, does not insist on separate production areas for its components, nor that its suppliers use the techniques and practices which Toyota insists on for all its other

Toyota way:
  PRICE (fixed) − COST (variable) = PROFIT (variable)

Traditional way:
  COST (variable) + PROFIT (fixed) = PRICE (variable)

Figure 4.1   Alternative sourcing strategies

Source: Robinson, 1991.

customers – though it would be disappointed if suppliers did not eventually embrace the Toyota Production System across its operations. Moreover, supplier firms themselves are adopting various co-operation strategies including joint ventures and the development of supplier clubs or associations. In Wales, the local state (in the form of the Welsh Development Agency) has played a key role in the formation of supplier associations for Llanelli Radiators (Calsonic) and Toyota (Hines, 1992).

The clearest statement on the development of new buyer–supplier relationships in the European automotive industry is from Lamming (1989a, 1989b, 1993), reporting work which formed part of the European research for the International Motor Vehicle Programme (IMVP) study of the global automotive industry, subsequently published in book form in Lamming (1993). The development of these new relationships can be understood as a move away from the adversarial buyer–supplier procurement regime of the past towards a more selective and co-operative regime. Lamming describes this as the 'post-Japanese model', which has several key features in terms of industrial structure:

- The industry will have fewer companies, which will be larger than at present, with greater capabilities.
- The suppliers will be structured in tiers, graded by the nature of their customer links, product technology and so on.
- There will be stronger vertical relationships throughout the tiers.
- Primary suppliers will develop stronger horizontal relationships through joint ventures, technology links and so on.
- Primary suppliers will focus on one key customer, but will have links to others.
- Suppliers will need a multi-market presence, e.g. aftermarket or non-automotive.
- Suppliers will need global production facilities to follow assemblers.
- Competition will be based on 'world-class' manufacturing.

As Lamming (1989a) notes, there is little evidence that the post-Japanese model has yet emerged in Europe. However, Lamming also provides an historical account of changes in procurement regimes in Europe over time. Briefly, these have moved from 'traditional' through 'stress' and 'resolved' to 'Japanese' (see Lamming, 1987, 1993). The two extremes of this argument are characterised in Table 4.9.

Table 4.9   Traditional and post-Japanese procurement regimes

	Traditional	*Post-Japanese*
In-house production	High	Low
Number of suppliers	2 000	300
Sourcing per item	Multiple	Single
R&D	In-house	In supplier
Relations	Adversarial	Partnerships
Contracts	Short-term	Long-term
Criteria	Price	Quality
		Price
		Delivery

Source: Authors' analysis.

Clearly, the above dualist distinction between previous and future procurement regimes is idealised and only of use as a general guide to the direction in which changes are occurring. If the vehicle assemblers are developing new 'governance structures', that is systems and methods to enhance the means by which suppliers are chosen and used, then it is likely that future procurement regimes will embody at least some of the characteristics indicated above. However, the model is insensitive to differences between assemblers, which remain highly significant, and between different technologies. With reference to the assemblers, the first point to note is that they have different historical experiences in terms of how the supply base was managed; they have an inheritance of suppliers from previous times. Thus at the very least it would take ten years (by which time the average assembler will have replaced most of the model range) to recreate the supply base along post-Japanese lines. The adoption of just-in-time deliveries is clearly conditional upon the existing spatial structure of the supply base (Mair, 1991). This means that firms such as Ford, Fiat and Rover are more concerned with developing mechanisms to reduce the numbers of direct suppliers (the Ford Q1 system appears to play this role, for example); the Japanese transplants with a 'clean slate' have been more concerned with developing purchase regimes that enable firms to be selected to be suppliers, and subsequently with direct intervention to improve the performance of potential suppliers.

In most cases, firms in Europe have developed formal quality measures from their suppliers: Ford has its Q1 system; Rover its RG2000 system and 'first choice suppliers'; PSA have three categories of firm – A, B and C; and so on. Table 4.10 shows how Ford have developed a uniform quality rating system for suppliers. Using this system, suppliers are given scores: less than 70 is unacceptable, 70–85 acceptable; with a minimum score of 85, and 12 points in statistical process control, the supplier is rated as excellent. The Ford system is very bureaucratic and statistically-driven, being concerned entirely to develop methodologies and systems to measure, identify and prevent from recurring, any production defects that appear. It stipulates performance parameters and required capabilities. These features are certainly important. Cole (1988), a senior Ford executive, considered that quality costs the firm between 5 per cent and 7 per cent of sales; if these costs could have been reduced by a third, overall profit in 1985 would have been up by $1bn. Yet, it also suppresses positive change. If a supplier wants to introduce a different material, or modify the production process, or alter the product design slightly to improve manufacture, it can be extremely difficult to get such changes accepted by the many parts of the Ford organisation which have to give approval. Thus certain quality levels are achieved, but in a static way with little direct intervention from the assembler to improve matters once the system has been established. There is little incentive for continuous improvement, and no long term support in terms of commitment to certain suppliers by Ford. Nissan, by way of contrast,

Table 4.10   The Ford uniform supplier quality rating system

		Number of points
1.	The adequacy of Supplier's quality systems (20 questions on the Ford Q101 survey)	30
2.	Quality awareness of management	15
	Quality Planning	(5)
	Training	(5)
	Management Control	(5)
3.	Response to quality concerns	5
4.	Ongoing quality performance	50
	Initial samples/first production	(5)
	Process potential studies	(5)
	Product quality	(40)
	Total possible	100

Source: Cole, 1988.

not only spend considerable time vetting potential suppliers to screen out 'unsuitable' candidates, but also will invest considerable corporate resources in direct, shop-floor intervention at the supplier. While it is true that UK suppliers have not yet reached Nissan's standards (NEDC, 1991), quality and productivity have benefited from this intervention, according to all the firms we have visited which supply Nissan. The GM procurement regime is different again. While they too have developed teams to send into suppliers with a view to improving performance, and have stated a commitment to 'partnership', they have retained elements of their previous cost-centred sourcing. In the case of one supplier in Germany, the firm had recently won a GM award for the excellence of its performance, and yet one part they were supplying was withdrawn because GM had found a cheaper source in Brazil. Ironically, the firm was subsequently given the part back again because the Brazilian firm could not sustain its output and quality.

Particular emphasis with the Japanese assemblers is placed on ensuring that prototype production accurately reflects volume production (that is, uses the same materials and processes) to enable problems to be 'engineered out' at an early stage. The example from Robinson (1991) shown in Table 4.11 is illustrative. Toyota takes its production philosophy of eliminating waste in all its forms into its suppliers with teams drawn from manufacturing, production engineering and quality control.

Table 4.11   Resolving production problems prior to volume production: an example from a new parking brake assembly line

	7/10	7/17	8/2	8/17 *Mass production*
Production cycle time 35 sec/	45 sec/ unit (day) 43 sec/ (night)	39 sec/ (day/ night)	35 sec	35 sec
Number of quality defects	3 cases	1 case	0 case	0 case
Number of workability improvements	25 cases	8 cases	2 cases	–

Source: Robinson, 1991.

A final feature of more recent procurement regimes which is so far very weakly developed is the concept of the supplier club or association. Here, all the suppliers of a particular end customer are grouped together to form a club. The club meets on a regular basis to exchange experiences and improve performance in meeting customer requirements. To date the only supplier club in the European motor industry that is actually running is that for Calsonic (Llanelli Radiators) in Wales (Hines, 1992). The key feature of supplier clubs is in fact non-involvement for the customer. Under the approach which Toyota is trying to develop clubs are spatially defined. Toyota benefits from a faster diffusion of its production system and requirements without carrying significant overheads, because it works with a selected few suppliers who then promulgate their experiences among the supply base as a whole.

We return to the differences in procurement regimes in the following chapters (see also Wells and Rawlinson, 1993b). Here, the point to note is that while all the European automobile assemblers appear to be moving towards at least parts of the post-Japanese model, individual procurement regimes at the level of the primary firm vary widely. This tends to lead to a proliferation of terminology. Black box engineering, corner engineering, simultaneous development and cluster engineering all mean roughly the same thing, and seek to express the idea that suppliers of at least some components are working differently from before.

The second major feature causing differentiation in procurement regimes is technology. Where a product and process technology is well established there are usually several suppliers available, firms are more likely to compete on price per unit, and there is less likelihood of co-development between assembler and supplier. In other areas the supplier may have proprietary components, designed by themselves, where co-development really only consists of adapting that product to suit a particular model – typical components of this type include clutches, starter motors and alternators. In our view, the first-tier suppliers, if they can be said to exist, are those with independent technological capabilities and sufficient market power to enable them to secure lifetime, single-source contracts. In this sense, there are many direct suppliers to the assemblers who cannot be considered to be first-tier, because the product they supply is simple and requires little by way of buyer–supplier interaction beyond price negotiations.

In pressings, the basic technology is well established, and there are a great many firms able to undertake a broad range of automotive and non-automotive presswork. Moreover, the vehicle assemblers have considerable knowledge of presswork costs. It remains the case today that the vehicle assemblers undertake most of the die design, and usually own the dies that the presswork components supplier uses to make the parts. Thus, in this area, although changes are occurring, it is still very common for suppliers to work with no written contract and with little sense of the partnership supposedly embedded in the post-Japanese model.

Clutches and brakes represent an interesting intermediate position. Generally, the technology is proprietary; Bosch, for example, has a powerful hold on the ABS market because it has developed the electronics and software technology required. In these cases, the assembler generates the performance parameters required of the product and the size/weight/cost package that would be acceptable, and the supplier seeks to meet those requirements. Thus there are varying degrees of co-development in this area, suppliers are brought in earlier in the model development process, and contracts (and future business) are more secure. On the other hand, brakes and clutches are both wearing parts – they generally have to be replaced (at least in part) during the lifetime of the vehicle. This has generated a complex supply structure for the aftermarket with many firms involved and rather different criteria for competitive success.

Engine management systems (EMS) in some senses represent one of the more advanced components technologies in the vehicle, though even here care needs to be taken. The core of EMS is the electronic chip and embedded software that controls the system, regulating the timing of the spark and so on. However, much of the actual system being controlled is well established in technological terms, comprising various sensors, spark plugs, coil and relays. However, in order to make EMS work it is necessary that the software be developed closely with the engine/transmission and overall vehicle package.

In all cases, the impact of new procurement regimes will be mediated by the mechanisms by which those new regimes are transmitted through the supply chain as a whole. This is not necessarily a case of those firms higher up the supply chain enforcing changes upon those lower down the chain; power relations in the industry as not as simple as this. In many product areas, including the three examined in this book, components firms may be caught between large customer assembler firms on the one hand, and large primary materials firms on the other. Thus in clutches and brakes, for example, the suppliers of these components have little knowledge of the 'art' of making friction materials, this resides in the hands of a few specialist firms. In this case, even where the friction materials supplier is vertically integrated into the clutch manufacturer, it is not clear who leads the process of technological change. In presswork, only a few components-supply companies are large enough (in terms of steel consumption) to warrant direct delivery from steel firms, and even here most of the technological developments in steel types and use derive from relationships between steel suppliers and vehicle assemblers. Components-supply firms in presswork do not have enough market power to influence the quality and reliability of their major purchasing cost.

4.4   PROCUREMENT REGIMES AND SPATIAL STRUCTURE

It is interesting to note that while much attention has been given to the spatial implications of just-in-time production and the supply base, little has been given to the Rover and Jaguar production system of the 1950s and 1960s which generated a dense and spatially localised cluster of suppliers. Before the labour unrest of the later 1960s and 1970s, this operated virtually as a just-in-time system. At this time the constituent firms which finally became Rover Group were remarkably unintegrated – even body pressings were bought from an independent supplier (Pressed Steel Fisher in Swindon). Under the old 'six quote' system, buyers would seek price-per-unit bids from a selection of suppliers, who would be expected to work to drawings and specifications supplied by the assembler. Frequently, this would occur at very short notice and be highly uneven. The UK assembler firms thus tapped into, and helped to sustain and develop, the general engineering capabilities in the locality. Rover was unusual in the relatively absence of vertical integration in operation at the time; it was putting out high volumes of work on a jobbing basis to a large number of small firms within its locality. Allied to this feature was a well-established specialist vehicle sector. Volumes thus tended to be low for components manufacturers in the UK when compared with those in Germany, Italy and France, a fact which meant that scale economies were not realised despite the low levels of vertical integration.

It is equally clear that the desire to use the 'best' sources of components implies a spatial extension of the supply base. Put simply, if firms want the best they may have to look Europe-wide rather than locally although instances of co-location to allow just-in-time delivery may occur. Equally, for the components firms, the prevalent strategy is to develop a tighter core of product-specific competencies but to spread this across a wider customer base (Barbaris, 1990). In practice, our research suggests that not only are assemblers seeking to develop preferred suppliers, those suppliers are themselves developing preferred customers and avoiding those who are not 'winners' or who involve, in the firms' analysis, insufficient reward for the work done. Given the dispersed production structure of assemblers across Europe, it is unlikely that components firms will be able to invest in nearby production locations for all assemblers, even if they have a preferred list of customers of, say, five firms. This is best illustrated in the case of Ford in Europe, the firm has to integrate production across three main countries with a European supply base (Wells and Rawlinson, 1992b).

As was noted earlier, Ford has been active in trying to reduce its numbers of direct suppliers in Europe, and in the five years to 1987 direct suppliers were cut from 2500 to 900 (House of Commons, 1987). However, suppliers do not equate with supply sites. Ford has many more Q1 site approvals than Q1 firms, because many firms have more than one site. Indeed the 'ideal' Ford supplier has at least three production locations (in Germany, Spain and the UK) with one point of contact for engineering, purchase matters and so on. Ford assembly plants tend to be located outside traditional spatial concentrations of suppliers, but still have to use tend to be in those concentrations. So, while Ford is able to compare costs and performance between firms in different locations, location as such is not a criteria for selection (see Wells and Rawlinson, 1992b). Equally, the Japanese in Europe have accepted that if they want to use the best suppliers they must draw on an existing and widespread industry across Europe. Toyota will be sourcing in twelve countries for its UK operations, for example, and some 50 per cent by value of all its components supplies will come from outside the UK.

4.5   SPATIAL RESTRUCTURING IN THE EUROPEAN COMPONENTS INDUSTRY

In general, we may say that, at least for the short to medium term, these developments in purchasing strategy will lead to a more widely distributed network of suppliers, one that extends beyond the national boundaries of the assembler firm. The subsequent relocation of suppliers to be alongside their assembler customers may occur, if the levels of business warrant it and if locational costs are not an issue. Certainly, the sourcing of components from outside Germany by the German-located assemblers appears to be based largely on cost grounds (principally labour cost) and in this case there would be no reason to expect non-German suppliers subsequently to move to Germany. One consequence of these changes in purchasing is that, for the UK at least, the importance of new assembler customers is increasing. Table 4.12 estimates the volume of purchasing by major assemblers in the UK.

In most cases, the volume of purchasing in the UK has increased in recent years. Mercedes increased international sourcing generally from 5 per cent by value of total sourcing in 1987 to 11 per cent in 1991, with

Table 4.12   Volume of purchasing by major assemblers in the UK, 1990 onwards (annual spend)

Firm	Spending
Rover	£1.8m, UK
	£300–350m, EC
	£35–40m, US
	£15–20m, Rest of world
	(total £2.3m)
Ford UK	£1.413m (1987), £2.4m (1990)
Ford (Non-UK)	£200m (1987)
Jaguar	£550m
Fiat	£200m
Toyota	c. £700m at full production 1994
	50–60% UK
Nissan	£850m by 1993 of which £655m with 122 UK suppliers.
Diamler	Dm1bn. Mercedes increased international spending from 5% (1987) to 11% (1991), with a target of 20%
Honda	£500m by 1994. 136 suppliers, of which 89 UK-based
Sogedac	£7m total p.a., of which £300m for Peugeot Ryton plant in UK. No specific UK spend

Source: Compiled from company reports, company press releases, press reports, and authors' estimates.

an eventual target of 20 per cent, some of which will go to the UK. It increased its UK spend from an average of £25m per annum in the 1980s to £72m in 1991. VW's 1991 spending in the UK, although small, was up 15 per cent on the previous year. Moreover, a substantial proportion of external-components spending by Japanese firms in Britain is going to suppliers within the UK. As the overall market and number of potential customers increases in the UK so further inward investment from non-UK automotive components firms may be expected. This cannot be expected to lead to rising employment in the automotive components sector in the UK. The EITB/SMMT study conducted in 1987 suggested that overall UK automotive employment had fallen from 448 000 in 1978 to 225 000 in 1987, (almost 50 per cent), of which the components sector accounted for a considerable portion (SMMT, 1990b). Inward investment, in so far as it occurs, will be alongside continued decline in the existing supply base. The long-term prognosis for jobs, in the UK and in Europe, is of continued overall decline coupled with a reduction in the share of total employment accounted for by unskilled manual and low-grade non-manual workers.

As was noted in the Chapter 3, the incidence of Japanese FDI in the components sector in Europe is currently quite low. Table 4.13 summarises the situation as it was in 1989, making clear that, first, the numbers of jobs involved are small – only 6654 manufacturing jobs across Europe by 1989. It also shows that Spain and the UK have been

Table 4.13   Japanese automobile components firms in Europe (service and manufacturing operations), 1989

Country	Service		Manufacturing		total	
	Sites	Employees	Sites	Employees	Sites	Employees
Belgium	3	222	1	331	4	553
Denmark	2	58	0	0	2	58
France	4	90	3	580	7	670
Germany	20	634	3	162	23	796
Italy	2	n.a.	0	0	2	n.a.
The Netherlands	10	207	3	646	13	853
Spain	2	94	7	2279	9	2373
UK	10	393	13	2666	23	3059
Total	53	1698	30	6654	83	8362

Source: Derived from DMC, 1990.

the prime recipients, with 2279 and 2666 manufacturing jobs respectively. Some of the Japanese arrivals have been 'high profile' and attracted some interest in the media. More notable firms include Nippon Denso and Calsonic. However, it is also interesting to note that some of the more vociferous opponents of the Japanese have also reached an 'accommodation' with Japanese suppliers. Renault, for example, have a joint venture agreement with Koyo Seiko to produce steering systems. Similarly, Magneti Marelli, 50 per cent owned by Fiat, has started a greenfield joint venture with Nippon Denso in Telford to produce air-conditioning systems. It is worth noting that the numbers of Japanese firms in Europe has continued to increase. An informed report (EIU, 1992) lists 82 firms (including subsidiaries of Japanese assemblers and joint ventures). A typical example is the entry of Press Kogyo. This Japanese firm is a leading producer of pressed components for vehicles, and recently acquired a 43.9 per cent stake in Press und Platgruppen of Sweden for $4.8m, with the intention of establishing a plant in Tongeren (Belgium) to supply pressings for the Volvo plant in Belgium (Griffiths, 1992). Overall, there is little to suggest the 'importation' of subcontracting complexes of the type identified by Morris (1989), although they may subsequently develop in a less pronounced form.

Internationalisation by European components firms is already well established in terms of the largest companies such as Valeo, Bosch, Lucas, BBA and Thyssen. Many German components firms followed Ford and GM into Spain in the late 1970s and early 1980s, at least partly because of governmental insistence on local content. The mode of internationalisation varies from licences all the way to full greenfield investments. In the case of European (principally German) firms investing in the UK, the preferred strategy appears to be one of acquisition of existing UK companies (Wells, 1992). Acquisitions are preferred in many instances because the acquiring firm can 'buy into' an existing customer base.

However, it is also apparent that widespread restructuring has involved considerable closures and job losses throughout Europe. In 1991 Magneti Marelli (Italy) spent L255bn on restructuring, including the closures of eight plants. Bosch (Germany) and Valeo (France) have also been cutting back on domestic plants and employment; the investment by Bosch in Wales to make compact alternators marked the largest ever by the firm outside Germany, and coincided with the announcement of 8000 redundancies in the group worldwide – mainly in Germany.

4.6 CONCLUSIONS

New procurement regimes in Europe are unlikely to alter the geography of the sector greatly in the short term because of the countervailing effects of other pressures. We might note, for instance, the impact of multiple customers in multiple locations, the importance of specific labour markets, and the scope which remains for acquisitions within the restructuring process. But distribution has become a key issue, with the further development of hybrid systems, rapid transit systems, and some local sub-assembly plants of bulky products.

Japanese transplants have already made a considerable impact in Europe in terms of their components purchasing, and will continue to do so. Up to now the UK has gained much in terms of the value of work outsourced, as Table 4.11 above shows, but this should not be taken to mean that UK firms are the beneficiaries. A significant number of the major UK-located suppliers to the Japanese transplants are not UK-owned firms. As borders become less significant within Europe so the major firms which have hitherto been considered to be French, Italian, German and so on will have a broad spread of sales and employment across several countries.

Finally, changes in the relationships between assemblers and their suppliers have highlighted the importance of the supply chain overall and the power relations within the chain. It raises questions as to where technological changes originate and how they are transmitted through the supply chain. It also raises questions about vertical integration along the various stages of the supply chain as firms seek to reposition themselves to capture higher value added – witness, for instance, the moves by Bosch, Lucas and Magneti Marelli to abandon previous core operations in vehicle electrics to concentrate on electronic sensors and systems.

5 The Steel Supply Sector

5.1 INTRODUCTION

Steel remains the most important material input for automobile manufacture and assembly. Although the European steel industry provides inputs to a wide range of industries outside the automotive sector, the fortunes of the two sectors (especially with respect to wide strip or coil steel) have been closely linked for many years. The typical modern automobile uses a wide range of types of steel in the form of castings, forgings, turned parts and pressings. In this chapter and Chapter 6 we shall be concerned with wide coil mild steel (also known as strip steel, and sometimes sold as cut sheets) which is used in the presswork industry. In this chapter we outline the scale of steel usage in the European automotive presswork sector; the structure of the steel production and supply sector; technological change in steels; and the nature of procurement regimes in the sector. The steel and presswork supply chain is detailed in Chapter 6.

5.2 STEEL USAGE IN THE EUROPEAN AUTOMOTIVE SECTOR

We have attempted to estimate the size of the sector and the flows through it in terms of steel consumption, concentrating on wide strip for pressed components in the body-in-white (the body-in-white comprises about 300–350 pressed parts welded together to form the basic body shape). Table 5.1 shows the average weight composition of a vehicle in 1985, in which it can be seen that sheet metal accounts for 39 per cent of the total.

Wide strip may be cut or slit (into narrow strip) or cut into pre-shaped blanks prior to delivery to press-shops. This aspect of the business is becoming increasingly important with the development of laser technology able to produce 'tailored' blanks that reduce on-line scrap levels. Estimation of the scale of the sector is made difficult by the intervening role of stockholders where the sectoral content of sales is not known. Table 5.2 summarises steel consumption in the European automotive sector. The estimates in the table may be taken

Table 5.1   Composition of the average autombile by weight (percentages)

Material	Proportion (%)
Sheet metal	39
Machined forged parts	13
Cast iron	13
Plastics	8.5
Aluminium	3
Electrical equipment	5
Rubber	4
Glass	3.5
Other	11.0

Source: Dawkins, 1991a.

Table 5.2   Estimated steel consumption in the EC automotive presswork sector, 1991

	Tonnes per annum
Vehicle assemblies	5 300 000
Presswork components	1 744 000
Total	7 044 000

Source: Wells and Rawlinson, 1992a.

as a guide to the aggregate scale of the sector and the size of independent producers compared to vehicle assemblers. It can be seen that independent presswork components firms account for about 20 per cent of total steel consumption in the sector, or to it put another way, in presswork the European assemblers are on average about 80 per cent integrated. The figure for vehicle assemblers was arrived at by multiplying the volume of vehicles produced by the weight of (wide strip) steel on average used per vehicle – 0.42 tonnes. This steel consumption figure is for material supplied rather than the average weight of steel on a vehicle – a firm that achieves a higher than average level of material utilisation – over, say, 55 per cent (ASPP, 1988), will need less steel to make each vehicle. If lighter (or thinner) steels are used, average weight per vehicle will also be lower. For example, the Rover 800 body shell (a large–medium saloon) contains 400 panels and weighs 324kg, but the firm estimates that the use of high-strength alloy mild steel for over 20 per cent of the total body weight retained structural integrity and saved about 10kg of body weight. This method does not account for the weight of pressed components from external suppliers. An alternative route to finding the size of the presswork market is to obtain plant level steel consumption figures for the vehicle assemblers; information on this is presented in Chapter 6, section 6.3.

5.3 THE STEEL PRODUCTION AND SUPPLY SECTOR

The whole European steel industry is not involved in supplying wide strip to the automotive industry, but all the major firms have an interest here. In this section we present a brief outline of the overall structure of the European steel industry in terms of those firms supplying wide strip to the automotive sector. Following this we comment on supply routes in the sector.

The steel industry is no stranger to state intervention in many forms, nor to intense political interest generally, with organised labour being an important feature of the industry (Hudson and Sadler, 1987; Warren, 1975). Apart from direct state ownership of steel production firms by the national and/or local state (a situation which persists in many instances, as is shown in the Table 5.3), the need to rationalise production on a pan-European basis was one of the original motivations for the creation of the Iron and Steel Community (forerunner to the EC). More recently, the so-called Davignon Plan saw through further cuts in capacity and employment over the period 1980–8. During this period, capacity of basic hot-rolled steel fell from 194.5 million tonnes (1980) to 165.0 million tonnes, while employment fell from 672 000 to 409 000. The industry benefited from the rationalisation process, largely financed by the EC, and in the boom conditions of the later 1980s some firms recorded profits for the first time since the early 1970s. However, the protracted recession of the early 1990s once again exposed over-capacity problems. The EC, and the industry federation Eurofer, failed to achieve the alignment of capacity with demand and has been unable to adjust to the appearance of cheaper imports from Eastern Europe on the market. Allied to this, the steel firms are facing ever-increasing demands from key customer sectors, notably in the automotive industry, for product innovation. Steel firms have responded in four main ways. First, there has been a general increase in downstream vertical integration into stockholders and further metal engineering companies; second, the steel firms have

Table 5.3   Main European suppliers of wide strip to the automotive sector, 1989

Company	Turnover £m	Crude steel production (m tonnes)	State (%)	Capacity utilisation (%)
Hoesch	3 467	4.10	0	87
Klockner	1 649	3.60	0	95
Krupp Stahl	2 718	4.60	25	85
Thyssen Stahl	3 429	10.50	0	98
Sollac	3 323	11.50	100	77
Cockerill-Sambre	2 914	4.40	88	65
Sidmar	935	3.60	33	95
Arbed	1 012	3.70	41	71
Hoogovens	2 597	5.40	19.5	70
Ilva	4 205	11.40	100	62
British Steel	5 113	14.20	0	79
Ensidisa	964	3.70	100	79

Notes: Hoogovens includes 5.9 per cent owned by City of Amsterdam; Krupp 25 per cent owned by Iran; Cockerill Sambre owned by Walloon regional government; Sidmar 67 per cent owned by Arbed, which in turn is 41 per cent owned by Luxembourg.
Source: Company reports and interviews.

sought to increase their capacity in terms of better substrates and coated steels (on which we give more details in section 5.4, below); Third, as we show in section 5.5, the steel firms have established customer-orientated R&D laboratories to enable closer interactive development of product and processing methods; and finally, there have been further moves towards mergers and alliances in the sector.

Levels of vertical integration in the industry vary quite widely as does dependence on the automotive sector – see Table 5.4. In the case of Sollac (the sheet metals division of the state owned Usinor-Sacilor of France), they used to own a presswork firm, Aubry, which they sold in the late 1980s to Arbel, a leading independent French presswork firm. On the other hand, the German firms Hoesch, Thyssen and Krupp as well as the Austrian firm Voest Alpine, all have extensive downstream metals engineering interests which have been expanded by acquisition in recent years (see Chapter 6). Indeed, Hoesch has deliberately sought to position itself as an automotive components system supplier specialist in the areas of suspension and under-body parts. Equally, the acquisition of downstream stockholder firms has

Table 5.4   Proportion of total turnover attributable to steel production, flat products and the automotive sector, 1991

Company	Percentage turnover, steel	Percentage turnover, flat products	Percentage turnover, automotive sector
Arbed/Sidmar	89	30	n.a.
Hoesch	25	n.a.	25[(e)]
Krupp	50	n.a.	n.a.
Thyssen	28	21	21
Voest Alpine	100	80	18
British Steel	100	50[(e)]	15[(e)]
Usinor	95	33	22[(e)]

Note: [(e)] = estimate.
Source: Company reports, interviews.

been seen by steel firms as an important means of increasing market share. Thus, for instance, Hoesch has bought Gwent Steel in the UK, while British Steel has made several such purchases in the UK (notably Walker Steel, a leading supplier to the automotive industry) and Europe (mainly Germany and Spain). It could also be argued that the development of metal-coating technologies by the steel firms represents a move downstream, and as we shall show later, this is a clear trend in the European steel industry.

The example of British Steel illustrates the sectoral spread of steel supply, as shown in Table 5.5. Two features are worthy of comment: first, about 10 per cent of prime markets for British Steel wide strip are automotive, though the largest single sector is the construction industry; and second, about half of deliveries are made to stockholders where the automotive content is unknown. The steel firms also differ in terms of the extent to which they are specialised in certain product areas or steel types. Only part of the output of the typical large steel producer is of 'flat products' (i.e. coil, sheets and so on). Much of the tonnage produced may be delivered as ingots, tubes or sections, for instance. Moreover, of the output of 'flat products', there is a mixture of different types and different market applications. To illustrate this, the cases of British Steel and Voest Alpine are shown in Tables 5.6 and 5.7. While British Steel represents the large generalist steel producer in which the automotive sector is one (albeit an important one) market sector served, Arbed/Sidmar probably represents the other end of this

Table 5.5   British Steel markets for prime deliveries, wide strip, 1990

Sector or type	Tonnes per annum
Automotive	262
Tubes	254
Re-rolled	122
Construction	283
Stockholders	1 163
Drums	89
Packing/shipping	62
Radiators	52
Domestic appliances	32
Total	2 423

Source: British Steel.

continuum as a smaller and more specialised producer (see Table 5.4). Sidmar only produces flat steels and, with its new 'Sikel' galvanising line, it is strongly orientated to supplying the automotive sector.

The continuing pressure on capacity has forced a restructuring of the European steel industry, notably in the form of a take over by Krupp of Hoesch in 1992, with many lesser joint ventures and interrelationships developing. Equally, there have been absolute

Table 5.6   British Steel sales, steel flat products, 1990

Product type	Tonnes per annum
Cold reduced	1 031
Hot dip galvanised	575
Electro-galvanised	300
Organic coated	338
Terne	19
Tinplate	838
Electricals	182
Aluminumised	48
Slab	258
Hot rolled (spd)	1 027
Hot rolled	544
Total	5 140

Note: spd = strip products division.
Source: British Steel.

Table 5.7   Voest Alpine sheet and strip steel production, 1991 (tonnes per annum)

Product type	Tonnes per annum
Hot rolled coil	693
Hot rolled sheet	160
Cold reduced sheet/coil	828
Hot dip galvanized	256
Re-rolled	253
Organic coated	89
Electro-galvanised	200
Blanks	10
Clad plates	4

Source: Voest Alpine.

capacity closures in internal restructuring by European leaders such as British Steel and Thyssen. British Steel finally announced the closure of the Ravenscraig works in Scotland in early 1992. From a peak of employment of 13 000 in the early 1970s (when £400 million was invested) the integrated steelworks at Ravenscraig struggled to fulfil its role as the hub of economic regeneration in the Motherwell area, and by the time the closure was made public only 1200 jobs remained. None the less, the closure is expected to save British Steel about £100 million per annum as the work from Ravenscraig is transferred to Llanwern and Port Talbot in Wales. In Spain, the state-owned Ensidisa is being merged with the large private steel group AHV to create the Integrated Steel Corporation, and it is expected that by 1995 9000 jobs will be lost out of an original 23 000.

5.4   TECHNOLOGICAL CHANGE IN STEEL

Steel itself is a high-technology product nowadays. Not only has the basic substrate material been subjected to continuous development leading to lighter, more easily formed and more consistent steel, but coatings technology has also developed. with many multi-layer combinations of surface treatment available to a surprising degree of accuracy. In terms of the steel substrate, the major developments have been in terms of high-strength low-alloy steels and interstice-free steels. These steels reduce the weight of the vehicle, but have implications for presswork because formability decreases as yield strength increases leading to increased die and press wear and greater 'springback' in pressed parts – which in turn has an impact on die design. Bake-hardening steels have also been developed. These steels are highly formable, but they harden under the temperatures experienced in the vehicle assemblers' paint-baking operations to produce impact-resistant panels. Another development of note, but which cannot be discussed further here, is surface laser etching to improve visual quality and handling properties.

There have been many developments in steel coatings. Indeed probably half the steels used on a modern vehicle were not available in the late 1980's – a feature largely attributable to the development of coated steels. Tables 5.8, 5.9 and 5.10 identify three broad categories of coated steel: hot dipped metallic coated; electroplated; and organic, and also provide an illustration of the pertinent properties of each coating and its common applications.

The various coatings can be combined with a range of steel types and paint finishes, as is shown in Figure 5.1, which gives an illustration

Table 5.8   Hot dipped metallic-coated steels used in the automotive sector

Coating	Trade name[a]	Features	Applications
Zinc	Galvatite Permazinc Durgrip	Standard Floor plan	Wheel arches
Iron–zinc alloy (7–12% Fe)	IZ Galvanised Perlite	Weldability Wet adhesive	Wheel arches Floor plan
Zinc–aluminium (55% Al)	Galvalame Aluzinc Zalutite	Corrosion/ heat resistant	Silencers Heat shields
Aluminium–silicon (7–12% Si)	Alutite Alsheet	Heat resistant Corrosion/ heat resistant	Exhausts Silencers Heat shields
Tin-lead (< 15% Sn)	Terne Weldability	Formability	Petrol tanks
Tin–lead–nickel (7–10% Sn)	Ternex Ni-terne	Formability Weldability	Petrol Tanks Radiator straps

Note: [a] trade name refers to British Steel products.
Source: Dasarathy and Goodwin, 1990.

Table 5.9   Electroplated steels used in the automotive sector

Coating	Trade name[a]	Features	Applications
Zinc	Zintec (EZ) Zincal Zinkote	Standard	Doors
Zinc–Chrome–chrome oxide	Zincrox	Corrosion resistant	Exterior panels
Zinc–iron	EZA Excell Zinc	Corrosion resistant	Exterior panels
Zinc-nickel	Nizec EZN	Corrosion resistant (unpainted)	Inner panels
Tin–lead (4% Sn)	Electro Terne	Corrosion	Petrol tanks

Note: [a] trade name refers to British Steel products.
Source: Dasarathy and Goodwin, 1990.

Table 5.10   Organic coated steels used in the automotive sector

Substrate (Metal coated)	Organic coating	Trade name[a]	Applications
Cold reduced (uncoated)	Zinc-rich paint	Zincirometal	Bonnet
Electrogenic	Zinc-rich paint	Bonazine Welcote	Bonnet
Zinc–nickel	Organic resin	Durasteel Welcote N	Door inner
Hot dip zinc	Zinc-rich paint	Benazine	Bonnet
Terne	1 side zinc paint		Petrol tank
Electrozine	Two-coat primer	Preprime	Exterior panels

Note: [a] trade name refers to British Steel products.
Source: Dasarathy and Goodwin, 1990.

of multiple-coated steel. In the past ten years or so, various forms of coated steel have become predominant in terms of vehicle weight. In contrast, basic uncoated steel has declined considerably in importance. The typical European car produced today has 60–70 per cent coated panels by weight. In fact, the type of coating may vary, as also may the

Primer – paint layers

Organic (sacrificial) coating

Metallic barrier coating

Alloy (sacrifical) coating

Adhesion zone

Steel substrate

Metallic undercoating

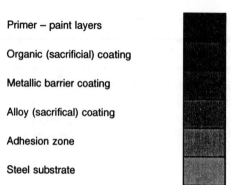

Figure 5.1   An example of coated steel

Note: Diagram of layers is not to scale.
Source: IISI, 1991.

substrate and the thickness, according to application, such that the typical car has different steels for the roof, boot, petrol tank, door sills, wheel arches and so on. An exception is Audi, which uses 100 per cent galvanised steel for its vehicle bodies, and some low-volume vehicles such as the Porsche 828 are made in aluminium. In general, coated steels are more difficult to work with: the coating tends to rub off on to the dies; it is more liable to surface damage such as scratching; and it is less easy to weld – all factors which increase the importance of automated handling of parts and of die maintenance. Coated steels are also heavier than uncoated, thus adding to vehicle weight. On the other hand, aluminium, because it is so soft, is also more difficult to press – any imperfections or dirt on the dies is readily revealed in the pressing – and joining technologies are less well developed.

The technical developments in steels discussed above have enabled this material to remain competitive compared with other potential substitutes, at least as far as high volume applications are concerned. The typical break-even point for steel parts is 100 000 units over four years. The extent of substitution is a dynamic balance between competing materials as product and process technology develop (see Wells and Rawlinson, 1994). For pressed steel panels there are relatively high investment costs for dies and press equipment, while the weight of steel is itself a significant disadvantage. However, for volume production those investment costs may be amortised over a high production level, leading to low 'per unit' costs. Other materials and other presswork/welding technologies are more viable in low volume work using either flexible technologies (for example, robotic welding and programmable stretch forming) or low-cost dedicated technologies with an inherently limited capacity (for example, glass-fibre mouldings). Moreover, unit costs may not be the sole criteria for choice: plastics or aluminium may be introduced to save weight, or where steel is less appropriate. While there is not space to permit a fuller discussion of these issues, we would note that in the medium term at least, volume vehicle production will continue to be dominated by steel, if only because of the high levels of investment during the 1980s in press technology equipment which (if maintained) can run efficiently for thirty years. Although Alcoa has invested $70m in the construction of an aluminium automotive components plant in

Table 5.11   Illustrative developments in coated steels capacity in the European steel industry

Company	Type of expansion
Sidmar-Kloekner	50/50 joint venture. 300 000 tpy electro-galvanising line at Ghent, Belgium (Sikel line)
British Steel	300 000 tpy HDG line (Zodiac line) at Llanwern, UK
	Organic coating line at Shotton, UK
Cockerill–Sambre	Phoenix plant, Liege. 1m tpy capacity HDG line, Belgium
Hoogovens	New HDG and organic coating lines at Ijmuiden, The Netherlands
Thyssen	400 000 tpy HDG line at Duisberg, Germany, also a 25% share in 300 000 tpy HDG line in Spain.
Sollac	200 000 tpy EZ line at Dunkerque. 100 000 tpy organic coating line at Florange. 250 000 tpy line for HDG at Florange, France.
Ilva	HDG line for 400 000 tpy, EZ line for 75 000 tpy, both in Italy.
Krupp	300 000 tpy HDG line in Bochum, Germany.
Hoesch	Expansion of existing HDG line at Ferndorf, Germany to 400 000 tpy (?)

Note: HDG = Hot dipped galvanised; EZ = electro-zinc; tpy = tonnes per annum.
Source: Company reports, press reports, interviews.

Germany (1991) to supply an all-aluminium top-of-the-range Audi model (using the so-called 'space frame' construction to replace the traditional steel-integrated monocoque), and has so far spent an estimated $250m on its 'aluminium-intensive vehicle', there are still major hurdles to the widespread adoption of aluminium. These would include the absolute price (about six times that of steel), price volatility, the structural weakness of aluminium with respect to impact forces, and the need to develop new means of joining panels.

For the steel firms, the move towards coated steels has raised new demands in both production and R&D. First, with respect to production, new capacity has had to be developed to supply coated steels to the automotive sector, necessitating downstream investment from core steelmaking activities. The dilemma for the industry is simple: investment in coating technologies is vital if sales to the automotive sector are to be sustained. On the other hand, there is a clear danger of over-capacity in coatings technology by the mid-1990s. British Steel has gained rapid access to Japanese assemblers not only because of their location in the UK, but also because the firm has licensed 'Durasteel', an organic-coated steel developed by Nissan in Japan.

Second, with respect to R&D, steel firms are working more closely with assemblers and major components firms to optimise the performance of the product. In this context, British Steel has recently established an R&D centre at Port Talbot dedicated to serving the motor industry which is equipped with its own press and diagnostic equipment. A similar example is the OCAS joint venture in Ghent (Belgium) operated by Cockerill-Sambre and Sidmar. These laboratories not only allow prototype testing of steel formability, corrosion resistance, and structural integrity, they may also be used in a 'fire brigade' role when rapid response diagnosis of press problems on the production line are required. As such, the development of customer-orientated laboratories reflects and reinforces the development of new materials in the steel industry. Both measures may be seen to be a deliberate strategy on the part of the steel firms to define and enhance core areas of competence; they thus cease to be 'commodity' suppliers and become 'partners'.

5.5   PROCUREMENT REGIMES IN STEEL SUPPLY

As a general rule, the steel producing companies only supply the vehicle assemblers directly with wide strip steel coils; for the presswork components sector, intermediaries such as stockholders or steel purchase agents form the dominant supply route. In consequence, the steel firms have only a partial picture of the sectoral or customer spread of sales, while stockholders also make it difficult to have a flow if information between the material producer and the user. However, in some instances the automobile assemblers do intervene in the supply structure between steel firms and presswork components firms: in France the steel consumed by the independent pressworkers for automotive applications is subsumed under a general negotiation between Sollac and the French vehicle assemblers. In terms of buyer–supplier relations, then, the links are mainly between steel firms and the automobile assemblers, but as was shown above, a number of the major steel producers also have wider metalworking and engineering interests, including presswork. This is important because it enables those firms to internalise the flow of information between the various key elements of the supply chain.

In many respects the procurement regimes in the steel supply sector are still very traditional. The increasing technological variety of the product is helping to differentiate firms more fully and thus fragment the procurement regime, and is also leading to more collaborative relationships at early stages of the design process (as noted earlier). Indeed, the development of such a range of steel types can be seen in part as an attempt by steel firms to escape the 'commodity' nature of their product with all the purchasing implications this entails. But in general all the automobile assemblers follow the same approach, an approach conditioned by the long history of steel–automobile firm relations, often overtly managed by direct state intervention, which laid great emphasis on domestic sourcing. A number of steel buyers in the automobile firms expressed the belief that the steel market was fixed by steel firms, who arranged prices and market share themselves. This view was strongly denied by the steel firms, but a 1991 EC judgement against the so-called 'Z Club' found that a cartel had been operating in the area of bright steels. In practice, the system that operated prior to the 1991/92 slump in the industry ensured that imports to any country were sold at the list price of the dominant domestic firm. For example, steel sold in the UK would take as its base price the British Steel price list for that type of steel. As we shall argue later, base price is only the starting point for actual price negotiations; none the less up to the 1990s there was a perception that unfettered competition did not prevail in the steel production industry.

Most of the vehicle assemblers, then, use three to four main suppliers of steel, though recourse to others for particular applications may occur. The normal approach is to have one primary supplier, based in the same country, for the bulk of production requirements (say up to 60 per cent). The second supplier, also usually domestic if available, takes a further 20–25 per cent. The third supplier takes perhaps 10–15 per cent, with others filling in the remainder. The third and subsequent suppliers are drawn on far more widely. However, the vehicle assemblers do not want to spread purchasing too widely or they will lack 'clout' with the steel firms whom they do business. The Toyota case is illustrative. The firm selects steels on the basis of the substrate performance for the applications it wants. It then draws up a matrix showing the performance of each steel supplier's steel for a particular application. In some applications there may be several firms able to meet the performance criteria, in others just one – although Toyota does not tell the steel firms whether or not they have sole source status for a particular part. In general, the firm would then seek more than one supplier against any one part or coil type. Toyota in the UK also have to import one particular steel type from Japan for a highly demanding body-exterior pressing.

In the early 1990s there has been some evidence that steel producers are becoming more prepared to attack the domestic markets of their rivals alongside strategies of traditional price cutting as the prospect of industry over-capacity again looms (Baxter, 1992). Table 5.12 indicates movements in the European price for hot rolled and cold

Table 5.12   Steel prices, Europe average real price, DM per tonne, 1986–92

Year	Price (DM per tonne)	
	Hot rolled coil	*Cold rolled coil*
1986	780	960
1987	620	825
1988	700	895
1989	800	975
1990	690	900
1991	585	795
1992	510	700

Source: Baxter, 1992.

reduced (wide strip) steel. It should be remembered that basic cold rolled or cold reduced steel declined considerably in importance over the 1980s in terms of use in vehicle bodies, and that coated steels of various types command a price premium. None the less, Table 5.12 shows that after the boom period of the late 1980s base prices have fallen by about a third. Moreover, the base prices are only the start of the negotiation process. There is considerable room for adjusting prices around the nature and extent of coating and production treatment (for example, different types of rinse may be applied to the steel) or post-production treatment (for example, the steel may be oiled and packaged in a variety of ways). With steel production "booked" three months in advance there is not a great deal of scope for daily flexibility in steel production for the automotive industry. For the steel buyers the greatest fear is of being let down by the steel firm and face having to resource significant quantities at short notice – again, this reinforces the domestic supplier who is expected to give priority to domestic customers.

Table 5.13 shows the geographical distribution of sales for selected firms. This data includes all activities, not just the sales of wide strip to the automotive sector, and can therefore only be taken as a rough guide. Apart from Voest-Alpine, which lacks a volume domestic vehicle industry, it is clear that for steel firms the domestic market remains of prime importance. The figure for Sollac is deceptive; the vast majority of sales classified as 'other' are, in fact, made in the EC. The relatively high proportion of sales enjoyed by Hoesch and Krupp in the USA are partly attributable to local subsidiary firms, but

Table 5.13   The spatial distribution of sales, selected steel companies, 1991 (percentages)

Company	Domestic	EC	Other Europe	Eastern Europe	USA	Other
Arbed	n.a.	72	8	2	9	9
Krupp	49	19	7	n.a.	15	15
Hoesch	68	15	n.a.	2	12	12
Thyssen	53	18	6	2	9	9
Sollac	50	n.a.	n.a.	n.a.	n.a.	50
BS	54	26	3	n.a.	4	13
Voest	35	47	4	4	n.a.	10

Source: Company reports.

sales of steel from these firms' plants in Germany to the USA are also quite important, reflecting strengths in 'special' steels.

Additionally, customer requirements are changing. In the steel sector the question of quality, as far as the automobile firms are concerned, revolves around how the steel performs in the press and (for visible applications) how it looks. In terms of press performance, all steel is produced to meet various national and EC grades of formability and strength. However, the adoption of automated press equipment has placed a premium on consistency of performance within these grades which are quite widely drawn. That is to say, administered standards, perhaps because of the time taken to create them on a pan-European basis, tend to be behind the capability and requirements of contemporary production technology. In negotiations the vehicle assemblers may define their standards rather more precisely. It is notable that the German steel firms were almost universally regarded by the automobile assemblers as being able to give consistent steel performance within a very narrow band. Again, with the drive towards low-inventory and right-first-time quality the consistency of material performance is as important as its absolute characteristics.

5.6   CONCLUSIONS

The European steel industry only partly fits the model of automotive components suppliers outlined in Chapter 4, and this is not surprising. The steel industry serves many sectors and yet has often been remote from end users and market applications, and has been protected from the more severe aspects of market operation by frequent state intervention. Moreover, many of the steel firms are very large businesses, able to ignore to some extent the pressures exerted by automobile assemblers in their normal relationships with suppliers. In some ways, therefore, the steel sector has been immune to the changes under way in the rest of the European automobile industry. While there have been some moves to decrease direct state involvement in the sector, at British Steel and Arbed for example, major firms such as Sollac and Ilva remain in state hands. Domestic customers remain the most important single market for steel firms supplying wide strip, while for the automobile firms the largest supplier is usually the domestic steel producer. Given the weight of the product, transportation over large distances is best avoided.

In other respects there is an increasing awareness of changes in the nature of relationships in the steel supply chain, at least in terms of relationships with the vehicle assemblers. Not only have steel firms sought to develop products more explicitly tailored to the needs of the automobile assemblers, they have also sought to develop expertise in production processes used by their customers. The growth of customer development centres is indicative of the attempt by steel firms to enter the vehicle development process at an earlier stage and thus, hopefully, to influence the nature of the product in such a way as to enhance their chances of supplying steel in the production phase. Additionally, the steel firms are taking on a 'fire brigade' role, with R&D centres to respond quickly to customer problems encountered in production.

Despite the existence of standards in terms of steel performance, the issue of quality was not as 'black and white' as may be supposed. First, the European standard specifications were too broad to be of any use except as a general guideline – partly because the definition of such standards lags behind actual production capabilities. Of more importance to the automobile firms was product consistency both within and between batches of steel, an issue of ever-increasing significance as press and welding processes become more automated. Second, other quality issues, especially with regard to surface finish, are difficult to describe in empirical terms. Rather, each firm has a body of practice which deems steel to be acceptable or unacceptable. Jaguar, for instance, place particular stress of surface quality on their body panels, and consequently they reject panels other firms would be prepared to accept. Moreover, the vehicle assemblers have to balance the demands for quality with the need to sustain the production process – quite simply, if the assemblers became too 'fussy' the steel firms would not be able to produce enough material to keep production going. When vehicle production is high, and steel capacity fully utilised, there is greater pressure to accept steel quality as delivered. This feature of the supply relationship is easily over-looked, and vehicle assemblers may be more prepared to fall back on 'traditional' purchasing practices when demand is low relative to supply. Consequently, quality is an ongoing and dynamic relationship involving both absolute and qualitative judgements.

It is also of significance to note that the steel industry has responded to the pressures put on it by vertical integration and, to a lesser extent, by diversification. The sort of 'one-stop shopping' offered by the integrated steel and engineering combines is in complete contrast to the vertical disintegration and tiering pattern evident in Japan. Even the firms such as British Steel which lack a metals engineering capability have sought to add downstream expertise in the form of customer development laboratories. In short, the steel firms have sought by a variety of means to shorten or bridge the supply chain between themselves and the automotive assemblers.

On the other hand, the steel industry as a whole remains highly vulnerable to cyclical movements in the economy as a whole, and the vehicle industry in particular. By 1993 all the major markets in Europe, with the exception of the UK, had registered declines of 20–25 per cent on the 1989 peak of sales. Combined with the overall recessionary conditions, this decline in vehicle sales (and hence vehicle production) has resulted in the whole European steel industry falling into losses. Attempts to increase the technological sophistication (and hence 'added value') of the product have failed to address the more basic question of over-capacity in the face of a long-term fall in the volume of demand. Further plant closures, company mergers and widespread redundancies are likely to be the most visible feature of the European steel industry in the 1990s.

6 The Presswork Sector

6.1 INTRODUCTION

Presswork is a key sector in the automotive industry. The work consists of the pressing or stamping of sheet metal (normally mild steel) to form panels which are then assembled (normally spot-welded) to create the basic body shell and structure. There are also a large number of smaller pressings used as brackets or stiffeners on the body shell, as well as embodied in other components, including brakes, engine components, seats, window mechanisms, and controls. It has always been considered a core activity by the vast majority of automotive assemblers – only low-volume firms such as Rolls-Royce and Lotus do not undertake their own presswork. However, as we shall discuss below, there has also been a long tradition of outsourcing various types of presswork and, more recently, the assemblers have been reappraising their levels of vertical integration in presswork in the light of new technology and the demands for leaner production structures.

The number of panels per car and the weight of sheet steel pressed parts varies quite widely. In general, there is a tendency towards reducing the number of pressed parts and using thinner, lighter steels, thus reducing overall pressed components weight in the vehicle. The Volvo 740 (a large saloon-type car) comprises 343 parts, of which 327 are made in-house, and the body-in-white weight is 332kg (the body-in-white is the welded body assembly to which all other parts are fitted); the Peugeot 605 luxury saloon has about 300 panels. Smaller cars tend to have fewer panels and weigh rather less; the new Renault Clio, for example, has only about 250 body-in-white pressed components. Pressings and assembly into body-in-white account for about 20 per cent of the final factory cost of the vehicle (ASPP, 1988). In some areas pressings may be replaced by other technologies – suspension systems, for instance, may be based on hydraulic technology (PSA) or tubular technology (Benteller). In general, for high volume applications, pressing technology is cheaper per unit than, say, casting or machining.

In the following section we examine key aspects of the presswork supply chain, then activities at the assemblers are considered and the

115

overall scale of the sector estimated. We compare two types of press-shop strategy: the regional centre and decentralised production, to show that considerable differences remain in Europe in terms of how presswork is integrated into assembly operations. In this section we also discuss vertical integration in presswork at the level of the assemblers. Subsequently we consider the presswork components sector: its size and structural composition, product and market segmentation, and national differences.

The forces for restructuring the sector are then considered. Major changes currently under way pose significant new competitive threats to firms in the sector. The introduction of non-steel materials to substitute for pressed components, changes in die design, reductions in the average numbers of panels per vehicle, and new forms of presswork technology, all have the potential to reduce the presswork components capacity requirements at an aggregate level. That is, in the future, fewer press stokes will be required to make the average vehicle. Coupled with the greater demands being placed on presswork firms in terms of R&D, quality, productivity, cost and delivery these technological changes lie at the heart of restructuring the sector across Europe. Finally, we draw out conclusions from the above analysis.

6.2   THE AUTOMOTIVE PRESSWORK SUPPLY CHAIN

Figure 6.1 summarises the presswork supply chain. In some cases, the flows of work through the presswork supply chain are quite simple. The greatest volume of work is also the most direct – steel firms supply wide strip direct to the vehicle assemblers who produce the majority of the presswork, especially of the larger and external panels which require the biggest presses, which then go on to a new vehicle to be sold on the market. On the other hand, supply routes may be more fragmented. In the case of aftermarket panels, for example, wide and narrow strip steel may go from the steel mill to a stockholder (usually one of several supplying the pressworker) and then the pressworker (either as pre-cut and shaped 'blanks' or as narrow strip coils). Depending on the product, secondary pressworkers may supply some components to the primary pressworker, and the product may be distributed through one of several routes. As we shall discuss further below, there are many categories of firm which come under the general heading of presswork; Figure 6.1 is simply intended to show the place

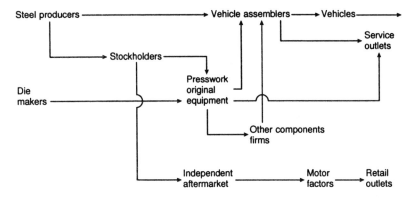

Figure 6.1   The presswork supply chain

Source: Authors' analysis.

of these firms within the wider industrial infrastructure which constitutes the supply chain.

Table 5.2 in Chapter 5 probably understates the relative size of the presswork components sector. First, there are firms producing for the commercial vehicle sector which are not included in the sector here. Second, there are inevitably an unknown number of firms supplying presswork which consume very small quantities of steel (i.e. less than 5000 tonnes per annum). Third, there is a danger that significant European firms may have been missed, although in most cases we have obtained from vehicle assemblers the names of their important presswork suppliers. Fourth, there are firms which, while not classified as pressworkers, may none the less use large quantities of steel. We have excluded firms supplying seats, radiators, sunroofs, wheels and other products where presswork is only a part (and not necessarily the critical part) of the overall business. By way of illustration, Fram Filters in the UK consumes some 30 000 tonnes of steel per annum in its production of oil and air filters, sufficient to be included in the largest presswork size category. Fifth, our research has concentrated on those supplying presswork to the vehicle assemblers (automobiles), not on those who supply other components firms. Finally, there is a surprising volume of business undertaken by vehicle assemblers for other vehicle assemblers. Until recently, Rover undertook all the major body pressings for Jaguar, for example; and both Volvo and Renault are active in the press-relief market. Thus, in aggregate it may be that the presswork components sector accounts for as much as half of all strip steel consumed by the automotive sector in any one country. The proportion of wide strip steel consumed by the vehicle assemblers is much higher; they probably account for 80 per cent of such usage.

Presswork components firms do not in general have a large supply base. The vast bulk of purchases goes on material (i.e. steel) and energy (i.e. electricity). Other production consumables may be bought in, for example welding gases and press lubricants as well as services (transport and office services, for example), but few components are bought in. The typical pressing jobbing-shop working to batch orders often did nothing else but presswork; downstream activities such as painting or plating would be subcontracted, and assemblers themselves did most of the sub-assembly. More recently, in response to new demands being made of them, there is an emerging trend for presswork companies to increase downstream levels of vertical integration by adding sub-assembly, welding, nutting, drilling and surface treatment activities – which in turn lead to a wider supply base. This was a very strong common theme among the firms we visited throughout Europe.

Frequently, the boundaries of the sector are by no means clear. While some firms are almost entirely concerned with presswork components for the automotive sector, there is a spectrum of firms with decreasing engagement in the sector. We thus had to identify a population of firms iteratively, using judgement to eliminate firms thought to be too small or too marginal to be of significance. Rover, for example, has some 97 presswork suppliers, though the vast majority are either small, or undertake presswork as part of wider engineering interests, or contribute only a limited amount to the components requirements of the assembler.

6.3   PRESS TECHNOLOGY

A press machine simply raises an upper die and then lowers it again to meet a lower die. Steel sheet is pressed between the dies to form a shape. Typically, the part is moved from one set of dies to the next to produce ever more complex shapes. For simplicity we may identify three main stages in the development of press technology: traditional; hybrid; and modern. The main operating differences are shown in Table 6.1.

In the *traditional* press-shop the presses were placed in line, with each line being six to ten presses long to accommodate the number of

Table 6.1   Comparative performance measures for three main types of press-shop technology

	Transfer	Automated tandem	Traditional tandem
Die change time (minutes)	10	45	180–360
Cycle time (days)	2–3	10–20	15–36
Parts output (units per hour)	800	600	180
Uptime (percentage of available time)	80	65	< 50

Source: Wells and Rawlinson, 1992a.

stages required to make a complete part. A distinctive division of labour was associated with traditional press-shops using this basic technology. First, there was a large number of unskilled manual workers to feed and remove sheet steel from the presses – typically four to each press, with others loading completed parts into racks. The space between the presses was large, to allow forklift trucks access to the presses to change the dies. Each press-shop had specialist die-change technicians, as well as separate staff categories such as electricians, materials handling, cleaning, press maintenance and toolroom staff. Typically, the press line (called a tandem line) could produce six parts per minute. Die change times were extremely slow, to change a line of tandem press dies would often require a full shift, as each die set had to be adjusted in turn by skilled setters.

Hybrid press technology consists of adding varying degrees of automation to the existing tandem line. At its most extreme the tandem line is entirely enclosed and automated (Mercedes at Sindlefingen have such a line, for example), but more generally there are several means by which automation may be achieved. The simplest is to put in belt transfer mechanisms to move panels between the presses. In some cases, dedicated mechanical transfer systems may be installed; in others, robotic, programmable handling arms may remove, transfer and place parts as they progress from one press to the next. The adoption of hybrid technology is a relatively inexpensive means of increasing labour productivity and machine flexibility. It is important to note that Toyota developed its rapid die-change approach (called 'single minute exchange of dies', or SMED) on fairly traditional tandem lines. Under SMED the basic principle was to reduce unproductive down-time by close analysis of the die-change operation itself, enabling a differentiation between internal and external set-up operations (Shingo, 1985). Internal set-up time was the time taken to perform operations when the press was stopped; external time refers to operations which could be undertaken while the press was running. Thus the Toyota approach was to shift operations from internal to external, so minimising press stoppage time. Dies were transported to position alongside the press and prepared for exchange while the presses were running, all required tools, cranes and so on were placed in position and only then were the presses stopped. In addition, many of these operations could be performed by the press-machine minders, thus reducing indirect labour. Moreover, Toyota pursued low-cost, low-technology solutions wherever possible. For example, to reduce the time required to adjust presses to different sizes of die, die heights were standardised by welding on plate steel backing plates. Equally, a variety of methods were adopted to enable the rapid fixing of dies to the press; for example, bolts were used that needed only a half turn to fix the die in place. These were all innovative ideas, but in practice, at least in many Western firms, changing the handling systems can take longer than changing the dies.

Modern press technology extends automation in both press operation and die-changing. It is interesting to note that transfer presses were developed by Nissan and Hitachi as a high-cost, high-technology solution to the problem of rapid die-change and complex parts-handling mechanisms. Transfer presses consist of five to seven stations and an associated parts handling system which can move in three dimensions. The space between the dies is minimal, thus reducing the time parts are in transit from one operation to the next. The handling system is directly linked to the press, ensuring perfect synchronisation of parts movement with die movement, enabling more rapid press action. Consequently, the transfer press has a much higher output rate than the tandem line. However, not only can it transfer presses be produced in greater volume, they are also more flexible than tandem lines. With rolling die bolsters on each side of the transfer press the new dies can be placed in position as the old ones are taken out. Internal set-up times are reduced to a minimum by push-button, computer-controlled and servo-operated set-ups; the operator simply has to select the programme number for the part to be produced. Moreover, the computer provides comprehensive monitoring and diagnostic facilities – which can be accessed on-line by the press manufacturers – thus improving quality, reducing the possibility of 'crashing' the dies, and enabling planned maintenance programmes.

For low-volume applications, a range of new technologies is currently being developed which could, in the future, compete with high-volume transfer presses on unit cost terms. Of these new technologies, the best established is the fluid cell press, the basic operation of which uses a neoprene layer to transfer hydrostatic pressure on to a lower die (no upper die is needed). Fluid cell presses have a relatively slow cycle time, about five minutes per part, but they can produce a complex pressing from just one lower die – including some shapes which cannot be achieved by conventional means. Currently they are used mainly for prototype work – they can even operate with a wooden lower die – although Mercedes uses its fluid cell press to produce low-volume panels for some commercial vehicles. After pressing, the panel has to be trimmed, which, again in low-volume applications, will be done by programmable laser. The attraction for vehicle assemblers is in the very low die costs required to produce a part which enables more possible vehicle configurations to be explored.

In terms of throughput efficiency, Western firms are broadly comparable with those from Japan. The number of parts produced per hour while the presses are running is a product of the technical parameters of the presses and associated handling equipment: for tandem presses this means six parts per minute and for transfer presses it means sixteen parts per minute on average. Most firms average about 65–70 per cent uptime – that is, the press runs for about 70 per cent of the available time per shift. But the critical difference lies in how the downtime is used. In Japan the downtime is accounted for by a large number of rapid die changes; in the West by a small number of slower die changes. For Japanese firms, this results in much smaller batch sizes, with consequent savings on inventory and associated personnel (Williams *et al.*, 1991b). It is these rapid die changes which lie at the heart of lean production in Japanese automobile assemblers, as pioneered at Toyota (Shingo, 1985).

6.4 DIE DESIGN

A set of large dies to produce a major panel can be very expensive. Firms tend to be guarded about die costs, but some idea can be gained from the following estimates: a die set for a progression press making small and not very complex parts will cost in the region of £20 000; that for a major, complex body panel may cost nearer £500 000. Differences in die design practice have been identified as a key variable in subsequent overall body-in-white performance and competitive success, contributing as much as 30 per cent of the overall cost differential between 'world best' and US standard performance (ASSP, 1988). Put simply, measures to reduce the fixed costs of dies lower the subsequent break-even volumes required (both for the individual part and the whole vehicle) and therefore allow greater product variety and a faster rate of new product introductions. Research in the USA and Japan suggests that 'world class' firms have die costs that are only 40 per cent of those of less efficient producers (ASPP, 1988) due to fewer press operations per part, the use of multiple parts per die, and lighter die standards. The press-shop manager at Mercedes Sindlefingen commented to us that his greatest problem was to encourage highly conservative Mercedes die engineers to accept fewer die sets per part, but was still a long way short of ensuring that each part required a maximum of five stages to produce.

Most vehicle manufacturers have sophisticated Computer-aided design (CAD) systems to design the vehicle and then derive die design – which can theoretically be linked subsequently to computer-aided manufacture, especially in terms of checking parts accuracy. In practice, however, none of the firms we visited felt confident enough simply to download design data from the design computer to a die-machining computer.

6.5   PRESSWORK BY THE VEHICLE ASSEMBLERS

As was indicated earlier, the automobile assemblers actually account for the majority of the presswork components business, at least in terms of volume supplies for the body-in-white. Levels of vertical integration can be very high – over 90 per cent by value in the case of Mercedes, for example, and even the Japanese firms do not normally outsource their core presswork needs. Nissan in the UK, when its captive small pressings supplier is included (Nissan Yamato, sited alongside the assembly plant), is also highly integrated. Traditionally, presswork has been regarded as a core area. The body and chassis not only define the vehicle as it is presented to the customer, but presswork also embodies high economies of scale and high-value added. The average new transfer press and associated handling equipment costs in the region of £20–30m and needs to be run 24 hours a day to gain full benefit from the investment. In other words, high absolute volume levels are a prerequisite for satisfactory commercial returns to made on the investment. Moreover, the technology embeds flexibility with automatic die change systems, reducing unproductive downtime considerably. Table 6.2 summarises the press-shop activities of the major vehicle assemblers in Europe.

Table 6.2 shows steel consumption and vehicle output at plant level. However, in practice the picture is somewhat confused by the production strategies adopted by the vehicle assemblers. The traditional strategy has been to establish very large press-shops serving several assembly locations (the so-called 'regional press-shop') and transport the parts as required. This has led to the development of some enormous press-shops. The Volvo plant at Olofstrom (Sweden) produces some 80 million body parts per year, consumes 180 000 tonnes of steel, employs 4600 people, and has over 200 press machines. Components and sub-assemblies (for example sub-assembled doors and boot lids) are produced in the plant and then shipped to production locations in Sweden (Gothenburg) and Belgium (Ghent) using 60 railcars a day. In turn, Gothenburg supplies assembled bodies to the low-volume Udevella plant. Equally, most of the pressings for the new Renault Clio are produced at Flins (France), although assembly will take place both at Flins and at other Renault plants in Spain, Belgium and Portugal. A variant on this practice is shown by Mercedes. For their highest-volume car (the 190 Series) half the pressings are made in Bremen, the other half in Sindelfingen – locations at opposite ends of Germany. Parts are then exchanged on a daily basis between the two sites, both of which contribute to assembly of the vehicles, with the state-subsidised Bundesbahn carrying the 'warehouse' costs. These strategies seek to reduce die investment costs: a calculation is made as to whether two sets of dies can be justified against the transportation cost of moving panels to assembly locations. Regional press-shops further allow vehicle assemblers to smooth the production process across their press capacity and to handle model change over time more easily. Typically, the large press-shop also has associated die design, production and maintenance facilities and staff. This pattern has been breaking down, however. Because modern transfer presses embody both greater flexibility and greater output than previous

Table 6.2   European automobiles assemblers' press-shop activities in Europe

Firm	Location	Steel (t/week)	Cars (per week)	Skin	Body	Chassis	Other	
BMW	Munich	?	3 750	*	*	*	*	
	Dingolfingen	?	5 000	*	*	*	?	
Citroën	Aulney	?	5 000	–	–	–	–	New press shop
	Rennes	?	6 700	–	–	–	–	
	Saint Ouen	?	n.a.	*	*	–	*	
Ford	Köln	2 600	?	–	*	–	–	Emp. 750
	Croydon	200	n.a.	*	–	–	*	
	Dagenham	1 956	6 000	–	*	*	–	
	Ghent	2 600	?	*	*	*	–	
	Halewood	1 956	?	*	*	*	–	
	Saarlouis	2 600	6 000	*	*	*	*	
	Valencia	2 600	6 000	*	*	*	–	
GM/Opel	Bochum	3 250	?	*	*	*	*	
	Kaiserslauten	3 250	n.a.	*	*	*	*	
	Russelsheim	6 000	?	*	*	*	*	
	Zaragossa	3 250	?	*	*	*	–	
Leyland Daf	Birmingham	450	480	*	*	*	*	
Mercedes	Sindelfingen	5 500	8 500	*	*	*	*	
	Bremen	?	3 000	*	*	*	*	
	Hamburg	200	n.a.	–	–	*	*	
Nissan Iberica	Barcelona	700	1 600	–	*	–	–	
Nissan MMUK	Sunderland	600	2 500	*	*	–	–	NB: Yamato
Peugeot	Mulhouse	?	6 370	*	*	*	*	
	Sochaux	?	7 320	*	*	*	*	

Renault	Poissey	?	5 805	*	*	*	*
	Douai	?	9 000	*	*	*	*
	Flins	?	6 000	*	*	*	*
	Sandouville	?	6 500	*	*	*	?
	Maubeuge	?	2 000	*	*	*	—
Rover	Swindon	1 956	n.a.	*	*	*	—
	Cowley	1 086	?	*	*	*	—
Seat	Barcelona	?	7 500	*	*	*	?
Volvo BV	Born	?	2 000	*	*	*	—
VW Audi	Ingolstadt	?	7 500	*	*	*	?	Roth Technik
	Neckarsulm	?	3 900	*	*	*	?
VW	Emden			*	*	*		New Press shop
	Kassel	?	n.a.	*	*	*	?
	Wolfsburg	?	?	*	*	*	—	NB: Magna

Key:
* = Yes
– = No
? = Not yet known

Note: Includes some light commercial vehicle operations.

Sources: Compiled secondary sources and original research.

approaches it is possible to have dedicated press-shops for each assembly plant, so long as die costs can be kept low. This is the case at Nissan in Sunderland for example. As we shall discuss later, changes in press and die design lie at the heart of new production configurations in presswork.

The introduction of transfer press technology into existing press-shops was undertaken in an incremental and piecemeal way throughout the 1980s. In 1992 we identified 45 transfer presses in the European automotive industry (with an unknown number in Fiat). Cash-poor Renault has none, GM Russelsheim, in contrast, has seven. However, the way these machines are used also varies. The most extreme contrasts are between Nissan in the UK, and GM. In Nissan UK, they changed the dies 120 times a month on average on each transfer press in order to exploit the flexibility in the technology. GM, on the other hand, appear more interested in the prospect of reducing labour content and improving unit output – thus they prefer to dedicate production of a few main components to one machine, and to move parts between locations as necessary.

6.6   THE PRESSWORK COMPONENTS SECTOR

As is indicated in the Figure 6.1 on page 117, the presswork components sector may be segmented according to the market focus and technological capabilities of the firms. Here we expand on the figure; in particular we identify the following categories of automotive components presswork suppliers, although some firms straddle more than one segment. On the question of vertical integration the vehicle assemblers all have systems for broadly categorising presswork as a guide to the make/buy decision. PSA, for instance, has the categories G1, G2 and G3, where G1 requires the heaviest press weight (1000 tonne double action or 600-tonne single action), and G2 and G3 have successively lower press weights. Mercedes adopts a similar pattern with A, B and C panels. Ford defines a cut-off point of parts requiring over 400 tonnes press-weight. In all cases the G1 or A panels are the largest, most difficult and most critical exterior body panels, and on these panels there is little prospect of abandoning vertical integration except in special circumstances. However, on G2 or G3 panels (or their equivalent in other vehicle assemblers) there is more scope and prospect for vertical non-integration.

6.6.1 Captive or in-house suppliers

Some firms, such as Ford at Croydon (UK) Mercedes at Hamburg (Germany) and PSA at Saint-Ouen (France) have captive suppliers of small pressings which are organisationally and spatially distinct from the main press-shops discussed earlier. These will usually concentrate on high-volume small pressed parts used in several assembly locations. They have not been included in the sector study, but typically they are comparatively small-scale operations – Ford in Croydon, for instance, consumes only 200 tonnes per week. In most cases, assemblers retain a section within the main press-shop which undertakes small pressings. In Germany, both GM Russelsheim and Mercedes Sindlefingen are interested in closing these production capacities and outsourcing the work, but in both cases have thus far been unable to do so. In the case of GM, resistance from IG Metal, who do not want to see work outsourced to non-unionised components suppliers, has succeeded in preventing change. In the case of Mercedes, the smaller presses (typically producing a simple part in one operation, usually manually controlled) are the only area on the shop-floor where disabled people can be employed. The firm thus retains its small pressings capability in order to achieve its quota of disabled people, which exempts them from certain local taxes.

6.6.2 High-volume independent suppliers of original equipment to vehicle assemblers

These firms form the core of the sector as we have defined it. In some cases they will be independent entities, more often they are part of wider groups but the presswork operation is run as a distinct business supplying external customers. In the UK, the best known example is probably GKN Sankey in Telford. Within this broad grouping there is an emerging trend for product area specialisation, which is increasing segmentation within the sector. Typical product specialisations could include vehicle jacks, pulleys, petrol tanks and oil filters, pedal boxes, and suspension arms. Production technology also tends to make this group of firms distinct. The presswork equipment needed for high volume small parts production is not economic for very small lot production. It was noticeable in our research that very few UK firms could meet production volumes of 3000 parts per day or more – the levels required for single sources on high volume vehicles such as the VW Golf.

An interesting variant to this pattern is a joint venture between assembler and independent components supplier: Venture Pressings in Telford was created by Jaguar and GKN to supply pressed parts for the Jaguar assembly lines, and makes a classic case study of the use of role models to change corporate working practices (Rawlinson and Wells, 1992a).

6.6.3 Design, styling and prototype firms

These firms often have a modest presswork capability; when measured by steel consumed per annum they are insignificant. However, they do undertake important prototyping work, and in some cases supply pressed components on a low-volume basis to external customers in the specialist car and commercial vehicle sectors. We have not included them in the subsequent analysis, but would note that they are often at the leading edge of flexible production technology and methods. Firms in the UK and Italy are particularly strong in this segment, with Airflow Streamlines and Pininfarina being globally recognised.

6.6.4 Low-volume independent suppliers of original equipment to vehicle assemblers

A number of firms are not in the high volume segment of the industry, but specialise in lower-volume production runs. The main customers are usually in the commercial vehicle sector. They may be capable of the largest body and chassis pressings. A typical example is Laepple of Germany. Mainly known for its die, tooling, and production technology, the firm also undertakes pre-production pressings and low-volume production work such as the aluminium Porsche 928 body. In the UK, a well-known example is Motor Panels of Coventry which supplies mainly to firms such as Rolls-Royce, Rover (for low-volume derivatives) and the commercial vehicle industry. In the subsequent analysis we have tried to exclude those firms dealing only with the commercial vehicle sector, notably those supplying chassis rails which, because of the high weight of steel involved, would distort our findings. In other cases, we have tried to apportion the extent of work outside the automobile sector.

6.6.5 Press relief specialists and original equipment aftermarket suppliers

This category of firm has the installed technological capability to replicate the work of the vehicle assemblers themselves. The European leader in this business, Polynorm BV of the Netherlands, is also one of the largest independent pressworkers overall. Two distinct types of work are undertaken. First, press relief is used by vehicle assemblers when, for whatever reason, it is necessary to outsource a pressed component which it had previously been making in-house. Typically, this occurs at model change-over time. Press relief firms essentially provide external, flexible capacity to smooth production planning. Second, and clearly related to the first, official aftermarket production may also be outsourced. Vehicle assemblers are legally obliged to provide replacement parts for up to ten years after production has finished, some parts have a 'high service content' (typically wings/ bumpers, front panels, etc.). Aftermarket supply can be highly profitable for the original vehicle assembler, and they will often retain the dies themselves for high-service parts.

It is worth noting that other vehicle assemblers also provide press relief capacity. The Volvo press-shop at Olofstrom (Sweden) is a major competitor in this market, and in general vehicle assemblers will undertake contract press relief work for other assemblers if they have the capacity available.

6.6.6 Unofficial aftermarket specialists

These firms operate in a 'grey' segment of the market, the unofficial aftermarket, supplying pressed panels to independent motor factors and parts retail/distribution firms. These firms typically will choose popular models and, two or three years after production has commenced, will start to produce copies of parts as replacements. Dies are designed by copying the original part, and are usually produced in low-cost countries such as Taiwan. The quality of the dies is certainly lower than that of the original equipment manufacturer, but so are die costs. Moreover, die design is different, enabling parts to produced in fewer operations but more slowly, and the steel used will not necessarily match that used in the original vehicle. Independent producers will often swap parts between themselves, acting as distribution agents, to enable greater levels of product specialisation. Within Europe, Italian firms dominate the sector, although they are threatened by current EC legislative actions designed by the vehicle assemblers to protect their ownership of the copyright on body parts, and by increased imports of parts from Brazil and Taiwan. A typical example is Rhibo of Bologna (Italy) which mainly produces replacement wings, bonnets and front grilles for VW cars (it does not produce replacement Fiat items!).

6.6.7   Generalist engineering firms with some presswork abilities

We have excluded these firms from the analysis below, but would note that in numerical terms they remain important.

6.6.8   Components firms with in-house presswork abilities

As we have already noted, some components embody significant presswork content. In many cases components firms will undertake some of that presswork themselves through a captive supplier or an in-house facility. For example, AP Pressings is part of the AP Group within BBA (in the UK) and supplies pressed components to AP Clutch and AP Lockheed (brakes). Until 1992, the AP Pressings operation did not attempt to supply the open market.

6.6.9   Low-volume derivative assemblers

Within Europe there are a few firms which provide a low-volume assembly service to the volume assemblers. Notable in this category are Karmann (Germany) producing the VW Sirocco and Corrado, and Heuliez (France) producing the Citroën XM estate. In both these above cases the firms have other areas of expertise: Karmann in die manufacture; and Heuliez in contract design and commercial vehicle assembly. Generally speaking, a high proportion of the parts on a low volume derivative vehicle are supplied by the vehicle assembler. However, some interior and exterior parts are different, including some pressed panels, and in this case the presswork is undertaken by the specialist assembler. As measured by annual steel consumption these firms are significant pressworkers and we have therefore included them in the analysis.

Table 6.3 summarises the comparative scale of the presswork sector in Europe. The data refer to aggregates derived by adding the

Table 6.3 National comparisons of industry structure in the automotive presswork components sector

Country	Total turnover (£m)	Average turnover (£m)	Total steel (tonnes per annum)	Average steel (tonnes per annum)	Turnover to steel ratio (£m/tonnes per annum)
Germany	1145	42.4	651	24.1	1.75
France	560	46.6	321	26.7	1.74
UK	519	19.9	409	15.7	1.26
Italy	209	11.6	159	8.8	1.31
Spain	206	10.3	173	8.6	1.19
Portugal	31	3.8	31	3.8	1.0

Note: Belgium and The Netherlands have been subsumed within Germany.
Source: Original research.

individual totals for firms identified by research. It is clear that German firms dominate the sector overall in terms of turnover, steel consumption and number of firms. The largest presswork firm in Europe is also German (Thyssen Unformtechnic), but Germany is also strongly represented in medium-sized firms consuming between 30 000 and 10 000 tonnes of steel per annum. When ownership is taken into account the dominance of the German industry (and to a lesser extent that of the French) is even greater – in comparison, there are few major independent UK presswork firms left. It is also clear that the French and German sectors have a larger average steel consumption and higher turnover-to-steel ratio. By using a rather crude proxy measure it is clear that these firms are adding more value in the presswork process whereas those in Portugal and Spain are more involved in the 'commodity' end of the sector.

6.7 NEW PROCUREMENT REGIMES IN PRESSWORK

Two basic features are worthy of note in respect to the outsourcing of pressed panels. First, the vehicle assemblers are all seeking to reduce the number of panels per vehicle. This reduces investment costs in dies. Second, all assemblers are seeking to reduce the number of dies per panel. Again, this reduces investment costs, as was noted earlier.

However, the effect of these two developments is to reduce the total number of press strokes required per vehicle. Given that the vehicle assemblers are also investing substantially in new transfer and progression press capacity there must be a diminishing volume of work in aggregate available for external suppliers.

Equally, both assemblers and components firms have indicated a move towards greater levels of sub-assembly work at the suppliers, though practice on this varies widely. Rover, for example, outsourced pressings on the R8 in clusters in order to reduce the total number of suppliers it dealt with; GM in comparison still tends to buy in large numbers of small components and undertake sub-assembly itself. On the other hand, many of the presswork components firms were expected to do more downstream work – typically in powder coating, painting, drilling and other operations.

In practice, the nature of component firm–automobile firm relations rather depends upon the nature of the product. In complex pressings such as suspension arms and folding vehicle jacks, the components firm will have a greater impact on and role in the design process, typically through linked CAD facilities. More typically the traditional situation still prevails – components firms are asked to quote a piece price and 'work to order'. The assemblers not only have the design copyright in most cases, but they also maintain ownership of the dies. Consequently, the generic strategy in the sector consists of differentiation by whatever means possible. For some firms, this entails product specialisation (for example, Tallent on suspension arms; Tubsa on vehicle jacks; and Cremsa on pulleys); for others, market segment specialisation (for example, Polynorm on press relief); for others still it entails developing distinctive technological capabilities (for example, Sigro on small progression press dies and presswork; and Thyssen on very large pressings).

However, we have found very few instances of major pressworkers subcontracting work out to smaller pressworkers, so tiering in this sense does not appear to be developing in the sector. One partial exception is Lebranchu, one of the larger French presswork firms, which manages 200 smaller firms on a subcontract basis for Renault – effectively the large firm acts as a purchase agent for the vehicle assembler. Equally, there was no evidence that presswork firms were passing on changes in procurement methods down into their own supply base. Only a few firms had established just-in-time steel supply, for example, though all reported that the number of suppliers they used was being reduced.

6.8 RESTRUCTURING THE AUTOMOTIVE PRESSWORK COMPONENTS SECTOR

As we showed in Table 6.3, German firms in Germany account for 37 per cent of total steel consumption in the independent presswork sector. During the late 1980s and early 1990s these firms have increased their hold on the sector through international expansion and acquisition. Table 6.4 summarises major restructuring activities in the European presswork components sector. This process of international expansion, in which the UK has been the main recipient, has

Table 6.4   Restructuring in the European presswork components sector, 1991–3

Firm	Activity
Lebrançhu (France)	Purchase of Coventry Presswork (UK)
Lebranchu (France)	Purchase of Barretts (UK)
Heuliez (France)	Establishment of Eurostamp (France)
GKN/Ford (UK)	Closure of Venture Pressings (UK)
Thyssen (Germany)	Purchase of Tallent Engineering (UK)
Thyssen (Germany)	Purchase of Albion Pressed Metal (UK)
Thyssen (Germany)	Purchase of IFA Ludwigsfelde (Germany)
Dr Meleghy (Germany)	Purchase of IFA Zwickau (Germany)
Laepple (Germany)	Establishment of greenfield site (Germany)
Plattenburg (Sweden)	Joint venture with Press Kogyo (Belgium)
Robinsons (UK)	Into receivership
Hoesch (Germany)	Purchase of Camford Engineering (UK)
Kutsch (Germany)	Purchase of 50% of Arjal (Portugal)
Kutsch (Germany)	Purchase of Sigro (Germany)

Sources: Interviews, company reports, specialist press reports.

been accompanied by consolidation within national boundaries. In the UK, groups (such as Benjamin Priest, and United Pressings and Fabrications) have formed to combine a range of metal processing interests. In France, the vehicle assemblers played a direct role in encouraging mergers in the supply base, thus mini-conglomerates such as SOFEDIT have been created from several previously separate entities. The international expansion adds a new dimension to this process.

With respect to German and French investments in the UK, in most cases the primary consideration has been access to Japanese assemblers (the exception is Sigro, a GM supplier). German firms in particular expressed concern at opening up their operations to Japanese assemblers, and were therefore attracted by the prospect of 'remote' learning through the market access attendant upon their acquisitions. In contrast, labour issues – whether involving pay, training, union representation, or working practices, did not appear to be a primary consideration except in so far as they formed a blockage to further expansion of output within Germany itself. Interestingly, Sigro's move to Ireland was motivated by labour cost and investment subsidy issues but, according to the firm, has yet to yield positive benefits – and the site does not even supply GM in the UK. It is notable that the British firms acquired by German firms were either large or highly thought of in the industry (for example, Albion has extensive cellular manufacturing; and Tallent has invested considerably on transfer press technology and specialises in suspension systems), and were considered by some commentators to be expensive purchases at the time. Quite how these operations will fit into a wider spatial division of labour controlled from Germany is not yet clear. What is clear is that German firms effectively control the European presswork industry, while independent British-owned firms are rapidly disappearing. The purchase of Coventry Presswork by Lebranchu is also an instance of market access; Lebranchu supplies petrol tanks to Toyota and a UK base makes sense for them as the product is bulky. However, Coventry Presswork itself was rather more typical of the state of the UK presswork sector overall, having lacked investment over the 1980s as its major customer (Rover) continued to decline in output.

6.9 CONCLUSIONS

As with the motor industry overall, the presswork sector appears to be one undergoing a process of de-maturity as new technologies and new working methods are introduced. An inevitable consequence of these changes overall will be a decline in the numbers of firms active in the sector in Europe, and the emergence of an economic structure dominated by large groups rather than smaller independent firms. With these changes are associated developments in the procurement regime within presswork. In general, there still appear to be substantial differences in the sort of regime firms face according to the type of presswork they may undertake, and the customer firm in question. For example, the Dutch firm Polynorm specialises in official aftermarket and press-relief work and as such it replicates in its production facilities the sort of equipment commonly found in the vehicle assemblers. Consequently, they are vulnerable to the customer taking back work on short notice should the customer develop surplus capacity in its own press-shops. In many cases, presswork is still outsourced on a capacity basis; vehicle assemblers decide which work they can do in-house and then outsource the rest. But this is still a long way from partnership. On the other hand, in components demanding a high engineering input and with firms which are more liable to outsource parts, it is the case that a closer and longer-term relationship is evident. This applies, for instance, to structural parts such as suspensions, and to 'black box' parts such as vehicle jacks.

7 Friction Materials

7.1 INTRODUCTION

Friction materials are widely used in the automotive industry in braking systems (where the friction material transfers kinetic energy into heat energy, thus stopping the vehicle) and in power transmission (where the friction material allows the smooth application of engine torque to the driven wheels via a clutch). Historically, the preferred friction material was asbestos impregnated with a resin polymer, but the health risks associated with its use forced the replacement of this material with metallic-resin compounds. For original equipment, the sector in Europe is dominated by just three main firms, though other firms also supply for original equipment they are small and generally concerned with specialist niche applications. There is also a much larger (but unknown) number of independent suppliers for aftermarket applications.

In this chapter we first outline the supply chain in friction materials before giving profiles of the three leading European firms. As in the steel industry, this apparently basic input is in fact a complex product embodying considerable technological development and new production methods. In the context of procurement regimes, we show that friction materials suppliers may often deal with two customers (the vehicle assemblers and the brake assemblers), while the aftermarket remains a significant consideration.

7.2 THE FRICTION MATERIALS SUPPLY CHAIN

Figure 7.1 illustrates the general dimensions of the supply chain only. Levels of integration down the supply chain vary widely, as do linkages across the chain between clutches and brakes. Table 7.1 illustrates these points with respect to the major firms in the sector in Europe. Clearly, some firms have extensive vertical linkages. BBA, for example, owns the largest friction material supplier in Europe (Mintex Don) which formed the original core business, as well both clutch and

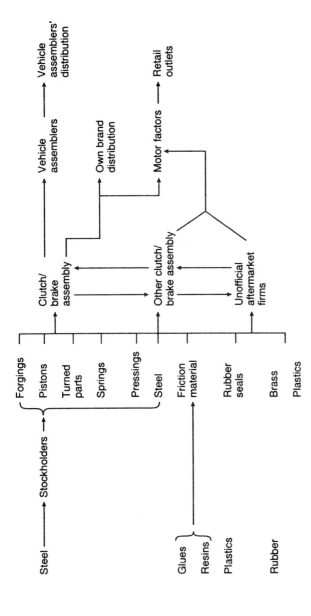

Figure 7.1   The clutch, brakes and friction material supply chain

Source: Authors' analysis.

Table 7.1   Vertical integration in friction materials, brakes and clutches

Company	Friction material	Foundation brakes	ABS	Clutches	Dist/AM
BBA	Mintex Don Textar	AP Lockheed	X	AP Borg & Beck	Yes
T & N	Ferodo	X	X	X	Yes
Allied-Signal	Jurid	Bendix	Yes	X	Yes
Bosch	X	X	Yes	X	Yes
ITT	X	Teves	Yes	X	Yes
Mannesman	X	X	X	F & S	Yes
LUK	X	X	X	LUK	Yes
Valeo	Valeo Friction	X	X	Valeo Clutch	Yes
Siemens	X	X	Yes	X	?

Notes: X = No activity.
         ? = Unknown.
Sources: Company reports.

brake assembly (AP Clutch, AP Lockheed). Equally, Allied-Signal
have a friction materials business and brakes business. T & N,
however, depend on friction materials for a high proportion of
turnover, but have no downstream interests in clutches or brakes.
Bosch, on the other hand, do not make 'foundation brakes' (i.e. the
basic physical components of brakes), friction material or clutches, but
specialise in the electronic control systems required for anti-lock brake
systems (ABS) in which they are the world leader.

7.3   THE STRUCTURE OF THE FRICTION MATERIAL SUPPLY SECTOR

Friction material supply is dominated by a few large firms who are
able to retain their control over the market through a combination of
economies of scale and considerable technological barriers to entry.
The main firms in the sector are Mintex-Don (BBA), Ferodo (T & N),
and Jurid (Allied-Signal). There are a few smaller firms in the sector,
but these are largely excluded from original equipment supply and
tend to specialise in aftermarket and/or commercial vehicle applications with much lower volumes of sales. An intermediary firm not
further considered here is Reutgers Pagid, which has plants in
Germany (including former East Germany), Italy and France.

7.3.1 Ferodo

Ferodo is part of the T & N group, one of the major UK automotive components firms which also has interests in pistons and rings (AE Piston Products); gaskets and valve train components (Coopers Payen, Brico); and bearings (Glacier Automotive Bearings). Ferodo has subsidiary firms in France (Abex Equipments); Italy (Ferodo Italia); Germany (Beral Bremsbelag); USA (Naturn); Spain (Ferodo Espanola and Garnecto); and long-standing plants in South Africa, Zimbabwe and India. The friction materials segment accounted for £252m out of a total £1188m turnover within T & N in 1989 (i.e. nearly 20 per cent). The firm has been increasing its presence in the friction materials area especially in Europe; both Abex and Garnecto were bought in 1989 while Beral Bremsbelag was bought in 1985 – though this division has continued to suffer operating difficulties despite new investment and restructuring. These acquisitions were seen as being important to capture business from vehicle assemblers who still tended to prefer purchasing within national boundaries.

In the case of France, T & N were excluded because of an arrangement with Valeo. T & N had a small shareholding in Valeo in exchange for promising not to enter the French market, but once that agreement lapsed, and Valeo decided to abandon friction materials altogether, T & N were able to make a direct entry. Thus by 1991 friction material accounted for £490m turnover out of group sales of £1.359bn. T & N involvement in friction materials and their spatial coverage was extended in 1992 with the purchase of Osinek AS, Czechoslovakia's sole supplier of friction material.

The extent to which the automotive sector is represented in friction material sales is not known; for example, Ferodo also supplies brake pads for railway trains, but automobiles are certainly the major market. As with the Lucas example shown later (Chapter 8, pages 230–235), T & N as a whole has an increasing proportion of turnover attributable outside the UK but this concentrates more on automotive business and has a greater proportion of UK employment, partly reflecting continuing growth by acquisition in the UK. Tables 7.2 and 7.3 show the distribution of friction material sales by major region of destination and origin, and spatial employment changes for the group as a whole.

The T & N group expanded rapidly in the UK with the takeover of AE in 1984, but since then most of the employment growth has been in Europe and the USA. This trend has continued into the 1990s with the

Table 7.2   Spatial distribution of T & N friction material sales, 1991 (£millions)

	Turnover by destination	Turnover by origin
UK	134	201
Europe	217	165
North America	104	105
Africa	21	21
Others	14	1
Totals	490	490

Source: T & N Annual Report, 1992.

Table 7.3   Spatial distribution of T & N employment, 1985–91

	UK	Europe	North America	South Africa	Other	Total
1991	15258	6393	4995	12757	977	40280
1990	16887	6547	3134	13268	991	40827
1989	17569	6390	1718	14217	1894	41788
1988	17318	5036	1371	14028	1924	40173
1987	16236	4594	1055	13514	1948	39404
1986	17984	1981	876	11279	2029	38532
1985	8379	1726	838	12467	2146	27248

Note: T & N bought AE (of the UK) and Beral Bremsbelag (of Germany) in 1985.
Source: T & N Annual Reports.

acquisition of the German firm Goetze, a producer of pistons, in 1993. Within the automotive components business, the overall share of the UK, Europe and the US markets rose from 44 per cent in 1984 to 76 per cent in 1987. T & N still have to put aside some £16m per annum for asbestos claims. This is a result of two features: first, the firm was more concerned with a broad range of asbestos applications than other friction materials firms – for example, in building materials, lagging for steam and ship engines, pipe insulation, fire retardant boards, etc.; and second, they had a much stronger presence in the USA than had other firms, and it is the USA which is the source of the most litigation with respect to asbestos. T & N also have their own in-house resins manufacture capability.

7.3.2 Mintex Don

The Mintex Don group is part of BBA, a British firm with diversified interests but also a strong representation in the automotive industry. Its primary friction interests consist of Mintex and Don in the UK, with subsidiary firms in Spain (Frenos y Embragues SA), Canada (Mintex Canada), Sweden (Svenska Bromsbandsfabriken AB) and Germany/Netherlands (Textar). It established a new factory in Virginia, USA (in 1991), while Pacific BBA has also engaged in a joint venture with Allied Signal for the co-production of friction materials. Within BBA as a whole, automotive sector sales, which include AP Lockheed (brakes) and AP Borg and Beck (clutches), amounted to £595m in 1991 (total group sales of £1.252bn), of which friction materials accounted for about 45 per cent – or around £300m – rather less than those of T & N.

The automotive sector within BBA is highly internationalised. Its non-UK earnings are especially boosted by Textar which has a powerful hold over the German friction materials supply industry. Table 7.4 summarises automotive sales and profits within BBA from 1987 to 1991. The dip in sales evident from the 1988 and 1989 periods reflect the downturn in vehicle sales generally at this time (especially in the UK), and such declines are to be found for most companies supplying automotive components. The squeeze on profits in the early 1990s, at a time when investment demands increased, is also a feature common to much of the European components industry. In terms of the spatial distribution of automotive sales, about 25 per cent were in the UK, 55 per cent in the rest of Europe, 15 per cent US and 5 per cent elsewhere. As with the other friction materials suppliers, BBA

Table 7.4   Sales and operating profit, BBA group automotive segment, 1981–91 (£millions)

	Sales	*Profit*	*Percentages profit*
1991	595.7	19.8	3.3
1990	631.8	34.6	5.5
1989	713.4	52.4	7.3
1988	707.0	53.8	7.6
1987	582.0	42.7	7.3

Source: BBA Annual Report, 1991.

has felt the need to engage in joint ventures. In 1991, the company entered a cross-licence agreement with Nisshinbo Industries of Japan to access their friction materials technology in order to supply Japanese transplants, in exchange for high performance, asbestos-free friction technology from BBA.

7.3.3   Jurid

Jurid is the principal friction materials producer in Europe for Allied-Signal, a US firm. In 1979, the then Allied Chemical was narrowly interested in the production of chemicals, fibres, oil and gas with a turnover of $3bn. Since then an aggressive diversification and expansion programme has been followed, most notably the acquisition of Bendix (a leading US brake producer with a strong European presence) in 1983 and the merger with Signal in 1985. As a group, the firm is one of the largest in the global automotive industry, as Table 7.5 illustrates.

The automotive sector in Allied-Signal encompasses the Automotive Systems Group (disc and drum brakes, ABS systems, boosters and master cylinders); Heavy Vehicle Systems Group – Garret (CV brakes and turbochargers); Friction Materials Group (disc brake pads and brake blocks); Aftermarket Group (filters and brakes); Safety Restraints Group (seat belts and air bags); and Autolite (spark plugs). The share of automotive markets in total turnover has risen slightly, from 31 per cent in 1987 to 34.6 per cent in 1991. Allied-Signal, and especially the Automotive Group as a whole, have been in some difficulties in the early 1990s and as a result have instituted a group-wide total quality programme. An automotive operating profit of $31m in 1991 was eradicated by restructuring costs of $257m. Between

Table 7.5   Allied-Signal Group turnover and employment, and automotive turnover and profit, 1988–91 ($millions)

	1987	1988	1989	1990	1991
Group turnover	11.1	11.9	11.9	12.3	11.8
Group employment (000s)	115	109	107	105	98
Auto turnover	3.54	4.10	3.84	4.18	4.09
Auto profit	0.10	0.09	0.11	0.03	(0.2)

Source: Allied-Signal Annual Reports.

1985 and 1991, the firm shed 45 500 jobs worldwide, or 31 per cent of the 1985 workforce. In 1991, Allied Signal announced its further intention to reduce the workforce by over 5000 jobs, or 16 per cent of the 1991 total. This is certainly a common theme in the automotive sector as a whole, in that labour tends to bear the costs of restructuring in the form of lost jobs.

As Table 7.6 shows, Allied-Signal is mainly dependent upon the US market, though this has declined slightly from 82 per cent of total sales in 1987 to 78 per cent in 1991. The exact contribution to turnover from the European automotive operations, and in particular the friction materials and car brakes businesses, is difficult to determine. The worldwide group figures are given in Table 7.7.

Global friction material sales of $463m (just over £200m) are broadly equivalent to those achieved by BBA. Of the total automotive sales, 59 per cent were as original equipment to the vehicle assemblers,

Table 7.6   Allied-Signal spatial distribution of sales to 1991 ($millions)

	1981	*1988*	*1989*	*1990*	*1991*
USA & Canada	9183	9621	9721	9736	9258
Europe	1468	1738	1663	2002	2079
Others	465	550	558	605	494

Source: Allied-Signal Annual Reports.

Table 7.7   Allied-Signal automotive sales, worldwide, 1990 ($millions)

	$millions	*Percentage*
Bendix automotive systems	1 679	40
Bendix heavy vehicle systems	471	11
Bendix safety restraints	328	8
Allied Signal aftermarket	754	18
Friction materials	463	11
Autolite spark plugs	66	2
Garrett Automotive	418	10
Other	2	–
Total	4 181	100

Source: Sleigh, 1991.

11 per cent original equipment service requirements, and 30 per cent independent aftermarket. Nearly 90 per cent of Allied-Signal turnover in Europe is attributable to the automotive sector, with Jurid Werke (Hamburg and Glinde, Germany), Allied-Signal Friction Materials (Rennegar, Germany) and Energit (Baden-Wurttemberg, Germany) major sources of friction material. The purchases by Allied-Signal of the former Valeo friction material plants in France and Spain (1989 turnover FFr1.14bn, employment 2,240) has extended their spatial coverage and increased industrial concentration in the segment. Allied Signal now has eleven friction materials plants in six countries.

7.4   NEW PRODUCT, MATERIALS AND PROCESS TECHNOLOGY

Although the basic ingredients of friction materials are well known, the development of application-specific material is widely regarded as a 'black art' in that it involves the mixing of up to 50 different ingredients. The friction materials industry, as previously mentioned, has its technical and locational roots in the British textiles industry in the early part of this century. The BBA group originated as a firm in Cleckheaton (Yorkshire) supplying drive belts to the textile industry, later expanding into conveyor belting and woven cotton. Then Frood, working in the Manchester textile industry, realised that woven asbestos, impregnated with resin, would make a far better friction material than the leather then used on vehicles such as coaches, and on pulley brakes (used in trawlers, for example). The Ford Model T was the first original equipment customer for the new product. Herbert Frood originated the Ferodo brand, now part of T & N. However, with the growing awareness of the health risks of asbestos in the 1960s came the development of moulded mineral textiles (hence the name Mintex) and the development of disc brakes.

Friction materials consist of the basic elements shown in Table 7.8. The resins are usually phenols, typically modified with the addition of chemical additives such as cashew nut shell liquid, elastomers, oils (for example, linseed oil), and inorganic chemicals (for example, boron, phosphorous); resins may be prepared in powder or liquid form and act to bind together the friction material while also making a contribution to friction performance. Typically, resins account for up to 25 per cent of the weight of drum brake pads, and up to 12 per cent for disc brake pads. Fibres may include asbestos, glass, poly-

Table 7.8   Constituent ingredients of friction materials

Material	Function	Example
Polymers	Binders	Glass Aramid Metal Natural
Fibre	Reinforcement	Phenolic resin Epoxy resin Silicone Rubber
Fillers	Inert medium	Barium sulphate Calcium carbonate Magnesium oxide
Modifiers	Alter performance	Graphite Antimony Zirconium silica

Source: BP.

aramidide pulp, ceramics, kevlar and steel, and in semi-metallic friction materials these may constitute up to 50 per cent of the weight. The fibres provide the bulk of the friction performance in a brake or clutch. The filler materials provide a low-cost medium to 'carry' and distribute the friction material. Conventional fillers (including, for example, talc, chalk, clay, vermiculite and wollastonite) also provide some reinforcement characteristics, and help in the processing of friction materials. Modifiers are essentially filler materials, though usually added in very small quantities, which also have important friction characteristics and usually cost more than conventional fillers. Organic modifiers include rubber crumb and cork particles; inorganic modifiers include graphite, metal particles and abrasives. The use of graphite and antimony trisulphide, for example, provides lubrication, helping to ensure that the brake blocks do not stick to the disc during use. Changing the balance of all of the above elements in the final friction material changes the performance of that material. Thus, for instance, a high total organic content gives increased fade and high temperature wear; high abrasive levels lead to increased wear on the brake rotor; and increased hardness leads to noise and vibration.

It can be seen that the resins used to bind together the friction material play a critical role in the composition and performance of the product. Chemical firms (notably BP in the UK and Hoechst in Germany) are leading suppliers of such resins. We return to relationships along the supply chain later. Here, it is sufficient to note that within the sector as a whole there is a long and extensive supply chain. It is also worth noting that brakes in particular are 'safety critical' items; that is, they must not suffer catastrophic failure in use. One consequence of this requirement is that quality testing and the creation of rigorous batch coding has long been a feature of the friction material production process – all original equipment brake pads must be traceable.

In this market segment we can see the pressures for technological innovation passed back all the way down the supply chain from vehicle assemblers to resin suppliers. While discrete innovations at each level may and do occur, there is evidence of more continuing technical involvement down the supply chain. At the top of the supply chain the vehicle assemblers are demanding ever greater levels of performance from clutches and brakes. With respect to brakes, for example, not only is the physical performance important – in terms of lack of fade and so on – but also the brake must fit into the space package allowed. Moreover, rather less measurable performance in the 'feel' of the brakes in operation will affect how customers respond to the vehicle overall. These technical requirements overlay the more general trends towards cost reduction, low inventories and frequent deliveries. Different assemblers may take different approaches to the same problem. For example, 'early morning grab' is caused by the build-up of deposits and water on the brake discs. Some assemblers prefer to use very hard disc pads which have the effect of slightly eroding the disc surface in use, thus cleaning the surface and ensuring smooth operation. Others prefer to use softer disc pads which are less liable to stick against uneven and damp surfaces.

Friction materials for original equipment must be tuned to the particular application. Each time a new product is considered, the friction material supplier will investigate a range of options for different mixes within the competence of the firms' manufacturing capabilities and cost targets. Friction materials firms will not release details of their mixtures to either the brake assemblers or the automobile firms; however, Mintex have recently entered a technical alliance with BP – their main supplier of resins – to improve the performance of resins in the mixture. In most cases, the vehicle assemblers also play a role in the friction material selection process, a role that has often increased in recent years. The sustained costs of product research and development provide a significant stimulus to industry restructuring in the friction materials sector. Essentially, the largest three firms have secured their hold over the original equipment market while smaller firms have either been acquired, forced into the aftermarket segment only, or gone out of business.

The traditional friction material production process is a hazardous and inefficient large-batch system. In a typical 1960s-generation friction material plant making brake discs, there are three stages: mixing; hot pressing (and curing); and machining. The mixing stage is highly automated, then drums of mixture are taken to the pressing area where operatives measure out the relevant quantities of loose material into dies (typically each press has a die with twenty spaces in), having first inserted the metal plates on to which the friction material is to be bonded. The mixture is then hot pressed for five minutes before being removed to the machining stage. Here each disc is baked for twelve hours, then trimmed and lacquered, the surface is ground and the batch code is marked on. Each batch is subjected to random testing to destruction of a few samples. More recently, this process has been replaced by automated and programmable machining centres, but such flexibility depends upon the development of new friction materials which can be 'wet'-mixed. Thus, although the friction materials area illustrates the general trend to replace the traditional production organisation of task-specific machines grouped together, it has only been possible with the developed of new friction technology that has changed the production parameters. Historically, friction materials suppliers in Europe have concentrated on the development of materials for the performance of the product rather than the processing technology, and in many instances have had to look to Japan to gain access to the latest in production technology.

7.5 PROCUREMENT REGIMES IN THE FRICTION MATERIALS SUPPLY SECTOR

As was suggested earlier, procurement regimes in the friction materials supply sector are not simply linear. That is to say, there is a triangular relationship, with friction material producers dealing with two customers: the vehicle assemblers and the brake manufacturers. All three have to be closely involved at the earliest stages of the design process, typically including sub-suppliers such as the manufacturers of the brake rotors (or discs as they are commonly known). Vehicle assemblers have tended to have particular preferences for compositions of friction materials and the supplier to use for that material, and have not in general been willing to relinquish total control over the choice of material to the brake assemblers. However, the pattern of sourcing has remained largely unchanged for a long period of time in that each vehicle assembler has a preferred source of friction material, and this preferred source recieves about 70 per cent of the total business available, with the majority of the remainder going to the second source. In this sense, the friction material sector has developed quasi-Japanese sourcing regimes ahead of other traditional sectors such as presswork, and ahead of more innovative sectors. In the future, it may be the case that the friction materials producer will play a more residual role as the brake system/chassis system supplier takes overall control over product co-ordination; however, our research with friction materials firms suggests that at present vehicle assemblers are reluctant to delegate all that work entirely to the brake assembler.

Of more interest in the friction materials sector is the question of the aftermarket and how that market is serviced. Brake pads tend to wear out long before the end of the useful life of the vehicle as a whole, and even though this performance has improved over time (especially in clutch friction material) it is still the case that for every pad sold as new on a new vehicle, the use of that vehicle over its lifetime will generate the consumption of three or four more pads. The market for such replacement parts is in distinct contrast to the structures prevailing in the original equipment sector.

We can distinguish several sources of supply to the replacement parts market. These are: the vehicle assemblers' own service and repair franchises; the branded products of the major friction material makers (for example, Ferodo); the 'own label' products of large retail and distribution firms (for example, Halfords); and the specialist aftermarket brands. Confusingly, the same friction materials supplier may make the pads for all these sources! Equally, it is the case that no single firm is able to make all the aftermarket range, the range is simply too large. There is thus a need to reach a critical mass of market coverage for any branded aftermarket product (typically 95 per cent of the market), which can only be done through the buying-in of pads from smaller, independent suppliers.

Obtaining hard information on this part of the friction materials businesses is not easy. Firms are reluctant to say what proportion of their range is bought in, what the levels of profit are, where their sources are, or to evaluate the relative importance of the different distribution channels noted above. Even the question of the composition of the friction material is not clear-cut. Typically, friction material sold to aftermarket applications is of the same quality as the original in that it will stop the vehicle as fast, but will not last nearly as long or will have other drawbacks because the mixture has had some of the more expensive ingredients excluded.

Equally, the geography of this industry remains obscure in the aftermarket sector. Friction materials may be supplied into the UK market from anywhere in the world, with Italy and Taiwan as major sources. Many suppliers of pads do not make the actual friction material itself, but buy this in from other sources and then process it. Most manufacturers of pads with strong brand names will also buy in a high proportion of their range, it is simply uneconomic to attempt to produce all types of friction material and brake pad required in a market as complex and varied as Europe's. We shall discuss the development of the aftermarket sector, using the illustrative example of Germany, in the Chapter 8.

7.6 CONCLUSIONS

The friction materials sector is one in which there has been a long process of industrial concentration accompanied by geographic extension via a process of acquisitions by the leading firms. The supply sector is now 'mature' in the sense that a relatively stable oligopoly exists within Europe to dominate the market overall. There are still some smaller firms making friction materials for more or less specialised applications, but in general the economies of scale in the industry are allied to those pertaining in much of the chemicals sector overall, of which friction materials can be considered a special case, and the demands for continued improvement in friction material performance will continue to demand large-scale suppliers. The pressures of the 1990s, notably those to reduce vehicle weight as a means of reaching other 'environmental' targets, will continue to place pressure on friction materials producers to develop highly innovative friction materials. It is possible that new firms with new competencies will arise, but the likely outcome is that friction materials will become ever-more 'high-tech' and dominated by the few leading firms.

8 Clutches and Brakes

8.1 INTRODUCTION

Clutches and brakes are both basic components of most vehicles, and are related in that both use friction materials in the physical operations they perform. Both are also mainly supplied to vehicle assemblers by external, independent firms. Unlike the presswork sector, the clutches and brakes markets for volume original equipment, as well as the friction materials markets, are dominated by a few multinational firms – although the aftermarket segment is much more fragmented. This chapter examines the supply chain in clutches and brakes, with the emphasis on the structure of the industry and the mechanisms by which change is transmitted through that structure. As we shall show later, product innovation by components firms has been a key facet of the sector; indeed, firms in this sector exhibit many more of the characteristics of the Lamming (1989a) post-Japanese model than do those in the presswork sector.

In both clutches and brakes, the components are essentially mechanical, but they are increasingly being integrated into electronic control systems and thus into the wider design process in vehicle development. Moreover, as in presswork, technological developments in materials, product design and process engineering are important in reshaping the industry, with the critical factor being which firm and which competencies take the role as systems integrator. As we shall show below, this sector illustrates more clearly the differences between assemblers in terms of how they source components, The components firms supplying clutches and brakes to vehicle assemblers are more fully developed in terms of their management of the supply base and lean production generally, compared with sub-sectors such as presswork. Both clutches and brakes involve the integration of several distinct types of material and technology and a large number of discrete components, with primary supplier firms decreasingly involved in manufacture, so the supply base in most instances is both quite broad and of greater significance than in presswork.

The data in Table 8.1 are supplied by a typical brake manufacturer to illustrate the nature of the supply chain, it is worth noting that in Table 8.1, of the 204 suppliers current in 1992 over half (113) were

Table 8.1   Number of suppliers by general category of part, typical brake
manufacturer

Steel	4
Rubbers	15
Plastics	21
Friction	13
Brass	2
Bundy	3
Castings	9
Forgings	6
Pressings	29
Springs	24
Turned parts	21
Pistons	1
Other	50
Total	204

Source: Personal interviews.

located within 40 miles. However, this does not necessarily illustrate a
propensity for local sourcing within the product area. The pattern is
very different for the two major brake assemblers in Wales, for
example, Teves and Lucas Girling. In both these cases, the extent of
component sourcing in Wales is minimal, despite these companies
being in the region since 1974 and 1947 respectively. It is also worth
noting that the firm whose data are shown in Table 8.1 has reduced its
supply base by over 50 per cent in just four years, an indication that at
least some of the elements of the lean production model have been
transferred down the production chain. A typical breakdown of
expenditure by product area is given in Table 8.2.

Table 8.2 clearly illustrates the relative importance of friction
materials in the overall spending of the firm; in clutches alone,
friction material is somewhat less significant overall. Pressings are
also important in brakes, and even more so in clutches, which explains
why BBA felt it useful to have a captive supplier of pressings to both
its clutch and brake divisions. Generally, there is a tendency for brakes
to be assembled from bought-in components, often even castings are
bought in ready-machined, whereas with clutches there are greater
levels of in-house machining and production prior to assembly. This is
largely a reflection of the view that, in clutch production, machining of
the clutch plates and clutch springs is so critical to product
performance that it must be considered a core activity.

Table 8.2   Distribution of spending on components and materials, typical brake manufacturer (percentage)

Plastics	4
Rubbers	13
Pressings	17
Turned parts	12
Steel	1
Springs	3
Pistons	1
Forgings	1
Friction	27
Brass	1
Castings/Bundy	14
Other	4

Source: Interviews.

8.2   STRUCTURE OF THE SECTOR

Measuring the size of this sector is extremely difficult, especially with respect to the aftermarket segment. Here we concentrate on identifying the main firms in the three parts of the sector of interest to us: friction materials; clutches; and brakes, and attempt to give some indication of the size of business involved in terms of units of output, turnover, employment and so on. Again, we concentrate on the main business of original equipment suppliers to high-volume automobile assemblers. Suppliers of low-volume products, including those for the commercial vehicle sector, are excluded where possible, as is the aftermarket. In practice, it is not always possible to make these distinctions – firms may not know, or be willing to make public, the extent to which their turnover and so on is attributable to the volume passenger car original equipment business. An illustrative case is Lucas. This firm has extensive UK and non-UK interests in aerospace, the automotive sector, and other technology areas. In terms of its automotive interests, the firm is largely concerned with brake systems and engine management systems for all types of vehicle. Thus while it is possible to identify some general changes in the structure of Lucas, it is not possible to disaggregate the data to show, for example, the value of its car brakes business, or the spatial distribution of automotive sales.

No clear pattern is evident in the structure of the sector. The diagram of levels of vertical integration in the sector (see Chapter 7) illustrates a diversity of firms which have varying degrees of specialisation, both in terms of product focus and in terms of geographic (and hence, customer) spread. In terms of product focus, LUK (Germany) appears to have the greatest degree of concentration, in this case on clutches, and the firm is not part of a larger group (but see the comments on Valeo in section 8.3.2). In brake manufacture the market in Europe is dominated by Teves (ITT) and Bendix (Allied-Signal). These firms are both part of much larger and more diverse groups. There appear to be few synergies between brake and clutch manufacture, only AP Lockheed and AP Borg and Beck are active in both markets, and even here the Lockheed brakes business is very specialised (see also EIU, 1993).

8.3 CLUTCHES

The European clutch market for original equipment on automobiles is dominated by just four firms: LUK (Germany); AP Borg and Beck (UK); Valeo (France); and Fichtel and Sachs (Germany). Of these, LUK is both the most recent entry and the most specialised in terms of clutch and transmission components, and in terms of its concentration on clutches for automobiles.

8.3.1 LUK

LUK was established in 1965. The firm now has an international production structure, as shown in Table 8.3. The firm's expansion into South America followed VW. Within Europe, production is concentrated in Germany and the UK. The firm was until the 1980s very dependent upon the main German vehicle assemblers, especially VW. As Table 8.3 shows, LUK is almost entirely concerned with clutch production, the majority being original equipment for automobiles. Tractor clutches account for a small proportion of output, while rebuilt clutches account for some activities. However, this degree of focus has enabled LUK to derive greater economies of scale and greater levels of automation. The firm does not produce an annual report, or make available figures on its financial performance. It is thought that Valeo has a 50 per cent holding in LUK, but under German company law the firm does not have to disclose any information. However, it is estimated that turnover in 1991 was in the region of £150m. The firm is interesting because of its product

Table 8.3   LUK production structure

Location	Output	Employees
Bühl Germany	HQ & R&D 6.0m car clutches 0.6m lock-up clutches 0.7m auto transmission bands 0.5m dual mass fly-wheels	1 100
Unna, Germany	0.5m rebuilt clutches	80
Largene, Germany	AM Distribution Centre 2500 clutch models	80
Werdahl, Germany	Electronic transmission systems	40
Eisenberg, Germany	Castings/engine blocks	550
Sheffield, UK	0.7m car clutches 0.3m tractor clutches	150
Hereford, UK	0.1m rebuilt double clutches	40
Worcester, UK	1.0m car clutches 1.5m lock-up dampers	300
Puebla, Mexico	0.4m car clutches	300
Sorocola, Brazil	2.0m car clutches 0.1m tractor clutches	400
Port Elizabeth, South Africa	0.6m car clutches	300

Source: LUK.

development strategy and for the high levels of automation in its German production facilities, both of which are discussed below.

8.3.2   Valeo

Valeo are one of the largest of the European automotive components firms (formed out of a merger of several French firms in 1980), clutch production is only part of their business, though the firm claims to be the largest clutch producer in the world (see Dawkins, 1989). It is also a rapidly changing firm which has a clear policy of concentrating on product areas where it enjoys a strong market presence – it is for this reason that Valeo sold its interests in friction materials to Allied-

Signal. It is interesting that Valeo should feel unable to retain a friction materials business. The friction materials division within Valeo recently expanded into Mexico and, via a joint venture, into South Korea, and has established a new research facility in France. The division supplies brake linings as well as clutch facings, although the clutch facings work seems to be of greater strategic importance. Clearly, Valeo considered the costs of retaining a global presence in friction materials to be too high in relation to the market they could achieve. In 1990, the firm undertook a major restructuring programme worldwide which involved the closure of fifteen plants and the loss of 3000 jobs. Table 8.4 shows the sales and employment for Valeo in its main component areas. Part of this strategy reflects a desire to escape dependence upon French customers: by 1991 56 per cent of Valeo's earnings came from outside France.

The firm has clutch production locations in Amiens (France); Birmingham (UK); two sites in Spain; Mondovi (Italy); Jedeida (Tunisia); Taegu (South Korea, a joint venture); Bursa (Turkey); and Reichenbach (Germany). The firm has also acquired a clutch-making facility in the former East Germany from the Treuhandanstalt. It is therefore well placed to serve all the major European markets, and has also expanded into the USA. As can be seen from Table 8.4, clutches accounted for about 10 per cent of Valeo employment and turnover in 1989 (Valeo is 100 per cent automotive), and is clearly an area where the firm intends to retain an interest. Technological

Table 8.4   Valeo sales and employment by major product area, 1989

Area	Sales (FFrbn)	Employees
Clutches	2.68	3 450
Friction material	1.14	2 240
Engine cooling	2.73	6 730
Climate control	2.71	4 460
Lighting	3.54	5 950
Electronics	1.00	2 120
Alternators and starters	2.38	2 750
Wiping systems	1.10	1 570
Security system	1.80	3 470
Distribution	2.97	1 340
Total	22.05	34 080

Source: Sleigh, 1991.

competition has been fierce in the Valeo product areas, and currently the firm spends about 4 per cent of turnover on R&D, employing 2000 staff, and made 490 patents applications in 1989 alone (EIU, 1993a). The firm completed a new, £4m clutch production site in Birmingham to serve new Japanese customers (notably Toyota). Globally, the firm produces 13m clutches per annum, and claims that its aftermarket range covers 94 per cent of vehicles in Europe.

8.3.3   Fitchel and Sachs

Fichtel and Sachs were acquired by the Mannesmann group (Germany) in 1987, but continues to operate independently of the parent company and produces its own annual report. The firm makes a broad range of clutches and related transmission products for cars and commercial vehicles, but it also has automotive components interests in shock absorbers, steering dampers, gas filled lifters and torque converters. The main production facility is in Schweinfurt (Germany) where most of the R&D work is also undertaken.

As with LUK, Fitchel and Sachs have been leading the process of technological innovation in their product area. This is partly a strategy to enable the firm to offset some of the costs of being based in Germany: by moving into higher 'value added' activities they change the terms of competition from one of price to one of performance.

8.3.4   AP Borg and Beck

AP Borg and Beck are a UK based firm, part of the BBA group. The clutch division has plants in Britain, Italy, Spain and France (original equipment production), Germany (sales only), and The Netherlands (clutch reconditioning). There are also R&D facilities in Britain and Italy, with smaller facilities in France. AP has a strong presence in Italy, with some 35 per cent of Fiat's demand for clutches, and in France, where the firm has about 30 per cent of the market (mainly from sales to Renault). It is interesting to note that AP in Italy currently outsource most of the pressings required for clutch assembly, but are currently considering bringing this activity in-house. Strangely, the assumed synergies of vertical integration do not necesserily materialise in AP Clutches. The firm's main customers (Rover, Honda, Saab and Volvo) prefer Ferodo or Allied-Signal friction material, so AP purchases very little from the Mintex Dom friction materials company despite being in the same group. It is also worth noting that AP have a strong interest in the aftermarket sector for clutches (up to 60 per cent of turnover) and in racing or high-performance vehicles.

8.4 BRAKES

In 1993, the estimated market for brake discs in Western Europe was 41 million units. Although dominated by the major firms noted below, it is a complex sector with a large number of small manufacturers and branders; in one estimate at least sixty-five such firms are active in the UK alone (EIU, 1993).

8.4.1 AP Lockheed

AP Lockheed are a long-established UK firm which for many years was the main supplier of brakes to the domestic motor industry. However, the firm is no longer in the volume brake foundation business and is now stronger in the low-volume original equipment market, commercial vehicles, and specialised high-performance brakes. The sporting links of AP Lockheed, together with the historic presence in the UK, have resulted in a strong brand image in the aftermarket sector. The firm is now part of the large BBA Group but still operates from a large site in Leamington Spa which also houses the AP Clutch factory. The parent company invested £16m on this site in 1992 for a new 'cellular production' factory and distribution centre.

8.4.2 Lucas Girling

Lucas Girling is part of the Lucas group, one of the largest European automotive components suppliers. As a group, Lucas has followed a clear strategy of first diversifying out of original business areas in automotive lighting, vehicle instruments, starters, alternators, wind-screen-wiper motors and electrics, and second reducing the importance of the UK as a production location and a market. Table 8.5 summarises the structure of the Lucas Automotive Division, while Table 8.6 shows the spatial and sectoral distribution of Lucas sales in 1992, and Table 8.7 summarises employment trends in the group.

In the period 1981–91, the automotive sector declined from 72 per cent of total turnover to 59 per cent, while the UK fell from accounting for 46 per cent of total turnover to 32 per cent. In the same period, the

Table 8.5 Lucas Automotive Division and product structure

Chassis systems	Car brakes
	Truck brakes
	ABS
Powertrain systems	Fuel systems
	Direct injection
	Petrol injection
	Engine Mgt system
Electrical systems	Wiring systems
	Body electronics
	Switch controls
	Heavy electrical
Lucas Electronics	Body computers
	Security systems
	Instruments
Aftermarket	All products

Source: Lucas Company Reports.

Table 8.6   The spatial and sectoral distribution of Lucas sales, 1992 (£m)

Share of related companies	2 370.2
Aerospace	642.5
Automotive	1 477.7
Applied technology	249.9
Total	2370.1
UK subsidiaries	893.9
Other Europe	769.4
North America	466.5
Other overseas	122.9
Share of related companies	117.4
Total	2 370.1

Source: Lucas 1992 Annual Report.

significance of the USA rose from 6 per cent to 21 per cent of turnover, while that of Europe grew from 29 per cent to 38 per cent. While the group as a whole has shed about 15 000 jobs over the 1985–92 period, as Table 8.7 shows, all of this job loss is attributable to the automotive sector. Following the stagnation of sales in the automotive sector over the 1989–92 period, and a near collapse in profits, Lucas introduced

Table 8.7   Lucas employment figures, 1985–91

	UK employment	Total employment	Auto employment
1991	29 498	54 942	38 045
1990	31 621	57 399	39 619
1989	32 208	55 957	38 709
1988	36 758	59 047	41 205
1987	42 866	62 572	45 802
1986	45 565	64 087	48 348
1985	46 854	64 855	49 429

Source: Lucas Annual Reports, 1986–92.

heavy cost-cutting and rationalisation in its UK automotive operations in 1991 and 1992. Once again, labour carried much of the costs of restructuring, with significant levels of redundancies. Lucas now concentrates its efforts in three main areas: diesel engine management systems (including fuel injection units); brakes and chassis systems; and body electronics. It is thought to have about 30 per cent of the European car brake market, and is the leading independent supplier of commercial vehicle brakes.

In October 1992, Lucas announced its intention to cut a further 5000 jobs. The attempt to develop ABS, at an estimated investment cost of £100m, appears to have failed to yield a positive cash flow despite partnership links with Sumitomo of Japan. Rather, Lucas appears to have a different strategy, one of concentrating on the mechanical and hydraulic elements of brake systems, and linking those systems via chassis control electronics. Lucas Girling is primarily an assembler of components and systems designer; as such it has pursued the establishment of a sophisticated supplier performance measurement system managed via a relational database. Table 8.8 illustrates contracts won by Lucas in the early 1990s where it is noteworthy that they have won supplier contracts to Nissan, Honda and Toyota in the UK, as well as Mercedes in Germany. Lucas have continued to develop a wider spatial presence in manufacturing through the development of a joint venture with a Czech firm, Autobrzdy, in which Lucas will invest £9m by 1996.

8.4.3   Teves

This German company, founded in 1906, was purchased by ITT of the USA in 1967 and is probably the second-largest producer of brake

Table 8.8   Vehicles launched since 1990 fitted with Lucas brakes

Vehicle model	Lucas components
Alfa Romeo 155	Front and rear disc brakes
BMW 316i/318i	Drum brakes, booster
Citroen ZX	Front discs, rear drums
Honda Accord	Front/rear discs, booster and master cylinder
Mercedes S Class	Front disc brakes
Nissan Primera	Front/rear discs, master cylinder, booster, valves
Renault Safrane	Front disc, rear drum
Rover 800	Front/rear discs, booster, master cylinder
Toyota Carina E	Rear drum brakes
VW Golf III	Front and rear discs

Source: Lucas.

systems in the world after Bendix. It has long been associated with the production of foundation brakes, but after the acquisition by ITT it expanded rapidly. The firm is based in Frankfurt, where it employs 3500 in production, administration and R&D – it also has major production facilities in Gifhorn (2700 staff) and Rheinbollen (1400 staff). Along with two further German production sites (and one recently acquired in the former East Germany), Teves has European plants in Belgium, France, the UK, Italy, and Spain – as well as many plants outside Europe. ITT's strengths in electronics, its substantial investment resources, and its openings into the US market all helped ITT to expand and move into the electronic ABS market. Teves now claims to hold 25 per cent of the ABS market in Europe, and 50 per cent of that in the USA.

The basic structure of Teves is shown in Table 8.9, though it should be noted that the position of Teves within the ITT group has changed dramatically since 1993, in response to continued economic pressures, in a manner which is evident for several of the firms in the brake and clutch industry. In essence, ITT has sought to absorb all its European automotive interests into one managment structure and one identity – in an attempt to reduce overhead costs and increase synergies between the various divisions of the corporation. With a turnover of DM2.6bn, 13 000 employees and eighteen production sites Teves is certainly a large firm in its own right. In 1989, Teves produced a daily output of 100 000 disc brake linings; 70 000 disc brakes; 25 000 vacuum brake boosters; and 3 000 ABS sets.

Table 8.9   Teves, main indicators, 1989

Total turnover (DMm)	2 656
Exports and sales of foreign subsidiaries (DMm)	1 517
Social expenses (DMm)	337
Investments (DMm)	190
R&D, Quality Assurance (DMm)	305
Total Workforce	12 893

Source: Teves.

As was noted above, Teves claims to hold 25 per cent of the European ABS market. Table 8.10 illustrates European models fitted with Teves ABS MkII and MkIV as standard or optional features. Table 8.10 also illustrates two features of the European components industry worthy of note. First, there is a broad spread of customers of different types and locations (though Ford have long been a key customer for Teves). Second, it is evident that new technologies 'cascade' down the model range. The MkIV ABS is available as standard equipment on only two models: a high-performance version of the latest BMW 3 Series, and the executive 'top of the range' Renault Safrane. The older generation MKII ABS is available as standard equipment or as an optional extra on many more models, though again they are high-performance vehicles. As an option, ABS can cost around 5 per cent of the purchase price of an executive-type saloon, but nearer 10 per cent of the price of a standard vehicle.

Teves has acquired a plant in the former East Germany at Reichenbach, with an estimated annual capacity of 1.5m brake boosters by 1993, and 300 000 disc brake calipers – with much of the production intended for just-in-time delivery to VW in Wolfsburg. Teves also has a plant in the UK, whose performance between 1986 and 1990 is illustrated in Table 8.11. A feature of this table, although it deals only with a relatively short run, is that profits have stagnated despite a doubling of output. Unusually, there is significant employment growth too, reflecting a strategy of decentralising production out of Germany to lower-cost locations.

8.4.4   Bendix

This US firm is part of the Allied-Signal group, and has many sites in Europe, with the majority of employment concentrated in France. It is thought to be the largest supplier of brakes in the world, with perhaps

Table 8.10   Vehicles fitted with Teves ABS MkII and MkIV (European models only)

Car model	MkII ABS	MkIV ABS
Alfa Romeo	0	
BMW 325i		S
BMW 3 series		0
Citroën BX	0	
Ferrari 348 TB	S	
Ferrari Mondial	S	
Ford Scorpio	S	
Ford Scorpio 4x4	S	
Ford Sierra	0	
Ford Sierra 4x4	0	
Ford Cosworth	S	
Ford Escort		0
Ford Orion		0
Ford Transit		0
Jaguar XJS	S	
Renault 21	0	
Renault 21 4x4	0	
Renault Clio		0
Renault Safrane		S
Saab 900	0	
Saab 9000	0	
VW Corrado	S	
VW Golf GTI	S	
VW Golf III Series		0
VW Passat	0	
VW Seat Toledo		0
Volvo 440/460	0	

Source: Teves.

Table 8.11   Teves in the UK, 1986–90

	1986	1987	1988	1989	1990
Turnover (£m)	23.2	22.3	27.1	31.5	41.0
Profit (AIBT)	2.3	2.1	2.2	1.6	2.9
Employees	268	323	365	425	469

Source: Company accounts.

30 per cent of the global market. Brake systems for the automotive market account for about 40 per cent of all sales for Allied-Signal (see Table 7.7 on page 143); if commercial vehicles, aftermarket and friction materials activities are included it can be seen that brakes for all markets account for 88 per cent of turnover.

Bendix has a strong European manufacturing presence; there are ten plants in France, two in both Spain and Italy, and one in both Germany and Portugal. There is a large UK plant in Bristol, although this produces brakes for the commercial vehicle sector. The Bendix brand is also well established in Europe, and the firm has a strong presence in the aftermarket sector. Despite the size of the parent firm and its very strong position in the European brake and friction materials sector, a further round of corporate reorganisation was introduced in 1993, which brought all the European aftermarket operations under one brand.

8.5 TECHNOLOGICAL CHANGE IN BRAKES AND CLUTCHES

8.5.1 Clutches

As noted above with respect to the AP ACTS approach, clutches too have been subject to further product innovation. Clutch manufacturers are under pressure to reduce costs, weight and complexity while at the same time improving performance. This results in a range of product solutions. In the USA, AP Borg and Beck have been producing pre-filled clutches with simple plastic connectors that greatly reduce the labour effort required to fit the part to the vehicle as it moves down the assembly line. Another technical development has been to replace clutch facing rivets with adhesive bonding. This is cheaper, reduces clutch weight, and necessitates fewer manufacturing operations.

The clutch usually has to do rather more than simply disengage the power train to enable gear shifts to be made. It plays a critical role in absorbing transmission irregularities and vibrations, thus reducing noise levels. Modern vehicles face greater demands for driver comfort, as well as vehicle weight reductions and higher transmission speeds, all of which result in greater demands being placed on spring damper systems in the clutch. In this sense, although many clutches look very similar, in practice each application on a particular model, gearbox and engine combination has to be fine tuned in the development phase.

LUK was the first European manufacturer to introduce the diaphragm spring clutch, which it now produces in volumes of some eight million per annum – the design has now virtually supplanted the traditional coil spring clutch in automobiles, but is not applicable to heavier vehicles. More recent innovations include the electronically controlled clutch and rivetless clutch plates. In the case of the former, AP Lockheed have the first volume production contract for its electronically controlled actuating system (ACTS), which will be going into a small car. This system uses the same clutch as in other models but is able to provide for automatic gear changes without the additional weight penalty that traditional automatics bear. Developing this clutch placed new demands on AP, and the firm has responded by developing strategic alliances to access related technologies, most notably with AB Electronics, and by developing their own in-house software skills. Other clutch firms have been pursuing the theme of electronics applications in clutch operation; Valeo, for instance, has tested a version on a Lancia rally car.

On the other hand, the clutch, even when controlled electronically, only exists to solve a particular problem – which could equally be solved via a continuously variable transmission (CVT). First developed by Van Doorne of the Netherlands (whose family at that time also owned Daf, the car assembler) CVT was initially applied on the Daf Variomatic. It consists of a series of interlinked belts and pulleys which act to transmit engine torque to the driven wheels, thus making the gearbox, though not the clutch, redundant. The technology, much refined and enhanced by the addition of electronic controls, has become more attractive in the 1990s – especially for small cars and urban driving. As installed in the Subaru Jesty the CVT drives a magnetic clutch (which uses no friction-material technology). The potential weight saving over conventional gearbox/clutch combinations and over conventional automatics is significant, especially for small cars. Should this technology continue to develop, the friction clutch may become as much a relic of automotive technology as the carburettor.

8.5.2 Brakes

Innovation in the product and material is critical to competitive sucess in this sector. The Lucas 'Colette' brake is a good example. Since its invention in 1971 (in the German division of Girling), the Colette brake has reached a cumulative production volume of 200 million units. It is strongly represented in Japanese models, and accounts for the majority of licensed production in Japan – where over 60 per cent of brake production is under licence to Lucas. In total, twenty-four brake supplier firms worldwide make Colette brakes, which can be used on a range of vehicles from cars (Rover Metro and Toyota Lexus rear, for example) to motorcycles (Honda Goldwing) and even light trucks. The innovation effectively gave Lucas a strong hold over the entire market for brake callipers.

Drum brakes have generally been superseded by disc brakes over the 1980s, especially at the front of the vehicle, where most of the actual 'stopping' is done. None the less, drum brakes are still substantially cheaper to manufacture, and have themselves been subject to further innovations in design which might enable the technology to regain market share. AP Lockheed, for instance, have developed a single-shoe rear brake which uses 50 per cent fewer parts compared with a conventional drum brake. The system, which is claimed to be as effective as disc brakes on a small vehicle, offers up to 25 per cent weight saving and 15 per cent cost saving, both attractive propositions for vehicle assemblers. Brake designers are under constant pressure to improve performance in the product by making it smaller, lighter in weight, more reliable, less expensive and with good working characteristics (i.e. lack of fade or lack of 'grab' in use).

The pace of technological change can be illustrated with reference to Teves. The company's first attempts at ABS began with prototypes in 1967 and the first (non-electronic) series version was ready by 1975. The first Teves MkII system was fitted to a US vehicle in 1984, and by 1988 one million MkII systems had been sold. By 1992, however, the fully electronic MkIV system was available – but it is interesting to note that the MkII system has not simply been deleted. In aggregate, the level of application of ABS in passenger cars has increased from 3 per cent in 1985 to 22 per cent by 1992, and an expected 55 per cent by the year 2000 (EIU, 1993), although the USA has seen greater levels of application than Europe.

8.6 PROCUREMENT REGIMES IN THE BRAKES AND CLUTCHES SECTOR

Table 8.12 summarises estimated market shares in the European clutch sector for original equipment only. A number of features emerge from

Table 8.12   Estimated market shares with the major vehicle assemblers, the European clutch firms (percentages)

	Valeo	*F & S*	*LUK*	*AP*
VW	10	45	45	0
Ford	40	60	20	0
Fiat	65	0	0	35
Renault	75	0	0	25
PSA	75	0	25	0
Opel	25	50	25	0
Mercedes	0	50	50	0
BMW	0	100	0	0
Volvo	0	100	0	0
Toyota	100	0	0	0
Nissan	0	0	100	0
Honda	0	0	0	100
Seat	70	25	5	0
Rover	50	0	0	50

Note: Daikin (Japan) have 6% of the original equipment market with Renault.
Source: Authors' estimates.

this table. First, only the Japanese firms single-source their clutches – and even here this refers only to the current model: Toyota may not use Valeo for their next model, for example. Second, while the clutch component firms have main customers with which they are associated, or alternatively the assemblers have main suppliers, there is a mixture of sourcing in most cases. That is, components suppliers will have many customers, and the assemblers will have two or three suppliers per component. This table does not show the extent of single sourcing by model or by assembly site, both of which are thought to be becoming more prevalent. However, the data on customers held by Lucas and Teves (shown in Tables 8.8 and 8.10) do indicate that at the system level each model is single-sourced, while at the component level there is a more fragmented structure, with different suppliers used for different parts within the same model.

It is clear that sourcing patterns and procurement regimes vary widely between assemblers. Nissan, for instance, source both front and rear brakes as complete sub-assembled units from just one supplier in one location (Lucas Girling), which also supplies the optional ABS. Ford, in their 1993 Mondeo model, source the front brakes from one firm, the rear brakes from another, and the ABS system to control it all from a third. GM will still source brake components from a number of suppliers and undertake sub-assembly itself. Such patterns are also evident in the clutch area. Opel (part of GM) may buy, for instance, an AP driveplate with an LUK cover, though one consequence of this policy has been high warranty costs for GM, and the firm is currently seeking to develop sourcing for complete systems from one supplier. In contrast, Honda in UK source all their clutches in Britain, and they are completely pre-assembled, balanced and tested prior to being dispatched in purpose-built trays.

However, in all three product areas it is clear that spatial presence in key markets is deemed to be vital, at least by the components firms. Market expansion has been achieved mainly via acquisition of existing enterprises. However, the use made of these new spatial configurations varies. In the case of AP Lockheed, the various national plants are 'stand alone' in character. However, the new UK factory is expected to produce a high proportion of exports. In the case of Teves, the Welsh subsidiary is used to take on declining items of work displaced from the main factory in Germany, usually using displaced older technology while the new investment goes into Schweinfurt. However, the firm has, changed from this pattern in the early 1990s, with its investments in the former East Germany (see Chapter 9) and reinvestments in its UK plant. Thus, there is a diversity of strategies in operation which go beyond the issue of simple local supply.

The second major feature of procurement regimes of interest in this sector do not concern the vehicle assemblers directly but are to do with the aftermarket sector. While supplier–customer relations in the original equipment sector are well established and relatively stable, this is not the case in the aftermarket sector. Before the provisions of 'Open Europe' and internationalisation of the components industry as a whole, the aftermarket sector tended to be very different in each major country. More important, for even the major firms, pan-European brand names were few and tended to be focused on a very narrow product range. Much of the corporate reorganisation of the early 1990s has been based around the desire to establish stronger brand presence across Europe, and to cater for the much wider vehicle stock in use that this end implies. Thus Lucas has dropped its Girling (brakes) and CAV (diesel injection units) brands while Allied-Signal has grouped all its aftermarket activities under one brand.

A virtually 'unseen' process of rationalisation is under way in the many firms that supply brake, clutch and friction material components to the aftermarket, and among those many firms involved in the distribution and sales of aftermarket components. The major original equipment firms are gradually consolidating their hold over the market and squeezing out the smaller independents, having suffered at the hands of those independents during the 1980s via reduced aftermarket profit margins.

The restructuring process can be illustrated with reference to Germany. The development of routes to the market in the German aftermarket segment, while unique to Germany, nevertheless shows how equipment manufacturers and importers have seen their strong hold over the market diminish. The development of supply structures to the German aftermarket segment is illustrated in Figures 8.1–8.5.

Initially, in the post-1945 period, the supply routes to the market were simple, with two main channels: one serving the vehicle assemblers' retail and service outlets; the other serving the accessory or independent retail sector via manufacturers' representatives (see Figure 8.1). The manufacturers' representatives were organised on a regional basis across Germany, and controlled all parts distribution other than that which went direct to the vehicle assemblers' retail and service outlets (that is, franchises). In an attempt to bypass the manufacturers' representatives (and thus capture more of the value-added), the parts wholesalers organised buying groups to deal directly with manufacturers and importers (see Figure 8.2). Wholesalers then attempted to do the same downstream by developing their own direct

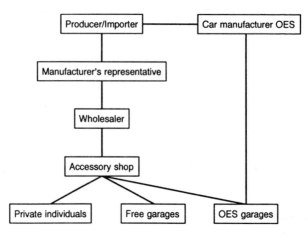

Figure 8.1   Aftermarket component supply routes, Germany, 1950.

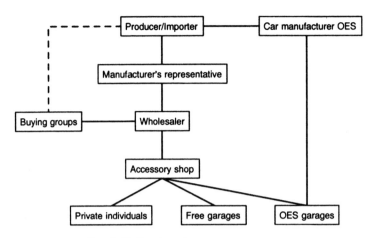

Figure 8.2 Aftermarket component supply routes: the growth of wholesale buying groups, Germany

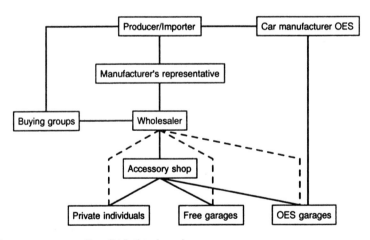

Figure 8.3 Aftermarket component supply routes: bypassing the retail outlets, Germany

market links with private customers, the independent garages, and the vehicle assembler service outlets (see Figure 8.3). Again, the intention was to exclude on stage in the chain, thus internalising more of the

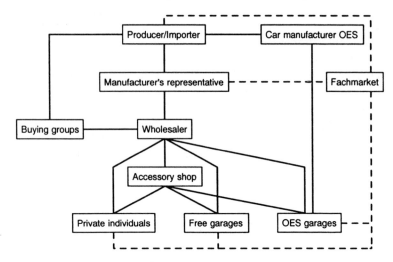

Key: – – – – – – New distribution channel

Figure 8.4   Aftermarket component supply routes, the growth of the 'Fachmarket', Germany

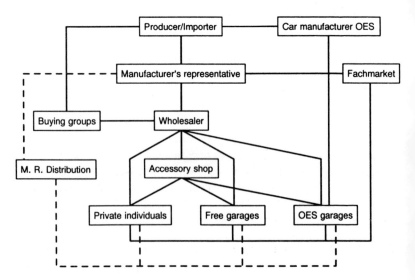

Key: – – – – – – New distribution channel

Figure 8.5   Aftermarket component supply routes: new supply routes from the 'Manufacturer's representatives', Germany

value-added and, as a result, offering lower prices to end users. A major de-stabilising force in the form of the Fachmarkets appeared in the 1980s (see Figure 8.4). These outlets are not found in the UK, for example, but have grown rapidly in Germany, where they both provide 'menu-based' servicing and sell spare parts and accessories. The Fachmarkets have significant purchasing power, and can deal directly with the equipment manufacturers and importers, effectively threatening the role of the wholesalers, accessory shops and manufacturers' representatives. Finally, the manufacturers' representatives have responded by creating shared distribution channels of their own, to increase purchasing power and develop stronger links to the independent garages, the vehicle assemblers' retail and service outlets, and to private customers (see Figure 8.5). Throughout this process, the equipment manufacturers and importers have seen their relative control over the distribution of their products reduced, with a detrimental effect on the profit margins enjoyed. On the other hand, consumers have a much greater choice of outlet and reduced prices in a more competitive market.

8.7 CONCLUSIONS

The brake and clutch sector in Europe is dominated by a few large firms, especially for the supply of original equipment. These major suppliers are increasingly taking on the role of systems integration to match long-established capabilities in independent product development. The application of electronics technologies, however, raises the issue of how the 'system' is defined and which capabilities are required to be the controlling firm that has 'first-tier' relationships with the vehicle assemblers. There is no simple answer to this issue, for the outcome will be the result of (unpredictable) competitive and technological changes. The firms in this sector will either have to internalise new capabilities or to forge linkages with appropriate other firms as the definition of the system is enlarged and a greater range of competencies is required. In the realm of brakes, for instance, R&D links with the producers of tyres, axles, suspension components and friction materials firms will all be needed as the system becomes defined in terms of overall chassis engineering.

There would appear to be little scope for spatial 'peripheralisation' in the brake and clutch sector, though new investments, either in existing plants or greenfield sites, will continue as cellular manufacturing systems replace the former flow systems. Greenfield sites are more likely to be established in connection with key clients (such as the Teves and Valeo investments in the former East Germany) but the wide supply base required mitigates against seeking out low cost locations at the European periphery. Opportunities for new entrants also seem slight, especially in the high-volume car market, given the entrenched position of the prevailing oligopoly.

9 Foreign Direct Investment, Investment Agencies and the Restructuring of the European Automotive Components Industry

9.1 INTRODUCTION

The motor industry has long been the subject of state regulation and intervention in almost all aspects of the business, and as such the state at national and international level is a key element in the context within which structural change in the industry occurs. Historically, the state has played a key, and direct, role in automobile production, notably since 1945. Not only do state laws on vehicle and petrol taxation have an impact, so too has direct ownership in the form of nationalised companies or strategic holdings in companies. The state fundamentally shapes production via laws on wages, working conditions, union and worker rights and so on. Moreover, the state fundamentally shapes car consumption through its investment policies regarding roads and other forms of transportation network, as well as through its fiscal measures. Through regional policies, national states have sought to influence the location of the automobile industry, both successfully (Volkswagen at Wolfsburg) and unsuccessfully (Chrysler at Linwood). Thus, while customer–supplier relations are a very important force for industrial spatial restructuring, the impact of state intervention in mediating those forces should not be neglected. The purpose of this chapter is to provide an account of one aspect of state intervention as it pertains to the automotive components industry in general, and to the case study sub-sectors in particular, that is, the attraction and support of foreign direct investment.

This is not to deny the significance of state intervention in other areas. In respect of the environment, in the longer term, the European

Community (EC), through such programmes as DRIVE and PRO-METHEUS, intends to influence the future shape of mobility and the place of the automobile within that future, while programmes such as FORCE are addressed at the skills needs of workers in the vehicle repair and distribution sector. Safety and environmental legislation has the potential to influence the long term development of the industry. However, in what follows we look at the nature of spatial competition for FDI – but the spatial scale on which this is done varies according to the main agency involved. On the one hand, there are the national level FDI attraction agencies such as the Industrial Development Authority for Ireland; and on the other there are very 'local' agencies such as the Black Country Development Corporation. In between are national–regional agencies such as the Treuhandanstalt in Germany, Locate in Scotland, and the Welsh Development Agency. At the local level, much of the concern has been with coping with employment decline. One feature of the new European automobile industry is that fewer people are going to work directly in it, and that some locations will be hit harder by decline than others. It is equally evident that the EC, through its decisions regarding allowable subsidy, itself helps define the investment climate across Europe and even beyond, while EC moves towards full economic integration have certainly provided additional impetus for the peripheralisation of production.

FDI in the automotive components sector is, of course, only part of the aggregate picture of FDI flows in Europe. As Thomsen and Woolcock (1993) show, direct investment levels into the EC, out of the EC and within the EC all showed strong growth during the 1980s, with a tendency for the relative value of all types of FDI to the economy increasing. Thus FDI inflows and outflows as a proportion of GDP have tended to increase for most countries. Similarly, mergers and acquisitions also showed a growing importance over the 1980s, but the economic conditions prevailing in the early 1990s has seen a curtailment of activity. This aggregate picture is supported elsewhere. For instance, in their annual survey and review of Japanese investments in Europe, JETRO (1992) showed that up to the late 1980s Japanese firms were arriving in Europe at the rate of 200 per annum, but that rate has fallen substantially in the early 1990s. The UK, according to figures from the IBB (1992), received 37 per cent of all US direct investment into the EC between 1951 and 1990, 39 per cent of all such Japanese investment between 1951 and 1990, and 18 per cent of all German FDI in 1990.

9.2 THE AUTOMOTIVE COMPONENTS INDUSTRY AND FDI

Foreign direct investment remains an important mechanism for firms in the automotive components industry to respond to competitive pressures. In this section, we consider the structural pressures which underpin FDI decisions. There is little doubt that the automotive sector is a significant part of the aggregate picture analysed by Thomsen and Woolcock (1993), and that in general it has followed the same trends as those in the aggregate picture. That is to say, there were increased levels of FDI of all types and from all sources throughout the 1980s; German, US and Japanese FDI has been prominent; the UK in particular has been the preferred recipient region in Europe; acquisitions take a high proportion of all forms of FDI; up to 85 per cent according to Thomsen and Woolcock (1993); and the early 1990s has seen a significant fall in automotive FDI activity, which remains highly sensitive to cyclical fluctuations in the economies concerned. However, examination of the automotive sector allows a closer appreciation of the reasons for FDI and the effect of agency intervention in FDI decisions.

In considering why FDI takes place, a wide range of causal mechanisms may be proposed. These may be grouped under two main headings: cost–push and demand–pull. However, account must also be taken of the structure of the sub-sector in question, the nature of the production technology, the nature of the product, and the relationship with the final customer (i.e. in this case the vehicle assemblers) which suppliers of those products enjoy.

In terms of cost–push mechanisms, it is clear that firms in comparatively high cost locations will, all other things being equal, face pressure from their customers to reduce costs by locating some or all of their production in a lower-cost location. Operating costs arise out of many factors, most importantly labour (including social overhead) costs, land purchase and rental, power, taxation regimes, and rates of inflation. Subsumed under 'labour' costs are a wide range of 'environmental' features which condition the relationship between capital and labour, including labour legislation, working hours, trade union activity, cultural norms and attitudes, and political conditions generally. Mediating between these costs and 'external' customers are currency exchange rates, which can be subject to large movements. The virtual demise of the European Monetary System in 1992–3 has reintroduced the problem of differential movements in currencies for the automotive components industry – in particular it has reinforced the domestic cost pressures facing firms in Germany. Of course, costs are only half of the equation, in the sense that productivity may also be higher in high cost locations. In so far as this is the case, higher productivity and higher quality may outweigh simple cost comparisons.

Historically, the pattern of sourcing within domestic boundaries by major vehicle assemblers in Europe tended to act against cost–push forces for international FDI. In the 1990s, however, this territorial allegiance can no longer be guaranteed: even Mercedes is prepared to dilute its 'Made in Germany' label by purchasing a greater proportion of components from outside Germany. Given that substantial and enduring spatial differences in costs remain, costs provide an impetus for 'peripheralisation' in the European components industry.

The 'demand–pull' side of FDI is rather more complex. In general, the European vehicle assemblers are seeking fewer suppliers with greater (systems) capabilities, and this has prompted a process of alliances, mergers and acquisitions in the European components industry. In so far as this is international in scope, FDI may be a result. A similar argument could be said to apply to the issue of economies of scale. Moreover, FDI is more likely to be undertaken by larger firms, so the consolidation process within national boundaries helps to create firms of the stature to undertake international FDI. Market access needs, or the demand for spatial proximity to customers, may also result in FDI. The influx of FDI into the UK in the period since Nissan first established operations is in part attributable to the desire of components firms to supply the new Japanese plants. New vehicle assembly plants in Europe have tended to include sites alongside, which are designated for key components firms to supply just-in-time products to the assembly line; for firms wishing to supply those components, a commitment to locate nearby is an important prerequisite. However, as Hudson and Sadler (1992) have argued, the demands for just-in-time are themselves not clear (just-in-time means different things to different people and firms), and have to be considered in light of the pre-existing structure of the European automotive components industry. The extent to which absolute or relative 'gaps' in the domestic supply base are perceived by the vehicle assemblers will also influence FDI. Initial contact with a non-domestic supplier for the purchase of components and materials may ultimately result in the request for FDI (from the assembler) so that the supplier may have a more local supply (this is exactly the case of Ryobi, for example, a Japanese manufacturer of Aluminium castings such as gearbox housings, who established their plant in Northern Ireland at the request of Ford).

To some extent, these are contradictory demands. On the one hand, the vehicle assemblers are interested in strategies, including FDI to peripheral regions, which will reduce costs; indeed, their own components operations (especially those of Ford and GM) feature in this process. On the other hand, an increasing demand for just-in-time delivery of components appears to imply a need for spatial proximity to customer sites. Those customer sites are, of course, still predominantly in the core industrial regions of Europe and cannot in general be considered low-cost. However, the newer assembly plants have tended to be located in the more peripheral regions (at the European scale), and have also tended to have space alongside for suppliers, which established plants may lack. Moreover, it is a part of overall policy for the vehicle assemblers that suppliers should (in general) win more business with other assemblers. Thus, for instance, Renault has actively encouraged its suppliers to work for Ford, GM, Rover, etc. on the understanding that this will result in greater economies of scale for the components firm, and that in consequence Renault itself will benefit. In most cases, the components firm is not in a position to establish separate (proximate) production sites for each customer, and given the dispersed nature of the vehicle assembly industry in Europe the least-cost single site solution would be to establish a plant somewhere in the region of the French/German/Dutch borders. This is clearly not an option for many firms.

It is also important to recognise that FDI depends upon the nature of the sector, the product, and the production technology. In terms of the sector, for example, the nature of the existing structure of production will make a difference. In the presswork sector there are a large number of supplier firms in the main automotive production regions, usually with a well-established customer base. In general, there is an over-capacity in the sector, which, combined with the large number of relatively small firms, creates the conditions for consolidation and rationalisation. Consequently, acquisition FDI is far more prevalent than greenfield FDI. In terms of the product there are also differences in propensity for FDI. Some products are relatively bulky or heavy and low-value, and hence expensive to transport; these are thus less suitable for peripheral locations. In contrast, products with a high value-to-weight ratio will be more suitable for peripheralisation. Some products are regarded as more important for just-in-time delivery than others. Typically, these products are items which will vary with the model type being assembled, are high-value items, and are bulky (for example, engines, trim items, seats, exhausts and large sub-assemblies). Some products are more complex and require more varied components than others. For instance, the case of the brake assembler supply base discussed previously (in Chapter 8) has an important implication; it may be less easy to develop a new brake assembly plant in a 'remote' region which would lack almost all the material and components inputs. In contrast, 'process'-based products of high value (for example, precision aluminium castings), which require few material and component inputs, may not require close contact with a broad industrial infrastructure. In terms of production technology, a critical issue is the 'divisibility' of technology. At one end of the scale, steelworks remain large and integrated undertakings, and it is difficult to separate and relocate a part of the production process to achieve a spatial–techical division of labour. On the other hand, it is possible in many sectors to relocate part of the production process to achieve lower cost; electronic components may be a case in point. Although it may be expected that labour-intensive operations would be relocated in peripheral locations, highly capital-intensive FDI does occur because of the level of investment incentives available, especially where the capital technology requires largely unskilled operatives.

The following sections examine the nature of competition for FDI in the European components industry through three case studies: the United Kingdom; East Germany; and the Republic of Ireland. These three locations have rather different operating environments for prospective firms, and rather different resources and incentives to deploy in order to win more investment.

9.3   THE UNITED KINGDOM

As has been noted above, the UK during the late 1980s and early 1990s was seen to be an attractive investment location because of the growing market for components created by the recently arrived Japanese assemblers. Relative total labour costs during this period were among the lowest in the EC, certainly in terms of the established industrial countries. Additional features which may have contributed to the relative attractiveness of the UK include a perception that quality levels in the UK in general were vastly improved, while trade union legislation was seen to be curtailing the power of organised labour to disrupt the production process. Our research indicates that in the period 1989–93 there were 92 cases of FDI into the UK attributable to the automotive sector. Of this investment, there was an even split between acquisitions (31 cases), in-situ expansions (30 cases), and greenfield investments (31 cases). The leading source locations were Germany (28 cases), Japan (25 cases), the USA (22 cases) and France (15 cases); other countries contributed only 6 cases. Because of joint venture investments, the number of source country cases is larger than the number of investment cases. Table 9.1 illustrates the regional distribution of this investment, although it should be noted that reinvestment in existing locations tends to be under-reported, and thus this account somewhat overemphasises the importance of greenfield and acquisition FDI.

The relative success of the West Midlands is clearly apparent here, a feature which may be reinforced by the activities of the Black Country Development Corporation (BCDC). In 1993 the BCDC established an 'Automotive Components Park' on a large, prime site alongside the M5 and M6 motorways. It comprises 115 acres of land with 1.5m square feet of floor space for manufacturing operations, constructed on the site of a former steelworks. Here the BCDC is acting in a traditional 'place marketing' role, seeking to sell the location on the basis of its claimed merits. The 'theme park' approach is an interesting

Table 9.1   Regional distribution of automotive components FDI into the UK, 1989–93

Region	Number
Yorkshire and Humberside	7
West Midlands	30
North East	17
Wales	11
East Midlands	2
South East	5
South West	7
Scotland	2
North West	4
East Anglia	1
Northern Ireland	2
Total	92

Source: Compiled from a wide range of press reports.

feature which incorporates some facilities that may have practical value (for example, shared waste recycling and laboratory facilities), though the merits of this theme are probably more to do with the marketing of the location. It is also most likely to capture two main types of investment: first, FDI based on the need for local proximity to key customers for key products such as seat assemblies, large injection mouldings and so on. The first major investment on this site fits this pattern exactly – the US seat manufacturing firm Johnson Controls has established a foam production unit there. Second, rationalisation and relocation investment within the UK, which will almost certainly have negative employment consequences overall.

Other regions in the UK have a rather mixed record in terms of attracting FDI. The North East region has clearly benefited from investments associated with the Nissan plant at Sunderland. Wales has a long history as a location for both US investment (firms such as TRW, making steering racks) and more recent Japanese investment (Calsonic and Yazaki). Indeed, the automotive sector in Wales is now the largest employment category within manufacturing. In contrast, Scotland has very few automotive components firms of note, and scant inward investment in this sector compared with the relative levels found in electronics. How deeply 'embedded' that investment is, how far the wider local economy can be said to benefit in the form of local purchases of materials inputs and so on is less clear. Turok (1993) argues that, in the case of the 'Silicon Glen' electronics sector at least, these investments have not become deeply embedded into an industrial infrastructure within Scotland.

It is also apparent that the UK institutional structure for attracting and supporting FDI is under some stress. Under the current system, the Invest in Britain Bureau acts to centralise and disseminate all FDI 'leads'; all 'regional' authorities such as Locate in Scotland' are supposed to report leads to the IBB. The intention is to attempt to eliminate unnecessary interregional competition. The early 1990s saw a vastly changed climate for those competing for FDI. Recession in the key capital exporting countries such as Germany, Japan and the USA had the effect of reducing the supply of forthcoming projects at a time when many regions sought greater reliance on external FDI as a key part of overall economic strategy. Tensions between the inward investment activities of agencies and their role in supporting indigenous industry have been combined with more intensive public scrutiny of the activities of investment agencies in the UK. A particular concern has been 'value for money' in agency activity, a greater emphasis on 'efficiency', and greater consideration given to the role of inward investment agencies within other policy frameworks (see Hood, 1993, for an informed account of the position of Locate in Scotland, for example).

9.4 FORMER EAST GERMANY

A rather different competitor location for FDI emerged with the disintegration of the 'Eastern bloc' during the late 1980s. Reconstruction of these economies has been premised on the basis of Western financial aid and capital investment. The political and social euphoria that accompanied the breaking down of the Berlin Wall, and the rapid reintegration of the formerly independent East Germany as five new Lander in the existing West Germany, was soon replaced by a more sober assessment of the economic difficulties of transition.

One aspect of the transition from Communist economy to capitalist, a transition which had never before been made on this scale, was the requirement to privatise the vast state combines which existed in East Germany. Initially, there were some 270 of these large, vertically-integrated, state-owned 'Kombinat' or holding companies, within which operated some 8000 Volkseiger Betrieb (VEBs, individual economic units). All of these passed into the ownership of the Treuhandanstalt, the organisation charged with the privatisation process – including the IFA Kombinat which embraced the vehicle manufacturing sector. The number of privatisations undertaken by the Treuhandanstalt is actually greater than the number of enterprises initially passed into the agency's hands, because the agency has followed a process of 'deconcentration' to break up larger units into more viable smaller ones. In the transport equipment sector, some 350 firms were inherited as 'stock' in mid-1990; as of June 1992, about 59 per cent had been privatised or liquidated (EAG, 1993). The IFA Kombinat included both final vehicle assembly (of both cars and commercial vehicles), as well as many of the key components such as brakes and clutches. There were also some production equipment makers in the IFA, including Erfurt, which manufactures presses.

The Treuhandanstalt was given impressive powers of discretion and very little time to achieve the most rapid privatisation possible – all assets were to be disposed of by the end of 1993. The political sensitivity of some of the work of the Treuhandanstalt was illustrated by the assassination of the first chairperson. Its role has two elements:

first, the restructuring of the inherited East German industry into appropriate units with Western accounting procedures; and second, the sale of those units to private capital – either Western companies or management buy-outs. The location has been sold as a unique and temporary business investment opportunity, a sort of 'buy now while stocks last' stance. Appeal has also been made to German industry to support the new Lander with investment, while the state itself has invested large sums in infrastructure. Various investment incentives are available for greenfield sites, amounting to as much as 50 per cent of the total cost of the investment. Equally, acquisitions may be made very cheaply in some instances, should the Treuhandanstalt decide that overall those investments will bring longer-term benefits (i.e. in terms of job creation). GKN, for instance, purchased IFA Gelenkwellenwerk Mosel for only DM4m in 1991, but also agreed to pay up to 20 per cent of the costs of environmental measures up to a limit of DM300 000 and to retain most of the original 1300 workers. Of note are the acquisitions shown in Table 9.2.

At first, the vast majority of the privatisations and greenfield investments in the former East Germany were undertaken without foreign participation. However, the Treuhandanstalt moved rapidly to a stance of supporting and encouraging FDI. According to EAG (1993), using Treuhandanstalt data, by June 1992 foreign investors accounted for 5 per cent of all cases (privatisations), 9.1 per cent of employment and 10.5 per cent of capital investment. In terms of source countries, the investments in the former East Germany have not

Table 9.2   Acquisitions in the former East Germany

Firm	Country	Investment
Dr Meleghy	Germany	Purchase of IFA press shop at Zwickau.
Thyssen	Germany	Purchase of IFA press shop at Ludwigsfelde
Krupp	Germany	Purchase of IFA Erfurt press manufacturer
Teves	Germany	Purchase of IFA Renak
GKN	UK	Purchase of IFA Gelenkwellenwerk Mosel
Valeo	France	Purchase of IFA Renak
Holset	UK	Purchase of Kompressorenbau Bannewitz

Note: Teves owned by ITT of the USA. Holset owned by Cummins of the USA. Both Valeo and Teves bought distinct parts of the IFA Renak organisation.
Source: Treuhandanstalt.

followed the global patterns described above. Rather, the major global source nations (Japan and the USA) are underrepresented in Treuhandanstalt privatisations, while European sources have been prominent, as shown in Table 9.3.

The moves by both GM and VW into the former East Germany have increased the attractiveness of investment by Western automotive components firms – this has mainly taken the form of acquisition of equivalent parts of the former IFA Kombinat. Although in aggregate the flows of inward investment have been dominated by large firms in commodity or very-high-volume products (for example, petroleum, chemicals and construction), there has been some FDI in automotive components and equipment.

In practice, the intuitive understanding that investments in the former East Germany are to service the new VW and GM plants, and prospective customers further into Eastern Europe, is only partly the case. Certainly this applies to the investments by Valeo and Teves, both mainly (but not entirely) established to serve the new VW plant at Mosel. In the case of Holset, a manufacturing presence in Germany in general was an important motive for investment (Baxter, 1993). For Thyssen, the investment in Ludwigsfelde is to service a new contract won from VW, in which Thyssen made all the aftermarket panels for the Golf II (since superseded by the Golf III). No proximity to the new VW plant is required for this operation. It does, however, allow

Table 9.3   Treuhandanstalt privatisations to foreign investors, by country, June 1992

Source	Cases	Jobs	Investment (DMm)
France	53	19 562	2 706
Switzerland	71	14 264	693
Austria	48	9 015	503
UK	69	14 437	1 631
Netherlands	33	5 854	910
USA	42	8 738	1 694
Sweden	20	3 741	104
Denmark	16	2 524	372
Italy	16	2 940	452
Belgium	9	2 804	87
Other	35	27 082	2 919
Total	412	111 691	12 026

Source: EAG, 1993.

Thyssen to achieve a spatial division of labour with its various presswork plants, enabling the high volume and technically complex production to be concentrated at its main site at Brackwede (Germany).

In most cases, the purchases have been relatively 'cheap', although one of the difficulties in the privatisation process has been the valuation of business. However, firms have often had to face heavy environmental clean-up costs, and at times have had to maintain a commitment to retain existing workers while investing in new capital production equipment. In the case of Valeo, the workforce at the IFA Renak plant was reduced from over 800 to just 108 following acquisition in July 1991. The plant used dated production equipment, and had to be entirely re-equipped by Valeo to produce 1.2m clutches per annum (Information du Vehicule, 1993). Previously, output was 30 parts per hour, with 4 hours needed to change tooling. By 1992 output was 70 parts per hour with only 20 minutes to change tooling, while the amount of floorspace has been substantially reduced. In the case of Teves, the factory purchased from the Treuhandanstalt had to be entirely re-equipped. To do so, Teves initially transferred two existing lines from a plant in Gretz (France), but the firm also installed a completely new assembly line for brake boosters that was claimed to the most modern in Europe (Information du Vehicule, 1992)

Not surprisingly, perhaps, the FDI projects into the former East Germany have tended to use existing Western suppliers. All previous suppliers have been dropped because of the poor quality and unreliability of materials and components in the former East Germany. For the firms that have invested in the region, a critical question is not that of suppliers but that of the cost and productivity of labour. Initially, agreement was reached with IG Metal on a phased programme of wage increases which would bring levels up to those prevailing in West Germany. The recessionary climate, together with the low productivity of East German factories, led the employers in the region to suspend that process in mid-1992, and a series of strikes ensued. A further compromise was reached, but the issue remains in the sense that, until greater productivity levels are reached, firms are going to resist claims for parity with the wages prevailing in the rest of Germany.

The Treuhandanstalt was closed at the end of 1993, but the attraction of inward investment, from other regions in Germany or from outside the country, will remain a key feature of the economic regeneration strategy overall. This can only intensify interregional competition for investment within Europe.

9.5   THE IRISH REPUBLIC

The Irish Republic has a surprisingly large automotive components sector (given that it lacks a vehicle assembly industry – apart from the kit assembly of commercial vehicles by Harris Hino) almost entirely comprised of FDI projects. The inward investment agency (the Industrial Development Authority for Ireland or IDA) has since the early 1980s made the automotive sector a distinct target for place marketing activities. Additionally, the IDA selected German small to medium-sized firms as the potential main source of FDI, and has assiduously sought to work with vehicle assemblers, notably GM. This highly focused approach has been supported by a network of offices in key regional locations in Germany and elsewhere. As a consequence, in the decade to 1990 exports of components from the Irish Republic grew at about 20 per cent per annum to reach IR£261m by 1990. In the early 1990s this industry employed about 10 000 people in about 100 firms. The export markets for the Irish components industry is illuminating, and is shown in Table 9.4.

Not surprisingly, the customer base reflects the bias of sales to Germany, with GM very much the dominant customer assembler. Table 9.5 shows the six leading customers. In fact, GM is also one of the largest employers in the Irish automotive components industry, with a 50 per cent share in the Packard-Rheinshagen joint venture which employs 1400 in the production of wiring harnesses.

Since joining the EC, the IDA have been able to deploy impressive grants and other inducements for prospective FDI projects. In 1991, the IDA paid out IR£65m to overseas firms in the form of grants;

Table 9.4   The geographic distribution of exports of automotive components from the Republic of Ireland

Destination	Percentage of total exports
Germany	62
UK	15
France	11
Sweden	5
Spain	4
Other	3

Source: IDA, 1991.

Table 9.5   The major customers for the automotive components industry in the Republic of Ireland

Company	Purchases (IR£m 1991)
GM	64
Mercedes	47
Ford	38
VW/Audi	21
BMW	19
Renault	13

Source: IDA, 1991.

the average cost per job created or sustained between 1985 and 1991 was IR£13 951. However, this figure includes domestic firms and all sectors. Jobs in overseas firms and in manufacturing were more expensive, at IR£19 684 and IR£17 471 respectively. In addition, the corporate rate of tax on profit is only 10 per cent to the year 2010, while in the Shannon Development Zone further grants and accelerated depreciation rates are available.

The Republic of Ireland has a young, well-educated and low cost workforce. On the other hand, it is remote from vehicle assembly sites (it takes 36 hours to reach Russelsheim in Germany), lacks some of the key skills for certain automotive components sectors, and lacks a broad industrial base. Consequently, a 'typical' FDI project in Ireland has distinct characteristics. That is, FDI investment in the automotive components sector tends to be capital intensive; to require relatively few material and components inputs (most of which are sourced outside Ireland); has a predominantly unskilled workforce of (often female) machine-minders; and exports finished and semi-finished products. In practice, the distance from customers does not appear to be a major problem, mainly because of the structure of the spatial division of labour in which the component firm maintains a final assembly operation much closer to the point of use by the vehicle assembler. Table 9.6 summarises the largest automotive components FDI projects in the Irish Republic.

Perhaps the prime example of investment in Ireland is that by Kostal – it has certainly been one of the most successful investors. It is worth considering the case of Kostal in some detail because the firm illustrates many of the (unsupported) points made above about the

Table 9.6   The largest automotive components FDI projects in Ireland

Company	Source	Product	Employees
Packard-Rheinshagen	US/Germany	Harnesses	1400
Kromburg	Germany	Harnesses	1200
Semperit	Germany	Tyres	750
Kostal	Germany	Electronics	600
Donnelly	US	Mirrors	350
Garrett	US	Turbochargers	350
Lapple	Germany	Press tools	340
Molex	US	Harnesses	350

Source: IDA interviews and site visits.

character of investment in Ireland (see also Tulip, 1993). This German family firm was founded in 1913 and, by 1992, employed some 7500 people worldwide, producing electronic switches and control systems in Germany, the Irish Republic, Mexico and Brazil. It established a plant in Abbeyfeale, a small town in the west of Ireland, in 1981 employing twenty-three people making wiring harnesses. The product was then changed to electronic switches, and since 1986 growth has been between 20 per cent and 50 per cent per annum. Critical to this growth were two factors: first, the tax and incentive regime allowed and encouraged reinvestment – the site is run as a profit centre and must generate its own investment funds; and second, the ability to install innovative shift patterns of a type which would be impossible in Germany allowed high capital-cost equipment to be more fully utilised.

On the other hand, the 'logic' of locational choice should not be over-emphasised. The instance of Lapple is illustrative. This plant was established by the German parent company in the 1970s as a low-cost die manufacturing location, mainly on the basis of the personal preferences of the owner. It subsequently won the contract to provide pressed panels for the ill-fated DeLorean plant in Northern Ireland. With the decline in orders for tools from the vehicle assemblers in the early 1990s, reflecting a decline in the rate of new model introductions as a response to recessionary conditions, Lapple sought to expand the amount of actual presswork done in the plant. The firm won a contract from Ford which defies all logic. Steel blanks are sourced from a stockholder in Birmingham, they are pressed in one operation in Ireland, and then are shipped to Southampton to be fitted to Transit vans.

9.6 FDI AND THE KEY SECTORS

From the above discussion of the three case-study areas it is already apparent that the key sectors treated in this book do feature to some extent in FDI. For steel firms, restructuring is more likely to be achieved by closure and rationalisation rather than FDI. Apart from the purchase by Krupp of ECO Stahl in East Germany, there have been no significant cross-border investments in the steel sector for the regions considered above. However, there have been FDI projects involving firms in presswork, friction material and brakes – some of these examples have already been noted above.

There has been some presswork FDI, but mainly in the form of purchases of existing businesses. However, two investments of interest are Nissan Yamato Engineering Limited (NYEL), and a joint venture between Press Kogyo (Japan) and Press und Plattenburg (Sweden). In the case of NYEL, the investment is very much tied to the supply of body-in-white pressings and assemblies to Nissan Motor Manufacturing in Sunderland, and the firm has occupied a site alongside the assembly plant since 1988. Some £60m has been invested in the plant, with the investment phases following the expansion of Nissan itself (by 1992 NYEL employed over 500 people). As with the Press Kogyo investment in The Netherlands, one vehicle assembly operation provides the main rationale behind the decision to build a new plant, and effectively determines the location of that investment. In the case of Press Kogyo, the firm will supply body-in-white pressings and sub-assemblies to Nedcar (the Mitsubishi and Volvo joint venture). The FDI activities of one typical medium-sized German presswork firm are also illustrative. The firm Kutsch specialises in small to medium pressings and sub-assembly for the body-in-white. In the late 1980s, it operated out of only one site in Germany, with Ford as the key customer. Faced with continued recruitment problems within its own locality of Attendorn, the firm also saw investment by its main customer in Portugal (in a joint venture with VW) as a major threat but also a potential opportunity. Kutsch responded by a search of firms in Portugal, eventually purchasing 50 per cent of one of the larger existing firms. It has subsequently been seeking a low-cost production location in Europe (notably in the UK), but again wanted to purchase existing facilities; ironically, the firm in 1993 purchased the plant of another German presswork firm, Sigro, in Ireland.

In the friction materials, brakes and clutches areas the main thrust of investment has been on acquisitions rather than greenfield sites. It could be argued that the purchases by Valeo and Teves in the former East Germany are effectively greenfield sites in the sense that the production equipment had to be entirely replaced, along with much of the existing workforce. In the relatively mature sectors that are the subject of enquiry in this book, it would appear that the scope for greenfield FDI is relatively restricted. The industrial structure in the clutches and brakes sector is very different from that for presswork, and the spatial structure of the firms reflects this. It is notable that all the leading firms have a production presence in most of the major production locations (i.e. the UK, Germany, France, Spain, Italy) and have had for some time.

9.7 CONCLUSIONS

It is tempting to try to identify a generalisable cause of FDI movements, a clear pattern which can be readily applied by investment agencies to capture new firms. While some general themes have emerged from the above discussion, there is not a single overriding imperative behind spatial–structural changes such as the product cycle or the demands of just-in-time. Perhaps the only general theme of significance (and even here this pattern is by no means universal) is for firms to establish remote or peripheral operations for part of their production and then have a final assembly site much nearer to their customer(s). Given the general trend to peripheralisation of vehicle assembly within Europe, this pattern is in any case distorted according to the locational preferences of the vehicle assemblers and their demands that some products be manufactured in close proximity.

For policy-makers in the investment agencies who are trying to capture new investments, the lessons are equally confusing. No single paradigm emerges, no single set of characteristics or attributes enables a location to emerge as distinct and successful. It is very difficult, if not impossible, to identify automotive components firms likely to relocate or establish new greenfield plants. Rather, our research suggests that the successful agencies are those that have sought (i) to focus on the automotive industry over a long period of time; and (ii) to focus on a particular aspect of locational difference and to 'match' it to the needs of particular types and categories of firm. Interviews with plant managers and with agency staff also reinforce the view that investment decisions are cumulative, and the long-run 'success' of any investment is critically dependent upon further agency intervention in a wide range of areas such as training, tax regimes, further incentives and local sourcing initiatives.

Few firms we interviewed pursued a rigorous and comprehensive location search strategy, though some employed consultants to provide this service. However, the overriding concern was with labour, and in particular labour attitudes to work. In this sense new locations provide firms with the opportunity to reshape working practices, to redefine labour–management relations. In so far as components firms are seeking to emulate the practices of 'lean' production, new locations offer an ideal opportunity to install those new practices. Thus, the successful investment agencies have emphasised (i) the flexibility of the available workforce; and (ii) the experiences of other inward investors in their region. On the other hand, it is not easy to establish how far investment agencies actually make a difference to the spatial structure of the industry. First, the flow of FDI activity in general is beyond the power of agencies to influence, depending as it does on the overall investment climate. Second, FDI is predominantly concentrated on acquisitions, where, again, agencies have traditionally not held a role (although there is a case to be made for some activities here). Third, many greenfield FDI projects will be located in one place out of an overriding necessity: for example, a plant built to serve a specific customer. Fourthly, for any one agency or region there will be FDI projects that are suitable (or 'winnable') and those that simply are not. Finally, agencies can only be expected to influence locational decisions where the firm in question is contacted and lobbied by the agency. Thus, while it may be the case that a particular region or country has attracted x investments leading to y jobs, how far that may be attributed to the actions of the agency cannot be shown. Even then, the rather more problematic issue of the longevity of jobs created has to be addressed.

Of course, the emphasis placed on inward investment agencies and policies reflects the prevailing weakness in the indigenous economic base. It could be argued that the long-term economic vitality of a region would be better served by policies directed at the indigenous economic base. As inward investment becomes ever harder to attract in the context of growing inter-locality competition, the rewards from promotional activities decrease, and so the importance of 'growing what you've got' becomes greater. These tensions are likely to become further evident in the 1990s.

10   Conclusions

10.1   GLOBALISATION AND NEW PROCUREMENT REGIMES

The process of globalisation in the automotive industry at the level of the vehicle assemblers has been accompanied by major new capacity additions within the EC. Much, though not all, of this new capacity has been established in locations which lack an extensive history of automotive manufacture. Plants such as Nissan in Sunderland and Toyota in Burneston (both UK), VW–Ford in Setubal (Portugal), BMW in Regensburg (Germany) all, to varying degrees, drew on workforces unused to vehicle assembly. On the other hand, there has been some new investment into established automotive localities, such as the latest Seat plant in Barcelona or the GM engine plant in Germany. Globalisation at the level of the vehicle assemblers has also been accompanied by industrial concentration, of which the Renault–Volvo merger of 1993 is perhaps the most conspicuous evidence. The arrival of Japanese transplant assembly operations in Europe has also provided a destabilising force in that some firms have been 'winners' in getting new contracts, but many others have been 'losers' in not doing so. Equally, the new Japanese transplants, together with the new investments of existing European firms, have been one of the features underpinning spatial restructuring in the automotive components industry.

Globalisation in vehicle assembly has been accompanied by, and partially realised through, significant changes in procurement regimes – although these changes are unevenly developed across assemblers and vary according to the component considered. One visible development has been the practice of new vehicle assembly sites having supplier locations alongside to facilitate just-in-time delivery. New procurement regimes have encouraged industrial concentration at national and, increasingly, international levels, while these practices are slowly becoming established further down the supply chain.

On the other hand, the industry's reaction in Europe to the slump in demand during the 1992–3 period suggests features of more traditional approaches to vehicle assembly. In particular, the established European and US vehicle assemblers have shown an overriding concern 'for basic cost-cutting and for passing on the demands for cost reduction on to their suppliers. This appears to be the main driving force behind new procurement regimes rather than quality *per se* (see Mair, 1992, who argues that this is the case for Ford of Europe). The development of 'post-Japanese' sourcing practices is highly uneven and contextual, so much so that it appears unrealistic to ascribe a single model to all situations. Even the Japanese transplants have different approaches to sourcing. Toyota, for instance, for its Burneston plant, will source about 50 per cent of the value of components purchases from continental Europe; spending by Nissan is more concentrated in the UK.

In the case study sectors discussed above there is little by way of a simple fit with the post-Japanese model based on the premise of lean production. While vehicle assemblers may indeed be moving towards the same general goals in this respect, the emphasis on different elements of the post-Japanese model varies widely. In general, the introduction of new models is also the time for the introduction of new purchase practices, and for a reconfiguration of the supply base. Thus, for the average assembler, it would take at least ten years – the time required to introduce new models across the whole range – for new procurement practices to become fully established. However, globalisation and new procurement regimes have conspired to introduce greater volatility in the environment facing the automotive components industry – particularly the shift away from national sourcing patterns. For the components industry, a greater spatial spread of production and markets provides a means of reducing these uncertainties.

Certainly, the major automotive components firms already have a substantial international spread of production and markets – though in general Western firms are weakest in Japan and South East Asia. However, as Chapter 4 showed, in the late 1980s the industry still included a large number of smaller (and often single site) firms which are certainly the most vulnerable to the consequences of globalisation in the vehicle assemblers.

10.2 PROCUREMENT REGIMES, VERTICAL INTEGRATION AND THE VEHICLE ASSEMBLERS

In the four case study sectors, a range of approaches to procurement and vertical integration was evident at the vehicle assemblers. As was noted in Chapter 4, there is a general move towards the 'post-Japanese' sourcing model, including the use of fewer suppliers, greater levels of outsourcing, the establishment of formal quality regimes, and greater responsibility for design and sub-assembly being passed on to suppliers. In the production of steel, friction materials, and clutches and brakes, the vehicle assemblers have ceased to play a direct role. However, in these areas effective integration has, in a sense, increased, as the vehicle assemblers exert control and influence in the design process and through their quality and delivery demands. Thus the disintegration of ownership in these sectors is accompanied by an integration of practice. In presswork, the introduction of transfer presses, coupled with design trends towards using fewer (and larger) panels, has increased the possibility of vertical integration in medium-to-large pressings.

Much of outsourced body-in-white presswork remains essentially as capacity contracting: contracts are awarded well into the pre-production phase after the vehicle assemblers have 'loaded' their own press-shops. Vehicle assemblers still tend to have a large number of presswork firms on which to draw, while the industry structure remains dominated by small to medium sized firms acting in a largely 'domestic' context. None the less, the sector has great potential for further rationalisation and internationalisation, a process which, as Chapter 6 showed, is already under way.

In the steel sector, the number of potential suppliers is much lower, but chronic over-capacity in the sector puts these suppliers in a weak position in relation to their customers. By virtue of the nature of the product, which is expensive to transport, indigenous national suppliers tend to win the bulk of contracts with indigenous vehicle assembly operations. In an industry which is heavily regulated by the state in all sorts of ways, the nature of relations between steel firms and the vehicle assemblers will always be, at least partly, 'political'. Moreover, the production technology available – which demands very large capacity investments and militates against small-batch production – means that steel firms cannot fit easily into a post-Japanese sourcing regime. Steel production is 'booked' at least three months in advance, and steel firms cannot be expected to establish sites alongside every customer! In this sector, while procurement regimes are of great importance, it is argualble that national and EC policies towards the sector (and especially with respect to the costs of capacity reduction) are the dominant concern for the firms and the most important influence.

In friction materials, brakes and clutches a mature oligopoly exists in the European automotive components industry. Relations between the supplier firms and the vehicle assemblers have long shown more elements of the post-Japanese model than, say, presswork. In these sectors, the suppliers have, for instance, retained an independent R&D capability, and are thus well placed to take even greater responsibility for the products. On the other hand, as was argued in Chapter 7, the vehicle assemblers are reluctant to abandon all control over the development process; equally, as was shown in Chapter 8, wide differences exist in terms of how these components are sourced. Firms in the sector also have a well-established multi-market presence, where, again, proximity (in the sense of being within the national boundaries of the customer) was recognised as being important for both economic and 'political' reasons. Firms in these sectors have been in the 'front line' of moves towards the post-Japanese model. Here, however, a critical concern is which product or sub-assembly constitutes a 'system', and consequently which firm with which competencies will take the role as systems supplier. As Chapters 7 and 8 argued, there is not one single, rational and universal answer to this question. It is also the case that the aftermarket constitutes an important, though often hidden, part of these sectors – as it does to a lesser extent in presswork.

10.3   TECHNOLOGICAL CHANGE IN PRODUCT AND PROCESS

The sectors studied in this book have illustrated that technological innovation in both product and process continue to underpin many of the structural changes in the automotive components industry. Technological innovation demands investment resources, of course, and components sector enterprises are thus in competition for investments. New generations of product and process technology have two effects for the innovating firm: first, they bestow absolute (though often short-term) techno-competitive advantage relative to other suppliers; and second, they raise further barriers to entry (or to continued presence) and firms which fail to innovate will not survive in the longer term. In the steel sector, R&D effort has gone into producing new coatings and substrates which offer particular combinations of performance improvement, with associated major capital investments in new steel coatings plants. In presswork, the development of transfer presses has transformed the economics of the sector (again with very large initial investment costs), especially in relation to the make–buy decision.

Here, the issue of vertical integration is critical, while supplier firms have attempted to develop niche specialities in pressed and fabricated components. In friction material, the replacement of asbestos in brakes was a major concern of the 1980s; this has been achieved mainly through the use of metal-based friction materials. New mixes of friction material, finely-tuned to specific applications, continue to be demanded. Additionally, the drive towards flexible, small batch production systems allied to just-in-time delivery has led to the development of cellular production plants employing 'wet mix' friction materials. For the clutch and brake sector, the process of technological change has been even more demanding, and even more of a threat. On the one hand, the application of electronic sensor and control systems to the basic mechanical components has greatly improved the performance of those components. On the other, the costs of these technologies and the competencies required has been beyond some firms in the sector, and in all cases has resulted in a process of alliance formation. Each leap in technology requires a larger market over which to amortise the development costs, and this is driving the process of industrial concentration allied with the spatial extension of the market. Moreover, for these sectors, especially for firms producing clutches, there is a danger that their product will become technologically redundant in the face of innovations in power transmission systems.

Additionally, in the more 'basic' and mechanical elements of brake and clutch technology, there is a pressure to introduce innovations to 'lock out' competition in the aftermarket. Two illustrations will suffice. First, firms producing brake shoes will frequently make minor design changes on different models (a practice originally developed in Japanese firms) in order to increase new tooling costs for independent aftermarket firms. Second, clutch firms have developed products which are much more difficult to rebuild without specialist equipment in order to restrict the market available to independent service outlets.

The major influence on product and process design for the 1990s and beyond will not, however, come directly from the vehicle assemblers or the structure of the automotive components industry. Rather, it will be governments and agencies taking 'environmental' measures which will offer the most profound technological challenges. The impact of the automotive industry and its products on the environment, and the impact of regulatory measures on the industry, are complex and multifaceted issues (see Wells and Nieuwenhuis, 1994). None the less, for the industry overall, and the case study sectors in particular, there is a real threat of technological redundancy arising from the need to meet new vehicle regulations. A simple example is the mechanical clutch, which would become obsolete were electric vehicles to become the dominant design. Similarly, for the steel industry, the traditional product virtues of strength and cost are less compelling when vehicle weight becomes the critical issue.

It will, of course, take many years for the effects of the emerging environmental concern to be realised. On the other hand, there is a clear potential for a significant proportion of the industry as currently constituted to become superfluous, while new industries and new firms may emerge in their place.

10.4   THE NEW EUROPEAN AUTOMOTIVE COMPONENTS INDUSTRY

There is, then, clear evidence of de-maturity in the automotive components industry generally and the case study sectors in particular. While much public attention has been directed towards the impact of sectors new to the automotive industry (for example, electronics, thin-film technology and so on), the more traditional sectors discussed in this book have faced profound changes in the nature of their product, the way it is produced, and their relationship with both original equipment and aftermarket customers.

Inevitably, these pressures have resulted in widespread changes in the levels of industry concentration, in the nature of competition, and in the spatial structure of enterprises. It is, of course, tempting to expect just-in-time delivery requirements to lead to greater spatial proximity between suppliers and their customers. There are instances where just such an event occurs, but the range of components and sub-assemblies concerned is limited, while the practice can generally only be applied to new assembler sites which have space provision for suppliers alongside. In any case, concepts such as just-in-time and proximity are elastic, subjective, and open to interpretation. Moreover, it would take many years to alter the spatial structure of the industry across Europe to a significant degree in the context of cumulative investment decisions.

Three general spatial trends can be tentatively identified. These are:

(i)   Europeanisation of production and sales;
(ii) Fragmentation and peripheralisation of production; and
(iii) Concentration of design and development.

With respect to the Europeanisation of production and sales, the larger firms within national boundaries have sought to develop an international presence. On the one hand, this strategy is one of risk-spreading. Having production sites in several countries enables a degree of insulation against, say, unfavourable cost or currency movements in another, or against labour strike action in another. Equally, having a broader base of customers provides against a firm being dependent upon one major customer. On the other hand, this strategy is also supportive of cost-reduction efforts. Having several production sites across Europe lowers overall transportation costs, especially if the customer base is spatially dispersed. Alternatively, having several plants can enable specialisation at plant level to occur, providing opportunities for economies of scale to be gained (though this mitigates against the risk-spreading strategy noted above). In the case study sectors, the overwhelming means of achieving spatial extension was acquisition. This enables further industrial concentration.

With respect to the peripheralisation and fragmentation of production, there is some evidence of an emerging spatial division of labour on a European scale which links together the desire to achieve lower costs with the utility of spatial proximity to customers. In this emerging pattern, elements of the production process are separated and allocated different spatial priorities. Thus final sub-assembly activities will still tend to occur in more central locations, nearer to the main source of demand, or alongside vehicle assembly plants where required and possible. These activities may then be supported by sub-components supplied from more remote and low-cost locations. This was not a pattern especially evident in the case study sectors.

In some product areas, the need for comparative cost advantage appears to be greater. Generally, this is the case for mature and/or labour-intensive activities, although, as was illustrated in the case of the Irish Republic it may also apply to capital-intensive projects. Typical product areas which show this pattern of development include tyres and wiring harness production. For these sectors, the attraction of low-cost labour is a prime consideration, although the locational cost calculations would also include the availability of grants, fiscal incentives and other measures which reduce operating costs. It is also the case that some product sectors are better placed to take advantage of the cost benefits of a more peripheral location without suffering from the negative effects which distance from customers and key suppliers can impose. A typical area is aluminium castings, where the material inputs and number and range of operations are few, and the product is of a relatively high value compared with its transportation costs.

With respect to the centralisation of product development activities, as part of the spatial division of labour generally, it must be admitted that the available evidence is less compelling. In the context of greater levels of co-development between suppliers and vehicle assemblers there is a case to be made for having development facilites in relative proximity. Despite the use of computer and telecommunications technologies which enable the design process to be conducted at a distance from the assembly point, there is still pressure for suppliers to be accessible. Seat, for instance, maintains a policy of requiring its major suppliers to have development engineers within a 'reasonable' distance of their own engineering facilities. On the other hand, Calsonic, a Japanese-owned supplier with plants in The Netherlands and Wales, decided to locate its main European R&D base in Wales simply because the firm already had engineering activities there and because no single European location was going to be ideal.

From the case study sectors, there is some evidence of this pattern emerging. In the case of friction materials, for example, BBA has centralised R&D activities in Germany and the UK while expanding production (mainly through acquisition) across several geographical locations. In the presswork sector, where in many cases firms are not large or multi-locational, the leading firms have the potential to create similar structures. Thyssen, for instance, can now concentrate high-volume and complex work (including R&D) at its main German site, while its new site at Ludwigsfelde can concentrate on lower-margin, lower-volume work.

The complexity and variety of the spatial structures in the automotive components industry in Europe defy generalisation. While the structural causes behind economic and spatial restructuring may be similar to all sectors and all supply chains, the nature of the outcome varies widely. Firms, for a variety of contextual and historical reasons, may react differently to the same imperatives to change. Locational change may be part of that response, and, as has been indicated above, some general features of spatial restructuring can be seen. Yet in the case study sectors, two features are worth underlining. First, procurement regimes which firms faced were diverse, and changing rapidly – if one of the key mechanisms for instigating economic and spatial restructuring is itself not fixed or uniform then it is hardly surprising that 'outcomes' are variable too. Second, the nature of the existing industry structure, levels of vertical integration at the assemblers, and the character of the product, all act to provide contingent mechanisms whereby wider structural forces are mediated, again yielding divergent outcomes.

10.5 NATIONAL AUTOMOTIVE COMPONENTS INDUSTRIES AND THE GLOBALISATION PROCESS

The dominance of Germany in the European automotive industry was demonstrated in Chapters 3 and 4. In the automotive components sectors in the late 1980s, and Germany accounted for the largest share of production; German firms were the most numerous of the largest firms. Yet it is difficult to escape the sense of crisis that gripped the sector in the early 1990s in the face of large reductions in volume, rising costs and increasing parity in quality across Europe. It is not surprising, therefore, that German firms have been at the forefront of internationalisation, as was illustrated both in the sector studies and in Chapter 9.

Equally, locations which have been more on the 'receiving end' of internationalisation have become characterised by external ownership of production facilities. It no longer makes sense to talk of 'The British components industry', rather it is 'The components industry in Britain'. This is equally the case with Spain, Portugal, the Republic of Ireland and, increasingly, France, Germany and Italy. The dissolution of national purchasing preferences and the demands for greater capabilities from suppliers has fostered the emergence of truly European firms in which the domestic or indigenous market is of rapidly declining overall significance. The forms of internationalisation adopted in the automotive components industry are varied, and this alone suggests that it would be simplistic to characterise the emerging structure as simply an extension of 'branch plant' strategies. Additionally, a feature of local economic development strategies in the early 1990s has been the growth of local sourcing initiatives by government agencies, with a view to augmenting local economic impact. These are increasingly being allied to the inward investment activities of agencies, as part of the overall 'package' put to potential investors.

It may be suggested that, in a truly pan-European industry, location no longer matters. Certainly, the location of ownership and of the higher-value activities remains dominated by Germany, and to this extent the internationalisation of German capital may be said to represent an extension of economic control over other locations. In terms of the location of production, place is clearly still very much an issue. While some investments are relatively 'footloose' and have a high degree of locational freedom, this is not so in the majority of cases. Each location consists of a series of interrelated and dynamic features which make it more or less attractive as a place to invest in production, or to continue in production. However, the spatial restructuring process is also constrained and shaped by the procurement regime which the supplier faces, and by the nature of the existing industrial base.

In this context, the efforts by national and regional agencies to attract and/or retain automotive components firms have relatively little scope to influence the industry. First, there is a relatively low proportion of total investments which result in a greenfield site; many investments are in-situ or consist of acquisitions. Second, of the greenfield sites, only a small proportion would be appropriate for the location in question. There is no point, for instance, in the Industrial Development Authority for Ireland seeking to attract a seat assembly operation. Third, a significant proportion of greenfield investments are essentially tied to one key customer. Thus, for Portugal, the key to the attraction of a components industry lay in the location of a high-volume vehicle assembly operation in the country. Investments which go to Portugal to serve that assembly plant are not locationally free, and would not therefore be susceptible to marketing endeavours by the investment agencies. Fourth, the nature of interlocational competition appears to be intensifying, as even traditional automotive components production regions join in the contest to attract new investment. Moreover, newer regions have joined in the competition to attract investment, notably Portugal and the former East Germany. Beyond the boundaries of the EC, Turkey and some of the East European countries have attracted investment. In the early 1990s, the effects of recession in the industry in Europe, and indeed globally, have been felt in a cyclical downturn in investment levels by vehicle assemblers and the components industry, with the result that the 'supply' of potential greenfield investors has declined. As a result of these features, investment agencies need to be much more knowledgeable about the sector overall, in order to better understand the investment requirements of firms. Locational competition for investment will not disappear, but will become more all-embracing. That is to say, while grants, incentives, labour costs and so on. will remain in the calculations, newer (and 'softer') features such labour attitudes, training provision and post-investment relations with government agencies will become more important.

Perhaps the outstanding feature of the new European automotive industry for the 1990s is how few people it will employ. Even during the relatively prosperous years of the late 1980s, jobs were being cut by both the vehicle assemblers and the components sector (during this period, for instance, Ford of Europe cut its employment levels by half). The pan-European slump of the early 1990s has accentuated and accelerated this process, notably in Germany, which up to that point had shown continued growth in employment in the sector for over thirty years. Employment in the industry overall could fall by 50 per cent between 1990 and the year 2000, and a revival resurgence in output is unlikely to alter the picture greatly. Whether, in the face of growing environmental pressures, the industry has embarked on long-term decline remains to be seen.

References

Abernathy, W. (1978) *The Productivity Dilemma: Roadblock to Innovation* (Baltimore, Md; Johns Hopkins University Press).

Aglietta, M. (1979) *A Theory of Capitalist Regulation: The US Experience* (London: New Left Books).

Aglietta, M. (1982) 'World Capitalism in the Eighties', *New Left Review*, 136, pp. 25–36.

Amin, A. and Robins, K. (1989) *Industrial Districts and Regional Development, Limits and Possibilities* (Centre for Urban and Regional Development Studies, University of Newcastle upon Tyne).

Amin, A. and Smith, I. (1991) 'Vertical Integration or Disintegration: The Case of the UK Car Parts Industry', in C. M. Law (ed.), *Restructuring the Global Automobile Industry*, pp. 169–99 (London: Routledge).

Arias, M. E. and Guillen, M. F. (1991) 'The Transfer of Organisational Management Techniques Across Borders: Combining Neo-institutional and Comparative Perspectives', paper prepared for INSEAD Conference, 'Organisational Theory at the Crossroads: European Contributions to the Science of Organisations', Fontainebleau, 29–30 November.

ASPP (1988) *Towards World Class Manufacture of Automotive Bodies*, status report prepared for the Tooling Task Force of the Auto/Steel Partnership Program (Ann Arbor, Mich.: University of Michigan).

Atkinson, J. and Gregory, D. (1986) 'A Flexible Future: Britain's Dual Labour Force', *Marxism Today*, 30(4), pp. 12–17.

Auster, E. R. (1987) 'International Corporate Linkages: Dynamic Forms in Changing Environments', *Columbia Journal of World Business*, XXII (2), pp. 3–6.

Baden-Fuller, C. W. F. and Stopford, J. M. (1991) 'Globalisation Frustrated: The Case of White Goods', *Strategic Management Journal*, 12(2), pp. 493–507.

Barbaris, A, (1990) 'Strategies for technology based competition and global marketing: The supplier's view', International Journal of Technology Management, 5, pp. 1–12.

Baxter, A. (1992) 'European Steel Prices Plummet', *Financial Times*, 10 September.

Baxter, A. (1993) 'Holset Buys into Eastern Germany', *Financial Times*, 5 April.

BCG (1991) *The Competitive Challenge Facing the European Automotive Components Industry* (London: Boston Consulting Group and PRS Consulting International).

Beamish, P. W. and Banks, T. C. (1987) 'Equity Joint Ventures and the Theory of the Multinational Enterprise, *Journal of International Business Studies*, 19(2), pp. 1–16.

Berggren, C. (1989) 'New production concepts in final assembly – the Swedish experience', in Wood, S. (ed) *The Transformation of Work* (London: Unwin Hyman) pp. 171–203.

202

Bernstein, P. (1988) 'The Learning Curve at Volvo', *Columbia Journal of World Business*, XXIII(4), pp. 87–95.

Bertodo, R. (1990) 'The Collaboration Vortex: Anatomy of a Euro-Japanese Alliance', *Japanese Motor Business*, June, pp. 29–43 (London: Economist Intelligence Unit).

Blois, K. J. (1972) 'Vertical quasi-integration', *Journal of Industrial Economics*, 20(3), pp. 253–71.

Bloomfield, G. T. (1981) 'The Changing Spatial Organisation of Multinational Corporations in the World Automotive Industry', in F. E. I. Hamilton, and G. J. R. Linge (eds), *Spatial Analysis, Industry and the Industrial Environment*, vol. II, (Chichester: John Wiley).

Bloomfield, G. T. (1991) 'The World Automotive Industry in Transition', in C. M. Law (ed.), *Restructuring the global automobile industry*, pp. 19–60. (London: Routledge).

Blum, P. (1991) 'A multi-purpose deal "for Europe"', *Financial Times*, 19 July.

Boynton, A. C. and Victor, B. (1991) 'Beyond Flexibility: Building and Managing the Dynamically Stable Organisation', *California Management Review*, 34(1), pp. 53–66.

Buckley, P. J. (1990) 'Problems and Developments in the Core Theory of International Business', *Journal of International Business Studies*, 21(4), pp. 657–65.

Carr, C. (1988) 'Strategy Alternatives for Vehicle Components Manufacturers', *Long Range Planning*, 21(4), pp. 86–97.

Carr, C. (1993) 'Global, National and Resource-based Strategies: An Examination of Strategic Choice and Performance in the Vehicle Components Industry', *Strategic Management Journal*, 14(7), pp. 551–67.

CEC (1991) *Panorama of EC Industry 1991* (Luxembourg: Office for Official Publications of the European Communities).

CEC (1992) *Panorama of EC Industry 1992* (Luxembourg: Office for Official Publications of the European Communities).

Chandler, A. D. (1966) *Strategy and Structure: Chapters in the History of American Industrial Enterprise* (New York: Doubleday).

Chandler, A. D. (1977) *The Visible Hand: The Managerial Revolution in American Business* (Cambridge, Mass.: Harvard University Press).

Chandler, A. D. (1986) 'The Evolution of Modern Global Competition', in Porter, M. (ed.) *Competition in Global Industries* (Boston, Mass.: Harvard Business School Press).

Child, J. (1987) 'Information Technology, Organisation, and the Response to Strategic Challenges', *California Management Review*, 30(1), pp. 33–50.

Clarke, S. (1989) 'Over-accumulation, Class Struggle, and the Regulation Approach', *Capital and Class*, 36, pp. 59–92.

Clark, K. B. and Fujimoto, T. (1990) 'The Power of Product Integrity', *Harvard Business Review*, 68(6), pp. 107–18.

Coase, R. (1937) 'The Nature of the Firm', *Economica*, 4, pp. 386–405.

Cole, G. S. (1988) The Changing Relationships between Original Equipment Manufacturers and their Suppliers', *Journal of Technology Management*, 3(3), 299–324.

Cooke, P., Moulaert, F., Syngedouw, E., Weinstein, O., and Wells, P. (1992) *Towards Global Localisation* (London: University College London Press).

Coopers and Lybrand Deloitte (1991) *The Knock-on Effects of Inward Investment in the English Regions*, in association with Benchmark Research (London: HMSO).

Corker, R. (1991) 'The Changing Nature of Japanese Trade', *Finance and Development*, June, pp. 6–9.

Cressey, P. (1993) 'Kalmar and Udevalla: The Demise of Volvo as a European Icon', *New Technology, Work and Employment*, 8(2), pp. 88–90.

CSCA (1988) *L'industrie automobile en France* (Paris: Chambre Syndicale des Constructeurs d'Automobiles).

Cusumano, M. A. (1985) *The Japanese Automobile Industry: Technology and Management at Nissan and Toyota* (Cambridge, Mass. and London: Harvard University Press).

Cusumano, M. and Takeishi, A. (1991) 'Supplier Relations and Management: A Survey of Japanese, Japanese-transplant, and US Auto Plants', *Strategic Management Journal*, 12(8), pp. 563–88.

Dasarathy, C. and Goodwin, T. J. (1990) 'Recent Developments in Automotive Steels', *Metals and Materials*, January, pp. 21–8.

Dawkins, W. (1989) 'Easing Off on the Accelerator', *Financial Times*, 25 September.

Dawkins, W. (1991a) 'Beckoned by the Afterlife', *Financial Times*, 3 July.

Dawkins, W. (1991b) 'Renault Stoppage Hits More Than 15000 Workers', *Financial Times*, 26 October.

Dawkins, W. (1991c) 'Renault Sees Profit in Spite of Strike Costs Near FFr2bn', *Financial Times*, 21 November.

Dawkins, W. and Blum, P. (1991) 'Matra Legal Action over EC ruling on VW–Ford', *Financial Times*, 5 July.

Dicken, P. (1988) 'The Changing Geography of Japanese Foreign Direct Investment in Manufacturing Industry: A Global Perspective', *Environment and Planning A*, 20, 633—53.

Dicken, P. (1990) 'The Geography of Enterprise: Elements of a Research Agenda', in de M. Smidt and R. Wever (eds), *The Corporate Firm in a Changing World Economy* (London: Routledge) pp. 234–44.

DMC (1990) *The Structure of the Japanese Automobile Parts Industry* (Tokyo: Dodswell Marketing Consultants).

Done, K. (1990) 'Volvo Prepares Itself for a European Battle', *Financial Times*, 31 August.

Done, K. (1991a) 'Jaguar to Stay in the Red with £70M Loss', *Financial Times*, 1 May.

Done, K. (1991b) 'Ford Feels the Drag from its British Plants', *Financial Times*, 23 December.

Done, K. (1992) 'Japanese Earn Highest Motor Industry Wages', *Financial Times*, 20 February.

Done, K. and Taylor, R. (1991) 'Skid On the Road to More Productivity', *Financial Times*, 11 February.

Dunning, J. H. (1988) *Multinationals, Technology and Competitiveness* (London: Unwin Hyman).

EAG (1993) *British Investment in a United Germany* (London: Economists Advisory Group). Copy obtained from the Anglo-German Foundation for the Study of Indsutrial Society, 17 Bloomsbury Square, London, WCIA 2LP.

EIU (1989a) *The East European Motor Industry: Prospects and Developments,* The Economist Intelligence Unit, Special Report No. 1167 (London: Economist Intelligence Unit).

EIU (1989b) 'Japanese Manufacturers in the USA', *Japanese Motor Business,* June, pp. 49–85.

EIU (1991) 'Strategic Update on the Volkswagen Group', *European Motor Business,* May, pp. 71–104.

EIU (1992) *The Future of Car Manufacturing: Implications for Component Suppliers,* July (London: Economist Intelligence Unit).

EIU (1993) 'The European Market for Braking Systems', *Europe's Automotive Components Business,* April (London: Economist Intelligence Unit).

Elkington, J. (1990) *The Green Wave: A Report on the 1990 Greenworld Survey* (London: Sustainability).

Elkington, J. and Hailes, J. (1988) *The Green Consumer Guide* (London: Victor Gollance).

Fisher, A. (1992a) 'Time to Become Lean and Mean', *Financial Times,* 23 June.

Fisher, A. (1992b) 'BMW Goes to America to Find the Smarter Buyer', *Financial Times,* 1 July.

Fisher, A. (1992c) 'BMW Has Target of 70,000 Cars a Year at US Plant', *Financial Times,* 24 June.

Florida, R. and Kenny, M. (1991) 'Organisation vs. Culture: Japanese Automotive Transplants in the US', *Industrial Relations Journal,* 22(3), pp. 181–96.

Froebel, F., Hinrichs, H. and Kreye, D. (1980) *The New International Division of Labour* (Cambridge University Press).

Gapper, J. (1989) 'GM Conditions for New Plant "Almost Met" ', *Financial Times,* 4 November.

Garrahan, P. and Stewart, P. (1991) 'Work Organisation in Transition: The Human Resource Management Implications of the "Nissan Way" ', *Human Resource Management Journal,* 2(2), pp. 46–62.

Gerry, C. (1985) 'The Working Class and Small Enterprises in the UK in Recession', in N. Redcliff and E. Mingione (eds), *Beyond Employment: Household, Gender and Subsistance* (Oxford: Basil Blackwell).

Ghoshal, S. and Nohria, N. (1991) *Distributed Innovation in the 'Differentiated Network' Multinational,* paper presented to INSEAD Conference, 'Organisational Theory at the Crossroads: European Contributions to the Science of Organisations', Fontainebleau, 29–30 November.

Glasmeier, A. and McClusky, R. (1987) 'US Auto Parts Production: An Analysis of the Organisation and Location of a Changing Industry', *Economic Geography,* 63(2), pp. 142–59.

GM (1991) *Initiatives for the Environment* (Zurich: General Motors (Europe) AG).

Grey, S. J. and McDermott, M. C. (1987) 'International Mergers and Take-overs: A Review of Trends and Recent Developments', *European Management Journal,* 6(1), pp. 26–43.

Griffiths, J. (1989) 'Honda Will Buy European Parts for UK-built Cars', *Financial Times,* 5 October.

Griffiths, J. (1992) 'Japanese Car Parts Maker Enters Europe', *Financial Times,* 21 July.

Grunwald, J. and Flamm, K. (1985) *The Global Factory* (Washington, DC: The Brookings Institution).

Hamel, G., Doz, Y., and Prahalad, C.K. (1989) 'Collaborate With Your Partners – and Win', *Harvard Business Review*, 89(1), pp. 133–9.

Hamill, J. (1988) 'British Acquisitions in the United States', *National Westminster Bank Quarterly Review*, August, pp. 2–17.

Hammarstrom, O. and Lansbury, R. (1991) 'The Art of Building a Car: The Swedish Experience Re-examined', *New Technology, Work and Employment*, 6(2), pp. 85–90.

Harrigan, K.R. (1987) 'Strategic Alliances: Their Role in Global Competition', *Columbia Journal of World Business*, XXII(2), pp. 67–9.

Henderson, J. (1989) *The Globalisation of High Technology Industry* (London and New York: Routledge).

Hill, R.C. (1989) 'Comparing Transnational Production Systems: The Automobile Industry in the USA and Japan', *International Journal of Urban and Regional Research*, 13(3), pp. 462–80.

Hines, P. (1992) *Supplier Associations: Creating World Class Manufacturing Performance in the Supplier Network*, paper presented at the conference, 'Boosting the Competitiveness of the UK Motor Industry', 30 November–1 December, Waldor Hotel, London.

Hirschhorn, L. and Gilmore, T. (1992) 'The New Boundaries of the "Boundaryless" Company', *Harvard Business Review*, 70 (3), 104–15.

Hood, N. and Young, S. (1982) *Multinationals in Retreat: The Scottish Experience* (Edinburgh University Press).

Hood, N. (1993) 'Inward Investment and the Scottish Economy: Quo Vadis?', *Royal Bank of Scotland Review*, Summer, pp. 17–32.

House of Commons (1987) *The Motor Components Industry: Minutes of Evidence*, Trade and Industry Committee, HC143 (London: HMSO).

Hu, Y. (1992) 'Global or Stateless Corporations are National Firms with International Boundaries', *California Management Review*, 34(2), pp. 107–26.

Hudson, R. and Sadler, D. (1987) 'Manufactured in the UK? Special Steels, Motor Vehicles, and the Politics of Industrial Decline', *Capital and Class*, 32, pp. 55–82.

Hudson, R. and Sadler, D. (1992) ' "Just-in-Time" Production and the European Automotive Components Industry', *Physical Distribution and Logistics Management*, 22(2), pp. 40–5.

Hyun, Y. and Lee, J. (1989) 'Can Hyundai go it alone?', *Long Range Planning*, 22(2), pp. 63–9.

IBB (1992) *Annual Report 1991–1992* (London: Invest in Britain Bureau).

IDA (1991) *Automotive Components from IRELAND* (Dublin: Industrial Development Authority for Ireland).

Imrie, R. and Morris, J. (1992) *Transforming Buyer–Supplier Relations* (London: Macmillan).

IISI (1991) *Innovations in Steel: Cars for the 21st Century* (Brussels: International Iron and Steel Institute).

Information du Vehicule (1992) 'Valeo Klupplingen is Setting up in Reichenbach for VW', *Information du Vehicule*, 199, p. 18.

Information du Vehicule (1993) 'Teves Bound for the Conquest of the East', *Information du Vehicule*, 200, p. 24.

IRES (1991) *Da indotto a sistema: la produzione di componenti nell'industria automobilistica* (Turin: Rosenburg & Sellier).

James, B. G. (1989) *Trojan Horse* (London: Mercury Books).

JETRO (1992) *8th Survey of European Operations of Japanese Companies in the Manufacturing Sector* (London: Japanese External Trade Organisation).

Johanson, J. and Vahlne, J. (1977) 'The Internationalisation Process of the Firm: A Model of Knowledge Development and Increasing Foreign Market Commitments', *Journal of International Business Studies*, 8, pp. 23–32.

Jones, D. (1990) 'Measuring Up to the Japanese: Lessons from the Motor Industry', *University of Wales Review: Business and Economics*, 5, pp. 23–38.

Jones, P. N. and North, J. (1991) 'Japanese Motor Industry Transplants: The West European Dimension', *Economic Geography*, 67(2), pp. 105–23.

Jonquires, G. de (1989) 'The New Kid on the Block', *Financial Times*, 27 June.

Jorde, T. M. and Teece, D. J. (1989) 'Competition and Cooperation: Striking the Right Balance', *California Management Review*, 31(3), pp. 25–37.

Kelly, J. (1983) *Scientific Management, Job Redesign and Work Performance* (London: Academic Press).

Klien, B. H. (1986)' Dynamic Competition and Productivity Advance', pp. 112–28 in R. Landau and N. Rosenberg, (eds), *The Positive Sum Strategy* (Washington, DC: National Academy Press).

Lamming, R. (1987) *The International Automotive Components Industry: Customer–Supplier Relationships Past, Present and Future*, International Motor Vehicle Programme (Cambridge, Mass.: Centre for Technology, Policy and Industrial Development).

Lamming, R. (1989a) *The Causes and Effects of Structural Change in the European Automotive Components Industry*, International Motor Vehicle Programme (Cambridge, Mass.: Centre for Technology, Policy and Industrial Development).

Lamming, R. (1989b) *The International Automobile Components Industry: The Next 'Best Practice' for Suppliers*, International Motor Vehicle Programme (Cambridge, Mass.: Centre for Technology, Policy and Industrial Development).

Lamming, R. (1993) *Beyond Partnership: Strategies for Innovation and Lean Supply* (London: Prentice Hall).

Lane, D. (1992) 'Partnership the Watchword', *Financial Times*, 14 July.

Law, C. M. (1974) 'Some Aspects of Post-war Geography of the West European Motor Vehicle Industry', *Geografisch Tijdschrift*, VIII(1), pp. 5–16.

Law, C. M. (1985) 'The Geography of Industrial Rationalisation: The British Motor Car Assembly Industry, 1972–1982', *Geography*, 70, pp. 1–12.

Lee, A. (1989) 'Breaking for Parts', *Purchasing and Supply Managment*, March, pp. 26–7.

Levitt, T. (1983) 'The Globalisation of Markets', *Harvard Business Review*, 61(3), pp. 92–102.

Lewchuk, W. (1987) *American Technology and the British Vehicle Industry* (Cambridge University Press).

Lipietz, A. (1984) 'Imperialism or the Beast of the Apocalypse', *Capital and Class*, 22, pp. 81–109.

Lovering. J. (1990) 'Fordism's Unknown Successor: A Comment on Scott's Theory of Flexible Accumulation and the Re-emergence of Regional

Economies', *International Journal of Urban and Regional Research*, 14(1) pp. 159–74.

Mair, A. (1991) *Just in Time Manufacturing and the Spatial Structure of the Automobile Industry*, Working Paper No.3 (Durham: Department of Geography, University of Durham, DH1 3LE).

Mair, A. (1992) 'Ford of Britain in the 1990s: Corporate Strategy in Europe and the Future of the Ford Locations', *Local Economy*, 7(2), pp. 146–62.

Mair, A., Florida, R., and Kenny, M. (1988) 'The New Geography of Automobile Production: Japanese Transplants in North America', *Economic Geography*, 66(4), pp. 352–73.

Mandel, E. (1979) *The Second Slump* (London: New Left Books).

Marginson, P., Edwards, P., Martin, R., Purcell, J. and Sisson, K. (1988) *Beyond the Workplace* (Oxford: Basil Blackwell).

Massey, D. and Meagan, R. (1982) *The Anatomy of Job Loss* (London: Methuen).

Millington, A. I. and Bayliss, B. T. (1990) 'The Process of Internationalisation: UK Companies in the EC', *Management International Review*, 30(2), pp. 151–61.

Morgan, K. and Sayer, A. (1989) *Microcircuits of Capital* (Cambridge: Polity Press).

Morris, D. (1991) 'Japanese Car Firms Make their Marque in Britain', *Anglo-Japanese Journal*, 4(4) pp. 4–6.

Morris, J. (1989) 'Japanese Inward Investment and the "Importation" of Sub-contracting Complexes: Three Case Studies', *Area*, 21(3), pp. 269–77.

Morrison, A. J., Ricks, D. A., and Roth, K. (1991) 'Globalisation Versus Regionalisation: Which Way for the Multinational?', *Organisational Dynamics*, 19(3), pp. 17–29.

Mueller, F. and Purcell, J. (1992) 'The Europeanisation of Manufacturing and the Decentralisation of Bargaining: Multinational Management Strategies in the European Automobile Industry', *International Journal of Human Resource Management*, 3(1), pp. 15–34.

Murray, F. (1987) 'Flexible Specialisation in the "Third Italy"', *Capital and Class*, 33, 84–95.

MVMA (1990) *World Motor Vehicle Data* (Detroit: Motor Vehicle Manufacturer's Association).

NEDC (1991) *The Experience of Nissan Suppliers* (London: National Economic Development Office).

Newman, R. G. (1990) 'The Second Wave Arrives: Japanese Strategy in the US Auto Parts Market', *Business Horizons*, 33(4), pp. 24–30.

Nieuwenhuis, P., Cope, P. and Armstrong, J. (1992) *The Green Car Guide*, (London: Greenprint).

Odaka, K., Ono, K., and Adachi, F. (1988) *The Automobile Industry in Japan: A Study of Ancillary Firm Development* (Tokyo: Kinokuniya and Oxford University Press).

Ohmae, K. (1985) *The Rise of Triad Power* (New York: Harper & Row).

Ohmae, K. (1989) 'The Global Logic of Strategic Alliances', *Harvard Business Review*, 67(2), pp. 143–54.

Ohmae, K. (1990) *The Borderless World: Power and Strategy in the Interlinked Economy* (New York: Harper).

Oliver, N. and Wilkenson, B. (1989) *The Japanisation of British Industry* (London: Harvester).

Peel, Q. (1992) 'Slump in Sales Drives Porsche Down Market', *Financial Times*, 26 January.

Pemberton, G. (1988) *The World Car Industry to the Year 2000*, Automotive Special Report No. 12 (London: Economist Intelligence Unit).

Perlmutter, H. V. and Heenan, D. A. (1986) 'Cooperate to Compete Globally', *Harvard Business Reveiw*, 64(2), pp. 136–52.

Peters, T. and Waterman, R. H. (1982) *In Search of Excellence* (New York: Harper & Row).

Piore, M. and Sabel, C. (1984) *The Second Industrial Divide: Prospects for Prosperity* (New York: Basic Books).

Pollert, A. (1988) 'Dismantling Flexibility', *Capital and Class*, 34, pp. 42–75.

Porter, M. E. (1980) *Competitive Strategy* (New York: Free Press).

Porter, M. E. (1985) *Competitive Advantage* (New York: Free Press).

Porter, M. E. (1986) 'Competition in Global Industries: A Conceptual Framework', pp. 15–60 in Porter, M. E. (ed.), *Competition in Global Industries* (Boston, Mass.: Harvard Business School).

Prahalad, C. K. and Doz, Y. L. (1987) *The Multinational Mission: Balancing Local Demands and Global Vision* (New York: Free Press).

PRS (1985) *Who's Who in Western European Automotive Components Markets 1985/86* (London: PRS Business Publications).

Rainnie, A. (1988) 'Your Flexible Friend? Small Firms in the 1980s', unpublished paper (Local Economy Research Unit, Hatfield Polytechnic, Hertfordshire).

Rawlinson, M. (1991) 'Subcontracting in the Motor Industry: A Case Study in Coventry', in C. M. Law (ed.), *Restructuring the Global Automotive Industry* (London: Routledge).

Rawlinson, M. and Wells, P. (1992) *Lean Production and Human Resource Management: An Example from the Presswork Sector*, paper presented at the conference 'The Challenge of Change: The Theory and Practice of Organisational Transformations', 9–10 September, Cardiff Business School.

Rehder, R. R. (1989) 'Japanese Transplants: In Search of a Balanced and Broader Perspective', *Columbia Journal of World Business*, XXIV (4), pp. 17–28.

Rehder, R. R. (1990) 'Japanese Transplants: After the Honeymoon', *Business Horizons*, 33(1), pp. 87–98.

Rehder, R. R. (1992) 'Building Cars as if People Mattered', *Columbia Journal of World Business*, XXVII(2), pp. 56–71.

Reid, N. (1990) 'Spatial Patterns of Japanese Investment in the US Auto Industry', *Industrial Relations Journal*, 21(1), pp. 49–59.

Rhys, D. G. (1972) 'Heavy Commercial Vehicles: The Survival of the Small Firm', *Journal of Industrial Economics*, 20 (3), pp. 230–52.

Rhys, D. G. (1974) 'Employment, Efficiency and Labour Relations in the British Motor Industry', *Industrial Relations Journal*, 5(2), pp. 4–26.

Rhys, D. G. (1989) 'Smaller Car Firms: Will They Survive?', *Long Range Planning*, 22(5), pp. 22–9.

Robinson, J. (1991) *The Importance of Customer–Supplier 'Partnerships'*, paper presented at the conference, 'Integrated Materials Management: The Key to Survival', Institute of Materials Management, Solihull, 29–30 September.

Rugman, A. M. and Verbeke, A. (1990) 'Multinational Corporate Strategy and the Canada–US Free Trade Agreement', *Management International Review*, 30(3), pp. 252–66.

Sandberg, A. (1993) 'Volvo Human-centred Work Organisation – the End of the Road?', *New Technology, Work and Employment*, 8(2), pp. 85–7.

Sayer, A. (1989) 'Postfordism in Question', *International Journal of Urban and Regional Research*, 13, pp. 666–95.

Sayer, A. and Morgan, K. (1987) 'High technology industry and the international division of labour: the case of electronics', ch. 2, pp. 10–36 in M.J. Breheny and R. McQuaid (eds), *The Development of High Technology Industries* (London: Croom Helm).

Scherrer, C. (1991) 'Seeking a Way out of Fordism: The US Steel and Auto Industries', *Capital and Class*, 44, pp. 93–120.

Scott, A.J. (1988) 'Flexible Production Systems and Regional Development: The Rise of New Industrial Spaces in North America and Western Europe', *International Journal of Urban and Regional Research*, 12, pp. 171–85.

Seiffert, U. and Walzer, P. (1984) *The Future for Automotive Technology* (London: Francis Pinter).

Servan-Schrieber, J.J. (1968) *The American Challenge* (New York: Atheneum).

Shingo, S. (1985) *A Revolution in Manufacturing: The SMED System* (New York: Productivity Press).

Shinohara, I. (1988) *NPS – New Production System: J–I–T Crossing Industry Boundaries* (Cambridge, Mass.: Productivity Press).

Shutt, J. and Whittington, R. (1984) *Large Firm Strategies and the Rise of Small Units: The Illusion of Small Firm Job Creation*, Working Paper 15, North West Industry Research Unit (University of Manchester).

Sleigh, P. (1989) *The European Automotive Components Industry: A Review of Eighty Leading Manufacturers*, Economist Intelligence Unit Special Report No. 1186 (London: EIU).

Sleigh, P. (1991) *The European Automotive Components Industry*, Economist Intelligence Unit Special Report No. 2107 (London: EIU).

Smidt, M. de and Wever, E. (1990) *The Corporate Firm in a Changing World Economy* (London and New York: Routledge).

Smith, M. (1989) 'GM Sets Deadline for Change to Working Practices', *Financial Times*, 1 November.

Smith, M. (1990a) 'Ford Wants Radical Revision of Pay Structure', *Financial Times*, 31 August.

Smith, M. (1990b) 'Jaguar Bares its Teeth at Outmoded Work Practices', *Financial Times*, 11 October.

Smith, M. (1992a) 'Demise of Clocking-on Winds up Rover Staff', *Financial Times*, 24 June.

Smith (1992b) 'Old Rover Learns New Japanese Tricks', *Financial Times*, 10 October.

SMMT (1990a) *The Motor Industry of Great Britain 1991* (London: Society of Motor Manufacturers and Traders).

SMMT (1990b) *Employment and the Motor Industry* (London: Society of Motor Manufacturers and Traders).

SMMT (1991) *The Motor Industry of Great Britain 1990* (London: Society of Motor Manufacturers and Traders).

Starkey, K. and McKinlay, A. (1989) 'Beyond Fordism? Strategic Choice and Labour Relations in Ford UK', *Industrial Relations Journal*, 20(2), pp. 23–8.
Starkey, K., Wright, M., and Thompson, S. (1991) 'Flexibility, Hierarchy, Markets', *British Journal of Management*, 2, pp. 165–76.
Taylor, R. (1991) 'Volvo US Sales Down Heavily', *Financial Times*, 4 October.
Teece, D. J. (1986) 'Profiting from Technological Innovation: Implications for Integration, Collaboration, Licensing and Public Policy', *Research Policy*, 15, pp. 285–305.
Teece, D. J. (1992) Foreign Investment and Technological Development in Silicon Valley', *California Managment Review*, 34(2), pp. 88–106.
Thomsen, S. and Nicolaides, P. (1991) *The Evolution of Japanese Direct Investment in Europe* (London: Harvester Wheatsheaf).
Thomsen, S. and Woolcock, S. (1993) *Direct Investment and European Integration* (London: Royal Institute of International Affairs and Pinter).
Thrift, N. J. and Leyshon, A. (1988) ' "The Gambling Propensity": Banks, Developing Country Debt Experiences, and the New International Financial System', *Geoforum*, 19(1), pp. 55–69.
Tighe, C. (1991) 'Nissan Favours North East Suppliers', *Financial Times*, 4 July.
Tulip, S. (1993) 'A Very Green Source of Supply', *Purchasing and Supply Management*, April, pp. 20–3.
Turnbull, P., Delbridge, R., Oliver, N. and Wilkenson, B. (1993) 'Winners and Losers: The Tiering of Components Suppliers in the UK Automotive Industry', *Journal of General Management*, 19(1), pp. 48–63.
Turok, I. (1993) 'Inward Investment and Local Linkages: How Deeply Embedded is "Silicon Glen"?', *Regional Studies*, 27(5), pp. 401–17.
VDA (1990) *Annual Report* (Verband Der Automobilindustrie E.V., Westendstrasse 61, 6000 Frankfurt/Main 1, Germany).
Vernon, R. (1966) 'International Investment and International Trade in the Product Cycle', *Quarterly Journal of Economics*, 80, pp. 190–207.
Waitt, G. (1993) 'Say Bye to Hyundai and Hi to Korean Autoparts? Restructuring The Korean Automobile Industry in the 1990s', *Tijdschrift voor Economische en Sociale Geografie*, 84(3), pp. 198–206.
Walker, R. (1989) 'Machinery, Labour and Location', ch. 3, pp. 59–90, in S. Wood (ed.), *The Transformation of Work* (London: Unwin Hyman).
Warren, K. (1975) *World Steel: An Economic Geography* (Newton Abbot: David and Charles).
Wells, P. and Cooke, P. (1991) 'The Geography of International Strategic Alliances: The Cases of Cable and Wireless, Ericsson, and Fujitsu', *Environment and Planning A*, 19, 87–106.
Wells, P. (1991) 'East–West Partnerships in Automobiles', *Long Range Planning*, 24(2), pp. 75–82.
Wells, P. (1992) 'European Foreign Direct Investment and Local Economic Development: The Case of the Automotive Sector', *Local Economy*, 7(2), pp. 132–46.
Wells, P. and Nieuwenhuis, P. (1994) *The Motor Vehicle and the Environment* (London: Belhaven).
Wells, P. and Rawlinson, M. (1992a) 'Technology, Procurement Practices, and Structural Change in the Automotive Presswork Sector', pp. 271–80 in B.

Shirvani and D. R. H. Baggs (eds), *Sheet Metal 1992* (London and Philadelphia: Institute of Physics Publishing).

Wells, P. and Rawlinson, M. (1992b) 'New Procurement Regimes and the Spatial Distribution of Suppliers: The Case of Ford in Europe', *Area*, 24(4), pp. 380–90.

Wells, P. and Rawlinson, M. (1993a) 'Playing the System', *Purchasing and Supply Management*, April, p. 19.

Wells, P. and Rawlinson, M. (1994) 'The Environment and a Traditional Sector: The Case of the Presswork Industry', in P. Wells and P. Nieuwenhuis (eds), *The Motor Vehicle and the Environment* (London: Belhaven).

Wells, P. and Rawlinson, M. (1993b) 'Japanese Globalisation and the European Automobile Industry', *Tijdschrift voor Economische en Sociale Geografie*, lxxxiv (5), 349–361.

Wickins, P. (1993) 'Lean Production and Beyond: The System, Its Critics, and the Future', *Human Resource Management Journal*, 3(4), pp. 75–90.

Williams, K., Haslam, C., and Williams, J. (1991) 'Ford versus Fordism: The Beginnings of Mass Production?', copy obtained from the authors, University of Wales, Aberystwyth.

Williams, K., Mitsui, I. and Haslam, C. (1991) 'How Far from Japan? A Case Study of Japanese Press-shop Practice and Management Calculation', *Critical Perspectives in Accounting*, 2, pp. 145–64.

Williams, K., Williams, J., and Haslam, C. (1987) *The Breakdown of Austin Rover* (Leamington Spa: Berg Books).

Williamson, O. (1975) *Markets and Hierarchies: Analysis and Anti-trust Implications* (New York: Free Press).

Williamson, O. (1985) *The Economic Institutions of Capitalism* (New York: Free Press).

Wormald, J. (1989) 'Manufacturer Integration and Supplier Relationships', *European Motor Business*, May (London: Economist Intelligence Unit) pp. 144–61.

Womak, P., Jones, D. T., and Roos, D. (1990) *The Machine that Changed the World* (New York: Rawson Associates).

Woot, P. de (1990) *High Technology Europe* (Oxford: Basil Blackwell).

Index